LIVERPOOL FC
THE GUIDE
2006

Sport Media
A Trinity Mirror Business

HONOURS

LEAGUE CHAMPIONSHIP
1900-01, 1905-06, 1921-22,
1922-23, 1946-47,
1963-64, 1965-66, 1972-73, 1975-76,
1976-77, 1978-79, 1979-80, 1981-82,
1982-83, 1983-84, 1985-86,
1987-88, 1989-90

DIVISION TWO WINNERS
1893-94, 1895-96, 1904-05, 1961-62

LANCASHIRE LEAGUE WINNERS
1892-93

FA CUP WINNERS
1964-65, 1973-74, 1985-86, 1988-89,
1991-92, 2000-01

LEAGUE CUP WINNERS
1980-81, 1981-82, 1982-83, 1983-84,
1994-95, 2000-01, 2002-03

FA CHARITY SHIELD WINNERS
(FA COMMUNITY SHIELD)
1966, 1974, 1976, 1979, 1980,
1982, 1988, 1989, 2001
(SHARED)
1964, 1965, 1977, 1986, 1990, 2001

EUROPEAN CUP
(UEFA CHAMPIONS LEAGUE)
1976-77, 1977-78, 1980-81, 1983-84, 2004-05

UEFA CUP WINNERS
1972-73, 1975-76, 2000-01

EUROPEAN SUPER CUP WINNERS
1977, 2001

SUPER CUP WINNERS
1985-86

INTRODUCTION

The Liverpool FC Official Guide 2006 will become the bible of club information for Reds fans everywhere. Every contact number you will ever need is included in this invaluable publication, from the Box Office to the Official Liverpool Supporters Club.

More than this, the Guide is packed full of facts and stats about the famous Mersey Reds. To achieve this we have utilised the finest statisticians and club experts to provide as much up-to-date information as possible that deadlines have allowed, prior to the new campaign.

Fittingly, there is a key section on Liverpool's exploits in Europe with comprehensive information about former opponents and famous games, up to and including the final game of the 2004/05 season, a certain final clash against AC Milan - incidentally, the first time the Reds have met the Italian giants.

There is a full Premier League section documenting our record since 1992/93, and the definitive guide to the club's FA Cup history. There is also a fascinating insight into Anfield managerial legends Bill Shankly and Bob Paisley. For instance, can you statistically compare the immortal Shankly and his famous partner in glory Paisley? The Guide provides an insight.

All of the 2004/05 playing stats come as standard. This is the kind of book that you will take down from your bookshelf time and again as a source of reference. To complete an outstanding package, it features some of the finest pictures from matches involving the Reds from the past year, not least the sensational Istanbul triumph and that remarkable Champions League semi-final victory over Chelsea.

It is a common theme for supporters to ask each other teasing questions about their favourite club. This book will help solve every pub or office quiz. Every year the official Liverpool FC Guide will be updated to make it a highly collectable source of reference for Liverpudlians everywhere. We hope you enjoy it.

CONTRIBUTORS

Ged Rea and Dave Ball are Liverpool FC's official statisticians. Ged's Liverpool FC records are second-to-none, while Dave is a key researcher for long-running BBC TV show 'A Question of Sport'. James Cleary has also played a major role in researching and writing key information.

Sport Media
A Trinity Mirror Business

Executive Editor: KEN ROGERS Editor: STEVE HANRAHAN
Art Editor: RICK COOKE Production Editor: PAUL DOVE
Sales and Marketing Manager: ELIZABETH MORGAN
Writers: JAMES CLEARY, ALAN JEWELL, GAVIN KIRK, DAVID RANDLES, CHRIS McLOUGHLIN, WILLIAM HUGHES
Designers: BARRY PARKER, GLEN HIND, COLIN SUMPTER, LEE ASHUN

ISBN 1905266022: Printed and finished by Scotprint, Haddington, Scotland

CLUB TELEPHONE NUMBERS

Main Switchboard	0151 263 2361
Ticket Office General Enquiries	0870 220 2345
Credit Card Booking Line	0870 220 2151
UEFA Booking Line	0870 220 0034
League/FA Cup Booking Line	0870 220 0056
Priority Booking Line (Priority Ticket Scheme members only)	0870 220 0408
24 hour information line	0870 444 4949
Mail Order Hotline (UK)	0870 6000532
International Mail Order Hotline	+ 44 1386 852035
Conference and Banqueting (for your events at Anfield)	0151 263 7744
Corporate Sales	0151 263 9199
Public Relations (inc. all charity requests)	0151 260 1433
Development Association	0151 263 6391
Community Department	0151 264 2316
Museum & Tour Centre	0151 260 6677
Membership Department	0151 261 1444
Club Store (Anfield)	0151 263 1760
Club Store (City Centre)	0151 330 3077

BECOME A MEMBER OF LIVERPOOL FC BY JOINING
THE OFFICIAL LIVERPOOL SUPPORTERS CLUB
To join, please call: 08707 02 02 07
International: +44 151 261 1444

SUBSCRIBE TO THE OFFICIAL LFC PROGRAMME AND WEEKLY MAGAZINE
To take out a subscription please call: 0845 1430001

Official LFC SMS alerts bring you all the latest LFC news, goals and match info wherever you are!
Simply text LFC 4U to 84414 (UK). Other packages include LFC MATCH (team sheet, goals, red
cards and results) or LFC NEWSPLUS (full time score, news flashes and team sheets).
For all packages and T&Cs visit www.liverpoolfc.tv.

Show your true colours and get LFC on your mobile by visiting www.liverpoolfc.tv/mobilezone and
choosing from LFC Wallpapers, Ringtones, Commentary Realtones and much much more.

Sign up for an e Season Ticket to see Premier League goals & highlights, on-line TV channels and
follow the team live through Turnstile.
To sign up go to www.liverpoolfc.tv

LFC Save & Support Account with Britannia
For more information visit www.britannia.co.uk/lfc, call 0800 915 0503 or visit any Britannia branch

Liverpool FC Credit Card in Association with MBNA
For more information call 0800 776 262

CONTENTS

THE BOSS

An analysis of Liverpool managers past and present, which includes a comparison of Rafa Benitez's first season in charge with that of previous men in charge at Anfield. There is also a special feature: Bill Shankly v Bob Paisley.

THE PLAYERS 05/06

A definitive guide to this season's squad, including appearances and goals for the club. Reserve, academy and ladies statistics are also present, including fixture lists for the new campaign.

THE TOP 10 MOMENTS 04/05

A pictorial reminder of the highs of the last campaign, culminating in the unforgettable Champions League final success in Istanbul.

THE ROAD TO ISTANBUL

From Graz to Istanbul - plus every Reds result in Europe.

THE 04/05 PREMIERSHIP CAMPAIGN

A look back at the domestic season, documenting the results, Liverpool's league progress and gems of wisdom from Rafa Benitez.

THE PREMIERSHIP

Liverpool's Premiership record, record appearance holders and goalscorers since 1992-93 are documented together with other facts and statistics.

THE FOOTBALL LEAGUE RECORD

Every championship triumph is analysed statistically, plus where the Reds finished in every league campaign, together with selected records.

THE CUPS

From the World Club Championship to every domestic cup competition, each game is listed including the Reds' FA Charity Shield/FA Community Shield record.

THE LFC RECORD

Selected information and statistics looking at playing records through the club's history.

PREMIERSHIP OPPONENTS

A look at who the Reds will be facing in the 2005-06 season, with useful information including how to get to the different stadiums, Liverpool's recent record against each team and other relevant information.

ESSENTIALS AND ENTERTAINMENT

From ticket details and how to join the Reds' supporters club, to selected pubs around Anfield and travel information, essential info for following the Reds.

FOREWORD

RICK PARRY
CHIEF EXECUTIVE

Liverpool supporters are amongst the most knowledgeable in the country. That's an indisputable fact. Based on our fan research we know that you have a real hunger for information about all aspects of the club. This is why our communication channels are so wide and varied.

* Our magazine – "LFC" – is the ONLY official weekly club publication in the country. This in itself demonstrates your insatiable appetite for exclusive interviews and features from the heart of Melwood and Anfield.
* Our website – liverpoolfc.tv – provides all of the breaking news coming out of the club and much more. Our e-Season ticket package, available through liverpoolfc.tv, strives to bring the match experience right into your home, even enabling you to view the manager's big match press conferences.
* We have a quarterly Official Liverpool Poster Magazine for younger fans and our award-winning This Is Anfield matchday programme is rated as one of the best in the country.
* We even have exclusive quarterly glossy magazines for both our junior and senior Official Liverpool Supporters Club members. The content focus in these publications looks at every angle of club life, from what the groundsman does to how our world-class Melwood training facility operates.

Now we have a brand new information tool and we believe it will once again support and help you to get the very best out of your favourite football club. Liverpool FC 'The Official Guide 2006' will be one of those little books that you will constantly be referring to, be it to secure a specific club phone number or to answer a teasing statistical query. As a fan myself and a Chief Executive who is constantly focusing on how we can reach out to our fan base, I know how useful Liverpool FC 'The Official Guide 2006' will become.

Thanks for your passionate and loyal support.

Rick Parry

KEY DATES 2005-06

(Dates are subject to change)

August

13	Premiership kick-off
25	UEFA Champions League group stage draw (3pm)
26	UEFA Cup first-round draw (12pm)
26	UEFA Super Cup final v CSKA Moscow (Stade Louis II, Monaco)
31	Transfer window closes (5pm)

September

13/14	UEFA Champions League group stage matchday 1
15	UEFA Cup first round 1st leg
27/28	UEFA Champions League group stage matchday 2
29	UEFA Cup first round 2nd leg

October

4	UEFA Cup group stage draw (11am)
8&12	World Cup qualifying final games (Europe)
18/19	UEFA Champions League group stage matchday 3
20	UEFA Cup group stage matchday 1
24 (w/c)	Carling Cup third round

November

1/2	UEFA Champions League group stage matchday 4
3	UEFA Cup group stage matchday 2
22/23	UEFA Champions League group stage matchday 5
24	UEFA Cup group stage matchday 3
28 (w/c)	Carling Cup fourth round
30	UEFA Cup group stage matchday 4
TBC	World Cup qualifying play-offs (European zone)

December

1	UEFA Cup group stage matchday 4
6/7	UEFA Champions League group stage matchday 6
9	World Cup draw (Leipzig, Germany)
14/15	UEFA Cup group stage matchday 5
15	FIFA Club World Championship semi-final (Yokohama Stadium, Japan)
16	UEFA Champions League first knockout stage draw (11am)
16	UEFA Cup first and second knockout stage draw (12pm)
18	FIFA Club World Championship final/3rd v 4th (Yokohama Stadium, Japan)
19 (w/c)	Carling Cup quarter-final
31	Transfer window re-opens

January

7	FA Cup third round
9 (w/c)	Carling Cup semi-final 1st leg

KEY DATES 2005-06

(Dates are subject to change)

January

23 (w/c)	Carling Cup semi-final 2nd leg
28	FA Cup fourth round
31	Transfer window closes (5pm)

February

15/16	UEFA Cup first knockout round 1st leg
18	FA Cup fifth round
21/22	UEFA Champions League first knockout round 1st leg
23	UEFA Cup first knockout round 2nd leg
26	Carling Cup final (Millennium Stadium, Cardiff)

March

7/8	UEFA Champions League first knockout round 2nd leg
9	UEFA Cup second knockout round 1st leg
15/16	UEFA Cup second knockout round 2nd leg
17	UEFA Champions League quarter-finals, semi-finals and final draw 11am)
17	UEFA Cup quarter-finals, semi-finals and final draw (12pm)
22	FA Cup sixth round (Wednesday)
28/29	UEFA Champions League quarter-finals 1st leg
30	UEFA Cup quarter-finals 1st leg

April

4/5	UEFA Champions League quarter-finals 2nd leg
6	UEFA Cup quarter-finals 2nd leg
18/19	UEFA Champions League semi-finals 1st leg
20	UEFA Cup semi-finals 1st leg
22	FA Cup semi-finals
25/26	UEFA Champions League semi-finals 2nd leg
27	UEFA Cup semi-finals 2nd leg

May

7	Premiership final day
13	FA Cup final (Wembley Stadium, London - TBC)
10	UEFA Cup final (Philips Stadium, Eindhoven, Holland)
17	UEFA Champions League final (Stade de France, Paris, France)

June

9	World Cup finals begin (Allianz Arena, Munich)

FIXTURE LIST 2005-06

August

10	UEFA Champions League 3rd qualifying round 1st leg	
13	Middlesbrough	(A) - 5.15pm kick-off
20	Sunderland	(H)
23	UEFA Champions League 3rd qualifying round 2nd leg	
26	CSKA Moscow	(N) - 7.45pm kick-off (UEFA Super Cup final, Monaco)

September

10	Tottenham Hotspur	(A)
13/14	UEFA Champions League group stage matchday 1	
18	Manchester United	(H) - 12pm kick-off
24	Birmingham City	(A) - 12.45pm kick-off
27/28	UEFA Champions League group stage matchday 2	

October

2	Chelsea	(H) - 4pm kick-off
15	Blackburn Rovers	(H)
18/19	UEFA Champions League group stage matchday 3	
22	Fulham	(A)
25/26	Carling Cup 3rd round	
29	West Ham United	(H)

November

1/2	UEFA Champions League group stage matchday 4	
5	Aston Villa	(A) - 12.45pm kick-off
19	Portsmouth	(H)
22/23	UEFA Champions League group stage matchday 5	
26	Manchester City	(A)
29/30	Carling Cup 4th round	

December

3	Wigan Athletic	(H)
6/7	UEFA Champions League group stage matchday 6	
10	Middlesbrough	(H)
17	Sunderland	(A) - 5.15pm kick-off
26	Newcastle United	(H)
28	Everton	(A) - 8pm kick-off
31	West Bromwich Albion	(H)

FIXTURE LIST 2005-06

January 2006

2	Bolton Wanderers	(A)
7	FA Cup 3rd round	
14	Tottenham Hotspur	(H)
21	Manchester United	(A)
28	FA Cup 4th round	
31	Birmingham City	(H)

February

4	Chelsea	(A)
11	Wigan Athletic	(A)
18	FA Cup 5th round	
25	Manchester City	(H)

March

4	Charlton Athletic	(H)
11	Arsenal	(A)
18	Newcastle United	(A)
22	FA Cup 6th round	
25	Everton	(H)

April

1	West Bromwich Albion	(A)
8	Bolton Wanderers	(H)
15	Blackburn Rovers	(A)
17	Fulham	(H)
22	West Ham United	(A)
	(FA Cup semi-final)	
29	Aston Villa	(H)

May

7	Portsmouth	(A)
13	FA Cup final	
17	UEFA Champions League final	
TBA	Arsenal	(H)
	Charlton Athletic	(A)

* All fixtures and dates are subject to change.

ANFIELD PAST AND PRESENT

There have been many changes around the fields of Anfield Road since Liverpool's formation in 1892. John Houlding owned the ground and established the club after Everton decided to move to Goodison Park over an increase in rent. From an original capacity of 20,000, the stadium now currently holds 45,522 – with this figure taking into account the press and disabled areas and all seating, some of which is not used due to segregation at the Anfield Road end.

THE KOP - Capacity 12,409

Built in 1906 after the Reds won the league championship for a second time. It was, of course, named 'Spion Kop' after a South African hill which was the scene of a bloody Boer War battle. In 1928 it was rebuilt and a roof was added with the capacity reaching close to 30,000 - the largest covered terrace in the Football League at that time. It was rebuilt in 1994 to its current splendour after an emotional 'last stand' against Norwich City.

CENTENARY STAND - Capacity 11,414

The original Kemlyn Road Stand incorporated a barrel roof and was fronted by an uncovered paddock. It was demolished in 1963 to make way for a new cantilever stand. In 1992 a second tier was added and the stand was renamed to mark the club's 100th anniversary.

MAIN STAND/PADDOCK - Capacity 12,277

The original structure was erected in the late 19th century, a 3,000-capacity stand with a distinctive red and white tudor style with the club's name in the centre. In 1973 it was redeveloped with a new roof and opened by HRH the Duke of Kent. Seats were added to the paddock seven years later.

ANFIELD ROAD - Capacity 9,045

In 1903 the first Anfield Road stand was built. Once a simple one-tier stand which contained a covered standing enclosure (1965), it was demolished to make way for a two-tier development in 1998 - the stand having been altered to accomodate seating in the early 1980s.

RECORD ANFIELD ATTENDANCES (Highs)

Overall: 61,905 v Wolves, 02/02/1952, FA Cup 4th round

League: 58,757 v Chelsea, 27/12/1949, Division 1
League Cup: 50,880 v Nottingham Forest, 12/02/1980, semi-final 2nd leg
Europe: 55,104 v Barcelona, 14/04/1976, Uefa Cup semi-final 2nd leg

RECORD ANFIELD ATTENDANCES (Lows)

Overall: 1,000 v Loughborough Town, 07/12/1895, Division 2
Record (post-war): 11,976 v Scunthorpe United, 22/04/1959, Division 2
FA Cup: 4,000 v Newton, 29/10/1892, 2nd Qualifying Round
FA Cup (post-war): 11,207 v Chester City, 09/01/1946, 3rd round 2nd leg
League Cup: 9,902 v Brentford, 25/10/1983, 2nd round, 2nd leg
Europe: 12,021 v Dundalk, 28/09/1982, European Cup 1st round, 1st leg

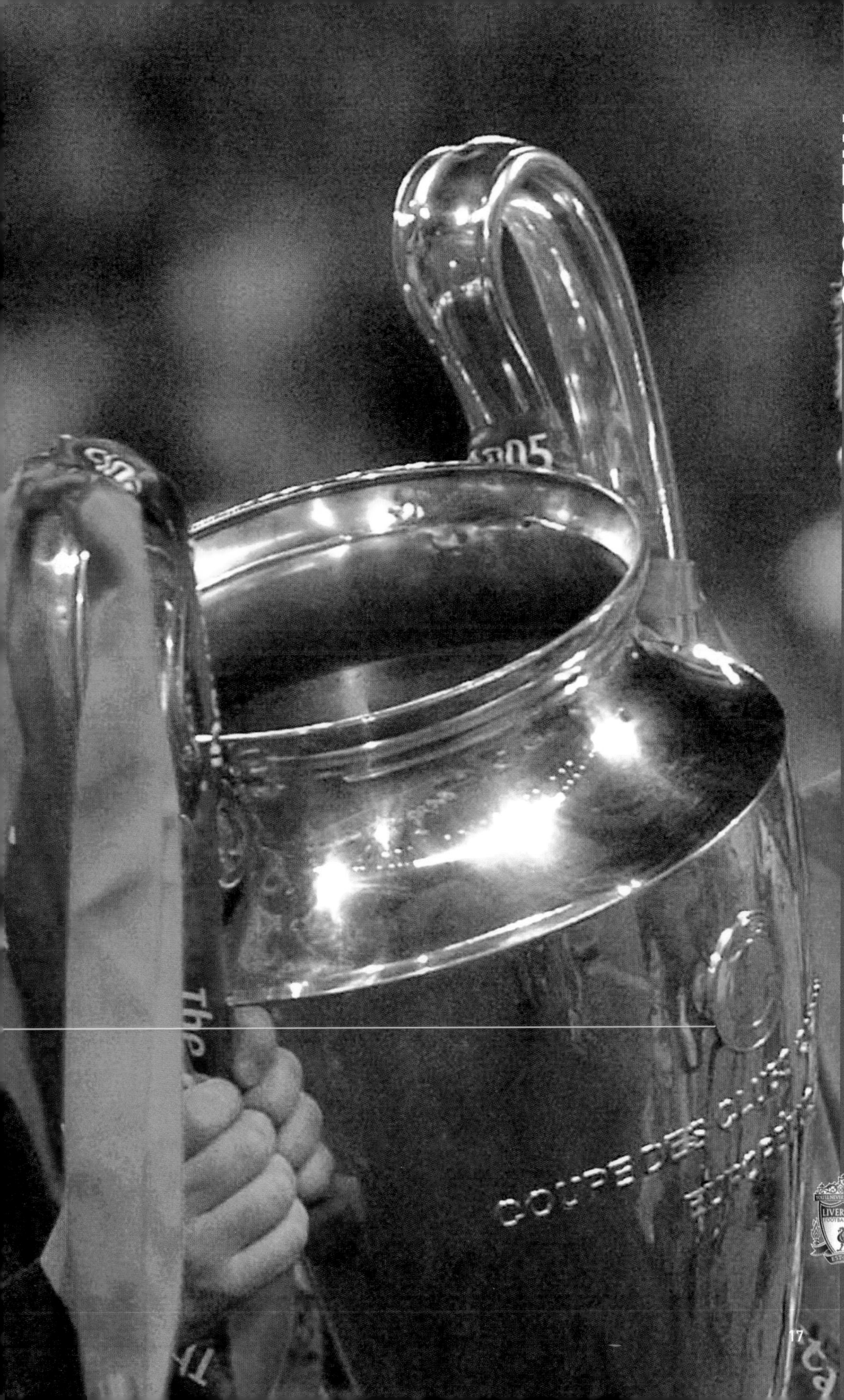
COUPE DES

LIVERPOOL'S MANAGERS

Liverpool have had 16 full-time managers. This figure does not take into account caretaker managers Ronnie Moran (who was in charge for 10 games following Kenny Dalglish's shock departure), and Phil Thompson (who spent just over six months in the role due to Gerard Houllier's illness).

Tom Watson oversaw the Reds' first championship success in 1900-01, Bill Shankly the first FA Cup triumph (1965), Bob Paisley the first League Cup success (1981) and European Cup win (1977) while Phil Taylor is the only Liverpool manager to have managed the club in Division 2 throughout his time in charge. Bob Paisley is the most successful in terms of silverware won, an impressive haul of 14 major trophies in nine seasons, although Kenny Dalglish, Liverpool's first player-manager, has the best win ratio - 60.91%.

The following list does not take into account W.E. Barclay (1892-1896), who was the secretary-manager of Liverpool while John McKenna was seen as the man in charge despite not holding down the official title of manager - in reality he performed many of the duties of the role.

RAFAEL BENITEZ	**June 2004-Present**
GERARD HOULLIER	November 1998-May 2004
ROY EVANS (joint manager with Gerard Houllier)	July 1998-November 1998
ROY EVANS	January 1994-November 1998
GRAEME SOUNESS	April 1991-January 1994
RONNIE MORAN (caretaker)	February 1991-April 1991
KENNY DALGLISH	May 1985-February 1991
JOE FAGAN	May 1983-May 1985
BOB PAISLEY	July 1974-May 1983
BILL SHANKLY	December 1959-July 1974
PHIL TAYLOR	May 1956-November 1959
DON WELSH	March 1951-May 1956
GEORGE KAY	May 1936-February 1951
GEORGE PATTERSON	February 1928-May 1936
MATT McQUEEN	February 1923-February 1928
DAVID ASHWORTH	December 1919-February 1923
TOM WATSON	August 1896-May 1915
JOHN McKENNA	August 1892-August 1896

RAFAEL BENITEZ'S RECORD

Few Reds fans could have expected the huge impact Rafa Benitez made at Anfield in his first season in charge. Appointed in June 2004 on the back of a trophyless campaign under Gerard Houllier, the likeable Spaniard immediately brought a new focus to the club. Despite a stuttering first campaign in the Premiership and FA Cup third-round disappointment as a much-changed Reds side went down at Championship side Burnley, the introduction of some much-needed flair courtesy of the likes of Xabi Alonso and Luis Garcia brought improvements which were felt in the other cup competitions - the Carling Cup and the UEFA Champions League.

Carling Cup final heartbreak, as Liverpool went down 3-2 after extra time to Chelsea in February had at least highlighted a battling spirit which would stand them in good stead for the UEFA Champions League resumption, the Reds having battled through to the last 16. Benitez, utilising his vast European knowledge gleaned through UEFA Cup success the previous season with Valencia, helped ease Liverpool past Bayer Leverkusen. Juventus were then installed as favourites to see off his side, but Benitez masterminded a famous 2-1 aggregate success. The 0-0 away result in Turin in the second leg came courtesy of Benitez's homework.

Premiership champions Chelsea were similarly undone, a 0-0 draw at Stamford Bridge the precursor to a 1-0 Anfield win in the return before THAT final in Istanbul against AC Milan - and ultimately European Cup glory for a fifth time. Benitez became the first manager to win the UEFA Cup and European Cup in successive seasons with different teams, and the second Liverpool manager after Joe Fagan to win Europe's premier trophy in his first season in charge.

The following statistics are a breakdown of Rafa Benitez's record in charge following his first campaign at the helm. Incidentally, the European Cup final triumph over AC Milan, despite the 3-3 scoreline (before Liverpool took the title on penalties), is recorded as an away win in the overall table, and a win in the other tables.

2004-2005 SEASON												
		HOME					AWAY					
	Pld	W	D -	L	F	A	W	D	L	F	A	GD	Pts
LEAGUE	38	12	4	3	31	15	5	3	11	21	26	11	58
FA CUP	1	-	-	-	-	-	0	0	1	0	1	-	-
LEAGUE CUP	6	2	0	0	3	0	3	0	1	7	4	-	-
CHAMPIONS LEAGUE	15	5	1	1	11	4	4	2	2	9	6	-	-
TOTAL	60	19	5	4	45	19	12	5	15	37	37	-	-

Season total:(all comps)					
Pld	W	D	L	F	A
60	31	10	19	82	56

RECORD IN ALL GAMES						
	Pld	W	D	L	F	A	Pts
LEAGUE	38	17	7	14	52	41	58
FA CUP	1	0	0	1	0	1	-
LEAGUE CUP	6	5	0	1	10	4	-
CHAMPIONS LEAGUE	15	9	3	3	20	10	-
TOTAL	60	31	10	19	82	56	-

Up to and including May 25th 2005

RAFA v THE REST

League success is often seen as the 'bread and butter', the indicator of domestic strength. Thus in analysing the influence of Rafa Benitez's impact at Anfield since taking over, we have utilised the league statistics of each of Liverpool's last eight managers, going back to Bill Shankly's first full season in charge.

Each of the seasons highlighted are that manager's first full campaign as boss, with Gerard Houllier, Roy Evans, Graeme Souness and Bill Shankly having first taken charge during the previous season. In this way we can give a fairer assessment of a manager's impact, marked by the '% Wins' column - which reflects the percentage of their games the team won in the league in that given season.

What the statistics do show is that the more settled a squad has been prior to a new manager's appointment, the greater the general level of success. The least successful, in terms of percentage of games won, Graeme Souness, was residing over a period of extreme change at Anfield while the more successful (Kenny Dalglish, Joe Fagan) made few changes to their squad prior to their first season in charge. Indeed, the figures show that Benitez is above only Souness in terms of his league record, although he achieved something Bill Shankly, Bob Paisley and Gerard Houllier failed to deliver in their first season - a major trophy.

BENITEZ 2004-2005   **(Premiership, three points for a win)**
TROPHIES WON   **European Cup**

LEAGUE RECORD								
Pld	W	D	L	F	A	Pts	Pos	% Wins
38	17	7	14	52	41	58	5th	44.74

Only five wins away from home ultimately proved the difference between 5th and a top-four finish, although a greater consistency in the League Cup and ultimate European glory showed positive signs for the future. However, only Graeme Souness achieved a lower league win ratio in his first season in charge.

HOULLIER 1999-2000   **(Premiership, three points for a win)**
TROPHIES WON   **None**

LEAGUE RECORD								
Pld	W	D	L	F	A	Pts	Pos	% Wins
38	19	10	9	51	30	67	4th	50

An impressive defensive record was the key difference in Liverpool's campaign (the best in the top flight that season), with the Reds just being pipped for a Champions League spot (only 3 teams qualified that season) by Leeds United. Having failed to qualify for European competition the previous season, there was disappointment in the domestic cups with a fourth-round defeat to Blackburn Rovers in the FA Cup (1-0 at Anfield) and in the third round at Southampton in the League Cup (2-1).

EVANS 1994-1995   **(Premiership, three points for a win)**
TROPHIES WON   **League Cup**

LEAGUE RECORD								
Pld	W	D	L	F	A	Pts	Pos	% Wins
42	21	11	10	65	37	74	4th	50

A first League Cup success in 11 years - Liverpool's fifth in the competition - was a satisfying start for Roy Evans, with a run to the quarter-finals of the FA Cup thrown in. Without European football that season, a return to UEFA Cup football would have been achieved through the league regardless of their cup success over Bolton Wanderers at Wembley.

RAFA v THE REST

SOUNESS 1991-1992 (Division 1, three points for a win)
TROPHIES WON FA Cup

LEAGUE RECORD								
Pld	W	D	L	F	A	Pts	Pos	% Wins
42	16	16	10	47	40	64	6th	38.10

With the lowest number of wins, the lowest win ratio and the least goals scored of the eight managers, 1991-1992 proved the least successful although despite this, Graeme Souness delivered the FA Cup - and with it qualification for the now defunct European Cup Winners' Cup. The Reds reached the last eight of the UEFA Cup, going down to Genoa although there was embarrassment in the League Cup, a 1-0 defeat at then Division 3 side (now League One) Peterborough.

DALGLISH 1985-86 (Division 1, three points for a win)
TROPHIES WON League title, FA Cup

LEAGUE RECORD								
Pld	W	D	L	F	A	Pts	Pos	% Wins
42	26	10	6	89	37	88	1st	61.90

Recognised as statistically the best first season of any Liverpool manager, Kenny Dalglish delivered the Reds' first-ever League and FA Cup Double with the most wins, best win ratio and highest number of goals scored. Everton were runners-up in both competitions, with the only 'shock' being a two-legged League Cup defeat to QPR in the semi-finals.

FAGAN 1983-84 (Division 1, three points for a win)
TROPHIES WON European Cup, League title, League Cup

LEAGUE RECORD								
Pld	W	D	L	F	A	Pts	Pos	% Wins
42	22	14	6	73	32	80	1st	52.38

An impressive haul of silverware ensures Joe Fagan as achieving the most of any Liverpool manager in his first season in charge, which culminated with European glory against Roma - in Rome. A fourth successive League Cup success (beating Everton in the final replay) and a third league title in a row were also delivered, with the only disappointment being an FA Cup fourth-round defeat at Division 2 (Championship) side Brighton.

PAISLEY 1974-75 (Division 1, two points for a win)
TROPHIES WON None

LEAGUE RECORD								
Pld	W	D	L	F	A	Pts	Pos	% Wins
42	20	11	11	60	39	51	2nd	47.62

The only season that Bob Paisley failed to deliver a trophy in his time in charge of Liverpool, Liverpool finished as runners-up behind Derby County (by two points), above Ipswich Town in third on 'goal average' as it was measured then, rather than goal difference. The cup competitions failed to yield much success too, with early-round defeats coming against Ferencvaros (European Cup Winners' Cup), Ipswich Town (FA Cup) and Middlesbrough (League Cup).

SHANKLY 1960-61 (Division 2, two points for a win)
TROPHIES WON None

LEAGUE RECORD								
Pld	W	D	L	F	A	Pts	Pos	% Wins
42	21	10	11	87	58	52	3rd	50

The only one of the managers who began their first full season in charge of Liverpool outside the top flight, Bill Shankly missed out on delivering promotion by six points, with only the top two being promoted (who that season were champions Ipswich Town and Sheffield United). There was little to celebrate in the domestic competitions, Shankly's Reds bowing out early on to Sunderland in the FA Cup and Southampton in the League Cup - both teams being in the same division as Liverpool that year.

SHANKLY v PAISLEY

Is it Bill or Bob? Being two of the most successful managers in the history of the game, arguments have raged for decades over the various merits of both parties. Who was the greatest Liverpool manager of all time?

From his appointment in 1959, Shankly led the Reds from Second Division obscurity to domestic and European success, laying the foundations of future glory at Anfield during nearly 15 years in charge, before stepping down in 1974.

Paisley meanwhile, groomed in the Boot Room philosophy started by the great man, is the most successful manager in Liverpool history in terms of honours scooped. Taking over from Shankly in 1974, the club failed to secure honours in his first season in charge – before leading them to a trophy in every season until his retirement in 1983, including six league championships and three European Cups.

So who's best – the Kop's messiah or Anfield's master tactician? You decide . . .

		HEAD TO HEAD					

BILL SHANKLY
BOB PAISLEY

	PLD	W	D	L	F	A	PTS
LEAGUE							
	609	319	152	138	1034	622	1109
	378	**212**	**99**	**67**	**648**	**294**	**735**
FA CUP							
	75	40	22	13	103	50	-
	36	**20**	**7**	**9**	**62**	**27**	**-**
LEAGUE CUP							
	30	13	9	8	51	35	-
	53	**32**	**13**	**8**	**98**	**31**	**-**
EUROPEAN CUP							
	18	8	5*	5	33	22	-
	41	**27**	**5**	**9**	**92**	**34**	**-**
EUROPEAN CUP WINNERS' CUP							
	13	6	2	5	16	11	-
	4	**2**	**2**	**0**	**13**	**1**	**-**
FAIRS CUP/UEFA CUP							
	34	20	6	8	65	21	-
	12	**8**	**3**	**1**	**25**	**9**	**-**
EUROPEAN SUPER CUP							
	-	-	-	-	-	-	-
	4	**2**	**1**	**1**	**10**	**5**	**-**
WORLD CLUB CHAMPIONSHIP							
	1	**0**	**0**	**1**	**0**	**3**	**-**
FA CHARITY SHIELD							
	4	1	2	1	5	5	-
	6	**5**	**1**	**0**	**7**	**2**	**-**
TOTAL							
SHANKLY	783	407	198	178	1307	766	-
PAISLEY	**535**	**308**	**131**	**96**	**955**	**406**	**-**

League Points are calculated as 3 points for a win
*Includes a replay decided by toss of a coin which is counted as a draw.

SHANKLY v PAISLEY

	PERCENTAGE WINS				
	LEAGUE	F.A. CUP	LEAGUE CUP	EUROPE	ALL GAMES
SHANKLY	52.39%	53.33%	43.33%	52.31%	51.98%
PAISLEY	**56.08%**	**55.56%**	**60.38%**	**63.93%**	**57.57%**

	AVE PTS PER LEAGUE GAME	AVE.GOALS PER LEAGUE GAME	
		(Scored)	(Conceded)
SHANKLY	1.82	1.7	1.02
PAISLEY	**1.94**	**1.7**	**0.78**

HONOURS WON

BILL SHANKLY	
FIRST DIVISION CHAMPIONSHIP:	1963-64, 1965-66, 1972-73
SECOND DIVISION CHAMPIONSHIP:	1961-62
FA CUP:	1965, 1974
UEFA CUP:	1973
FA CHARITY SHIELD:	1964 (shared), 1965 (shared), 1966

BOB PAISLEY	
FIRST DIVISION CHAMPIONSHIP:	1975-76, 1976-77, 1978-79, 1979-80, 1981-82, 1982-83
LEAGUE CUP:	1981, 1982, 1983
EUROPEAN CUP:	1977, 1978, 1981
UEFA CUP:	1976
EUROPEAN SUPER CUP:	1977
FA CHARITY SHIELD:	1974, 1976, 1977 (shared), 1979, 1980, 1982

WHO'S THE GREATEST?

In terms of trophies won, the unmatchable Paisley is the more successful, although the inspirational Shankly was a god-like figure to the fans at Anfield . . .

- Liverpool won nearly 4% more of their games under Paisley;
- Over 2% more FA Cup games were won under Paisley;
- Paisley enjoyed 17% more success in League Cup games;
- European success yielded an 11% greater success rate for Paisley;
- 0.12 more points were won under Paisley;
- Shankly's Liverpool averaged the same number of goals per league game as Paisley's men (1.7) - despite Shankly residing over more than 200 league matches more than Paisley;
- Liverpool under Paisley conceded less than goal a game on average (0.78) - compared to Shankly's 1.02.

THE SQUAD 2005/06
All statistics correct up until start of 05/06 season

Scott Carson

Position	Goalkeeper
Born	Whitehaven
Age (at start of 05/06)	19
Birth date	03/09/85
Height	6ft 3ins
Other clubs	Leeds United
Liverpool debut	05/03/05 v Newcastle United - Premiership
Liverpool appearances	5
Liverpool goals	0
International caps	0
International goals	0

Jerzy Dudek

Position	Goalkeeper
Born	Rybnik, Poland
Age (at start of 05/06)	32
Birth date	23/03/73
Height	6ft 2ins
Other clubs	Sokol Tychy, Feyenoord
Liverpool debut	08/09/01 v Aston Villa - Premiership
Liverpool appearances	173 + 1 as substitute
Liverpool goals	0
International caps	50
International goals	0

Chris Kirkland (on loan at West Brom)

Position	Goalkeeper
Born	Leicester
Age (at start of 05/06)	24
Birth date	02/05/81
Height	6ft 3ins
Other clubs	Coventry City
Liverpool debut	09/10/01 v Grimsby
Liverpool appearances	45
Liverpool goals	0
International caps	0
International goals	0

Jose Manuel Reina Paez

Position	Goalkeeper
Born	Madrid, Spain
Age (at start of 05/06)	22
Birth date	31/08/82
Height	6ft 2ins
Other clubs	Barcelona, Villarreal
Liverpool debut	-
Liverpool appearances	0
Liverpool goals	0
International caps	0
International goals	0

Antonio Barragan

Position:	Defence
Born:	Sevilla, Spain
Age (at start of 05/06)	18
Birth date	12/06/87
Height	N/A
Other clubs:	Sevilla
Liverpool debut	-
Liverpool appearances	0
Liverpool goals	0
International caps	0
International goals	0

Jamie Carragher

Position	Defence
Born	Bootle, Liverpool
Age (at start of 05/06)	27
Birth date	28/01/78
Height	6ft 1ins
Other clubs	-
Liverpool debut	08/01/97 (as a sub) League Cup
Liverpool appearances	344 + 16 as substitute
Liverpool goals	2
International caps	17
International goals	0

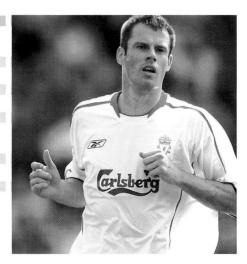

Steve Finnan

Position	Defence/Midfield
Born	Limerick, Republic of Ireland
Age (at start of 05/06)	29
Birth date	20/04/76
Height	6ft 0ins
Other clubs	Welling, Birmingham City, Notts County, Fulham
Liverpool debut	17/08/03 (as sub) v Chelsea - Premiership
Liverpool appearances	72 + 11 as substitute
Liverpool goals	1
International caps	36
International goals	1

Sami Hyypia

Position	Defence
Born	Porvoo, Finland
Age (at start of 05/06)	31
Birth date	07/10/73
Height	6ft 4ins
Other clubs	Pallo-Pelkot, Ku Mu, My Pa Anjalankoski, Willem II Tilburg
Liverpool debut	07/08/99 at Sheffield Wednesday - Premiership
Liverpool appearances	313
Liverpool goals	24
International caps	68
International goals	4

Jose Miguel Gonzalez Rey (Josemi)

Position	Defence
Born	Malaga, Spain
Age (at start of 05/06)	25
Birth date	15/11/79
Height	6ft 0ins
Other clubs	Malaga
Liverpool debut	10/08/04 at Graz AK
Liverpool appearances	19 + 4 as substitute
Liverpool goals	0
International caps	0
International goals	0

Carl Medjani (on loan at Metz)

Position	Defence
Born	Lyon, France
Age (at start of 05/06)	20
Birth date	15/05/85
Height	6ft 0ins
Other clubs	St Etienne, Lorient
Liverpool debut	-
Liverpool appearances	0
Liverpool goals	0
International caps	0
International goals	0

David Raven

Position	Defence
Born	Wirral
Age (at start of 05/06)	20
Birth date	10/03/85
Height	6ft 0ins
Other clubs	-
Liverpool debut	01/12/04 at Tottenham Hotspur - League Cup
Liverpool appearances	2 + 1 as substitute
Liverpool goals	0
International caps	0
International goals	0

Djimi Traore

Position	Defence
Born	Laval, France
Age (at start of 05/06)	25
Birth date	01/03/80
Height	6ft 3ins
Other clubs	Laval, Lens
Liverpool debut	14/09/99 at Hull City - League Cup
Liverpool appearances	104 + 13 as substitute
Liverpool goals	1
International caps (Mali)	2
International goals	1

Zak Whitbread

Position	Defence
Born	Houston, USA
Age (at start of 05/06)	21
Birth date	04/03/84
Height	6ft 2ins
Other clubs	-
Liverpool debut	26/10/04 at Millwall - League Cup
Liverpool appearances	4
Liverpool goals	0
International caps	0
International goals	0

Xabi Alonso

Position	Midfield
Born	Tolosa, Spain
Age (at start of 05/06)	23
Birth date	25/11/81
Height	6ft 0ins
Other clubs	Eibar, Real Sociedad
Liverpool debut	29/08/04 at Bolton Wanderers - Premiership
Liverpool appearances	27 + 5 as substitute
Liverpool goals	3
International caps	16
International goals	0

Bruno Cheyrou (on loan at Bordeaux)

Position	Midfield/Forward
Born	Suresnes, France
Age (at start of 05/06)	27
Birth date	10/05/78
Height	6ft 1ins
Other clubs	Lille, Marseille
Liverpool debut	11/08/02 (sub) v Arsenal - FA Community Shield
Liverpool appearances	28 + 20 as substitute
Liverpool goals	5
International caps	3
International goals	0

Salif Diao

Position	Midfield
Born	Kedougou, Senegal
Age (at start of 05/06)	28
Birth date	10/02/77
Height	6ft 1ins
Other clubs	Monaco, Epinal, Sedan, Birmingham City
Liverpool debut	28/08/02 (sub) at Blackburn Rovers - Premiership
Liverpool appearances	35 + 26 as substitute
Liverpool goals	3
International caps	39
International goals	4

Steven Gerrard

Position	Midfield
Born	Whiston, Merseyside
Age (at start of 05/06)	25
Birth date	30/05/80
Height	6ft 0ins
Other clubs	-
Liverpool debut	29/11/98 (sub) v Blackburn Rovers - Premiership
Liverpool appearances	257 + 26 as substitute
Liverpool goals	41
International caps	34
International goals	6

Dietmar Hamann

Position	Midfield
Born	Waldsasson, Germany
Age (at start of 05/06)	31
Birth date	27/08/73
Height	6ft 3ins
Other clubs	FC Wacker Munchen, Bayern Munich, Newcastle United
Liverpool debut	07/08/99 at Sheff Wed - Premiership
Liverpool appearances	230 + 21 as substitute
Liverpool goals	11
International caps	59
International goals	5

Harry Kewell

Position	Midfield/Forward
Born	Smithfield, Australia
Age (at start of 05/06)	26
Birth date	22/09/78
Height	5ft 11ins
Other clubs	Leeds United
Liverpool debut	17/08/03 v Chelsea - Premiership
Liverpool appearances	70 + 10 as substitute
Liverpool goals	12
International caps	17
International goals	5

Luis Javier Garcia Sanz

Position	Midfield
Born	Barcelona, Spain
Age (at start of 05/06)	27
Birth date	24/06/78
Height	5ft 10ins
Other clubs	Valladolid, Toledo, Tenerife, Atletico Madrid, Barcelona
Liverpool debut	29/08/04 at Bolton Premiership
Liverpool appearances	40 + 4 as substitute
Liverpool goals	13
International caps	1
International goals	0

Darren Potter

Position	Midfield
Born	Liverpool
Age (at start of 05/06)	20
Birth date	21/12/84
Height	6ft 1ins
Other clubs	-
Liverpool debut	10/08/04 (sub) at Graz AK - European Cup
Liverpool appearances	5 + 5 as substitute
Liverpool goals	0
International caps	0
International goals	0

John Arne Riise

Position	Defence/Midfield (L)
Born	Molde, Norway
Age (at start of 05/06)	24
Birth date	24/09/80
Height	6ft 1ins
Other clubs	Monaco
Liverpool debut	12/08/01 v Manchester United - FA Community Shield
Liverpool appearances	179 + 25 as substitute
Liverpool goals	22
International caps	43
International goals	4

Mohamed Sissoko

Position	Midfield
Born	Rouen, France
Age (at start of 05/06)	20
Birth date	22/01/85
Height	6ft 2ins
Other clubs	Auxerre, Valencia
Liverpool debut	-
Liverpool appearances	0
Liverpool goals	0
International caps (Mali)	N/A
International goals	N/A

Stephen Warnock

Position	Midfield
Born	Ormskirk, Lancashire
Age (at start of 05/06)	23
Birth date	12/12/81
Height	5ft 9ins
Other clubs	Bradford City, Coventry City
Liverpool debut	10/08/04 (sub) at Graz AK Champions League
Liverpool appearances	17 + 13 as substitute
Liverpool goals	0
International caps	0
International goals	0

John Welsh (on loan at Hull City)

Position	Midfield
Born	Liverpool
Age (at start of 05/06)	21
Birth date	10/01/84
Height	5ft 7ins
Other clubs	-
Liverpool debut	04/12/02 (sub) v Ipswich Town - League Cup
Liverpool appearances	3 + 7 as substitute
Liverpool goals	0
International caps	0
International goals	0

Boudewijn Zenden

Position	Midfield
Born	Maastricht, Holland
Age (at start of 05/06)	28
Birth date	15/08/76
Height	5ft 10ins
Other clubs	PSV Eindhoven, Barcelona, Chelsea, Middlesbrough
Liverpool debut	-
Liverpool appearances	0
Liverpool goals	0
International caps	0
International goals	0

Djibril Cisse

Position	Attack
Born	Arles, France
Age (at start of 05/06)	24
Birth date	12/08/81
Height	6ft 1ins
Other clubs	Auxerre
Liverpool debut	10/08/04 at Graz AK - Champions League
Liverpool appearances	14 + 11 as substitute
Liverpool goals	5
International caps	20
International goals	5

Peter Crouch

Position	Attack
Born	Macclesfield
Age (at start of 05/06)	24
Birth date	12/08/81
Height	6ft 7ins
Other clubs	Tottenham Hotspur, QPR, Portsmouth, Aston Villa, Norwich City, Southampton
Liverpool debut	-
Liverpool appearances	0
Liverpool goals	0
International caps	1
International goals	0

Robbie Foy

Position	Midfield/Forward
Born	Edinburgh, Scotland
Age (at start of 05/06)	19
Birth date	29/10/85
Height	5ft 11ins
Other clubs	Chester City
Liverpool debut	-
Liverpool appearances	0
Liverpool goals	0
International caps	0
International goals	0

Anthony Le Tallec (on loan at Sunderland)

Position	Forward
Born	Hennebont, France
Age (at start of 05/06)	20
Birth date	03/10/84
Height	6ft 1ins
Other clubs	Le Havre, St Etienne
Liverpool debut	13/09/03 (sub) at Premiership
Liverpool appearances	11 + 19 as substitute
Liverpool goals	1
International caps	0
International goals	0

Neil Mellor

Position	Attack
Born	Sheffield
Age (at start of 05/06)	22
Birth date	04/11/82
Height	6ft 0ins
Other clubs	West Ham United
Liverpool debut	04/12/02 v Ipswich Town
	- League Cup
Liverpool appearances	15 + 7 as substitute
Liverpool goals	6
International caps	0
International goals	0

Fernando Morientes

Position	Attack
Born	Caceres, Spain
Age (at start of 05/06)	29
Birth date	05/04/76
Height	6ft 2ins
Other clubs	Albacete, Real Zaragoza, Real Madrid, Monaco
Liverpool debut	15/01/05 v Manchester United - Premiership
Liverpool appearances	14 + 1 as substitute
Liverpool goals	3
International caps	38
International goals	25

Florent Sinama-Pongolle

Position	Forward
Born	Saint-Pierre, Reunion Islands
Age (at start of 05/06)	20
Birth date	20/10/84
Height	5ft 7ins
Other clubs	Le Havre (and on loan)
Liverpool debut	15/10/03 (sub) v Olimpija Ljubljana - Uefa Cup
Liverpool appearances	18 + 31 as substitute
Liverpool goals	6
International caps	0
International goals	0

SQUAD NUMBERS
2005/06

1 Jerzy Dudek
3 Steve Finnan
4 Sami Hyypia
6 John Arne Riise
7 Harry Kewell
8 Steven Gerrard
9 Djibril Cisse
10 Luis Garcia
14 Xabi Alonso
15 Peter Crouch
16 Dietmar Hamann
17 Josemi
19 Fernando Morientes
20 Scott Carson
21 Djimi Traore

22 Mohamed Sissoko
23 Jamie Carragher
24 Florent Sinama-Pongolle
25 Jose Reina
28 Stephen Warnock
30 Boudewijn Zenden
31 David Raven
33 Neil Mellor
34 Darren Potter
36 Antonio Barragan
37 Zak Whitbread
42 Robbie Foy

* (Correct as of 23/08/05).

Liverpool (v FBK Kaunas, Champions League qualifying round two, 02/08/05):
Top row, from left: Dietmar Hamann, Zak Whitbread, Mohamed Sissoko, Peter Crouch,
Fernando Morientes, Scott Carson. Front row, from left: Stephen Warnock, Luis Garcia,
Boudewijn Zenden, Sami Hyypia, Steve Finnan

RESERVES

RESERVES LEAGUE NORTH TABLE 2004/05

		Pld	W	D	L	F	A	Pts
1	Man Utd	28	19	6	3	68	23	63
2	Aston Villa	28	16	6	6	62	38	54
3	Man City	28	16	6	6	55	32	54
4	Blackburn	28	11	12	5	45	28	45
5	B'ham City	28	12	7	9	37	36	43
6	Wolves	28	9	9	10	32	32	36
7	Middlesboro	28	10	6	12	41	42	36
8	Everton	28	8	11	9	23	34	35
9	Sunderland	28	8	9	11	38	44	33
10	Bolton	28	8	9	11	32	41	33
11	West Brom	28	6	13	9	29	36	31
12	Newcastle	28	8	7	13	30	41	31
13	Leeds Utd	28	7	7	14	31	52	28
14	**Liverpool**	**28**	**6**	**8**	**14**	**27**	**47**	**26**
15	Notts Forest	28	5	6	17	21	45	21

RESERVES LEAGUE FIXTURES 2004/05

			Result*
09.08.04	Manchester City	H	0-1
18.08.04	Middlesbrough	A	0-1
01.09.04	Nottingham Forest	H	0-0
07.09.04	Blackburn Rovers	A	2-2
16.09.04	Sunderland	H	1-0
23.09.04	Birmingham City	A	1-2
30.09.04	West Bromwich Alb	H	4-1
04.10.04	Newcastle United	A	0-0
12.10.04	Everton	H	0-1
21.10.04	Manchester United	A	2-5
25.10.04	Bolton Wanderers	H	1-2
01.11.04	Aston Villa	H	1-6
15.11.04	Wolverhampton W	A	1-0
25.11.04	Leeds United	A	1-1
13.12.04	Nottingham Forest	A	2-1
24.01.05	Birmingham City	H	2-0
29.01.05	Aston Villa	A	0-4
02.02.05	Middlesbrough	H	2-1
07.02.05	West Bromwich Alb	A	1-3
14.02.05	Newcastle United	H	1-1
01.03.05	Manchester United	H	0-1
08.03.05	Bolton Wanderers	A	1-2
24.03.05	Everton	A	1-1
29.03.05	Wolverhampton W	H	0-2
06.04.05	Leeds United	H	0-1
14.04.05	Sunderland	A	0-0
18.04.05	Blackburn Rovers	H	2-0
26.04.05	Manchester City	A	0-5

* Liverpool score shown first

RESERVES APPEARANCES & GOALS 2004/05

	Appearances	Goals
Xabi Alonso	1	0
Paul Barratt	5	1
Igor Biscan	4	0
Chris Butler	2	0
Scott Carson	4	0
Salif Diao	1	0
Robbie Foy	14	3
Steven Gerrard	1	0
Danny Guthrie	10	0
Adam Hammill	2	0
Paul Harrison	14	0
Stephane Henchoz	3	0
Adam Hitchen	2	0
Stephen Hogg	1	0
Josemi	3	0
Harry Kewell	1	0
Chris Kirkland	3	0
Anthony Le Tallec	6	4
Patrice Luzi	7	0
David Mannix	22	0
Neil Mellor	11	7
Karl Noon	4	0
Antonio Nunez	4	0
Danny O'Donnell	19	0
Jon Otsemobor	14	0
Richie Partridge	18	2
Lee Peltier	4	0
Conal Platt	6	0
Florent Sinama-Pongolle	3	0
Mauricio Pellegrino	3	0
Darren Potter	20	1
David Raven	24	0
Vladimir Smicer	4	1
Danny Smith	3	0
James Smith	14	0
Mark Smyth	15	3
Phil Townley	4	0
Djimi Traore	4	0
Stephen Warnock	11	1
John Welsh	19	2
Zak Whitbread	23	1
Ryan Wilkie	16	0

FA PREMIER RESERVE LEAGUE NORTHERN SECTION FIXTURES 2005-06

AUGUST

16 Everton (H)
22 Newcastle United (H)
30 West Bromwich Albion (A)

SEPTEMBER

14 Wolves (H)
19 Bolton Wanderers (A)
27 Leeds United (H)

OCTOBER

19 Wigan Athletic (A)
25 Blackburn Rovers (H)

NOVEMBER

01 Manchester City (H)
08 Aston Villa (A)
23 Birmingham City (A)
29 Sunderland (H)

DECEMBER

05 Manchester United (A)
13 Everton (A)

20 Manchester United (H)

JANUARY

09 Newcastle United (A)
17 West Bromwich Albion (H)
24 Wolves (A)

FEBRUARY

02 Middlesbrough (H)
09 Bolton Wanderers (H)
22 Leeds United (A)

MARCH

01 Sunderland (A)
07 Wigan Athletic (H)
14 Manchester City (A)
23 Aston Villa (H)
28 Middlesbrough (A)

APRIL

04 Birmingham City (H)
10 Blackburn Rovers (A)

The Racecourse Ground: Where Liverpool will play their 2005-6 Reserve fixtures

THE ACADEMY

The Academy Director is Steve Heighway. Six players have graduated from the Academy to Melwood for the 2005/06 season under the wing of U18s coach John Owens. These are: U18 captain Danny O'Donnell, Lee Peltier and James Smith (defenders); Danny Guthrie and Ryan Wilkie (midfielders); and goalkeeper Paul Willis.

After an excellent 2004/05 campaign, 14 boys will begin a full-time scholarship having impressed for Dave Shannon's U16s side. Only five were offered such contracts 12 months ago.

FA PREMIER ACADEMY 2004/05 Group C

	P	W	D	L	F	A	Pts
1 Blackburn	28	19	4	5	57	24	61
2 Man Utd	28	17	6	5	61	41	57
3 Everton	28	14	9	5	46	34	51
4 Man City	28	13	10	5	66	37	49
5 Crewe	28	13	6	9	53	44	45
6 Stoke City	28	10	9	9	39	46	39
7 Wolves	28	8	13	7	38	39	37
8 Bolton	28	6	7	15	38	53	25
9 Liverpool	**28**	**5**	**7**	**16**	**24**	**52**	**22**

UNDER-18s' LEAGUE FIXTURES 2004/05

21.08.04	H	Crystal Palace	1-3
28.08.04	A	Charlton Athletic	1-2
4.09.04	H	Leeds United	0-3
11.09.04	A	Middlesbrough	1-0
18.09.04	H	Newcastle United	2-4
25.09.04	A	Nottingham Forest	2-1
2.10.04	A	Blackburn Rovers	1-3
9.10.04	H	Bolton Wanderers	1-0
16.10.04	A	Wolverhampton W	0-2
23.10.04	H	Manchester City	0-3
30.10.04	A	Everton	1-1
13.11.04	H	Crewe Alexandra	1-1
20.11.04	H	Manchester United	1-2
4.12.04	A	Stoke City	0-2
11.12.04	A	Manchester City	0-0
22.01.05	A	Crewe Alexandra	0-2
5.02.05	A	Manchester United	0-1
12.02.05	H	Stoke City	1-1
19.02.05	H	Blackburn Rovers	0-1
26.02.05	A	Everton	1-1
5.03.05	A	Bolton Wanderers	1-4
12.03.05	H	Wolverhampton W	1-3
19.03.05	H	Crewe Alexandra	4-4
31.03.05	H	Everton	2-1
2.04.05	A	Sunderland	0-2
9.04.05	H	Sheffield United	1-1
16.04.05	H	Barnsley	1-0
23.04.05	A	Sheffield Wed	0-4

UNDER-18s APPEARANCES & GOALS 2004/05

	Appearances	Goals
Chris Ashton	1	0
Mitchell Bailey	1	0
Charlie Barnett	4	0
Paul Barratt	26	2
Stephen Behan	3	0
Michael Burns	4	0
Luke Coleman	3	1
Robert Dalley	1	0
Stephen Darby	4	0
James Frayne	20	1
Danny Guthrie	24	2
Adam Hammill	21	2
Adam Hitchen	9	0
Jordan Holmes	5	0
John Paul Kelly	4	1
Paul Lancaster	11	0
Craig Lindfield	3	0
David Mannix	4	0
Josh Mimms	1	0
Karl Noon	24	7
Danny O'Donnell	23	2
Caleb Patterson	2	0
Lee Peltier	9	0
Conal Platt	17	4
Jonathon Pringle	5	0
Mark Roberts	2	0
Danny Smith	22	0
Francis Smith	7	0
James Smith	23	0
Jay Spearing	5	0
Robbie Threlfall	11	0
Phil Townley	18	0
Ryan Wignall	1	0
Ryan Wilkie	22	1
Paul Willis	14	0
Calum Woods	7	0
Lee Woodward	3	0

FA PREMIER ACADEMY LEAGUE
FIXTURES 2005-06

AUGUST

20 Cardiff City	(A)
27 Ipswich Town	(H)

SEPTEMBER

03 Middlesbrough	(A)
10 Leeds United	(H)
17 Huddersfield Town	(A)
24 Stoke City	(A)

OCTOBER

01 Everton	(H)
08 West Brom	(A)
15 Bolton Wanderers	(H)
22 Crewe Alexandra	(H)

NOVEMBER

05 Blackburn Rovers	(A)
12 Manchester United	(A)
19 Manchester City	(H)

DECEMBER

03 Wolves	(A)
10 Stoke City	(H)

JANUARY

07 West Brom	(H)
14 Bolton Wanderers	(A)
21 Crewe Alexandra	(A)

FEBRUARY

04 Blackburn Rovers	(H)
11 Manchester United	(H)
18 Manchester City	(A)
25 Wolves	(H)

MARCH

04 Everton	(A)	
08 Sheffield United	(A)	(A)
11 Derby County	(H)	
18 Sunderland	(A)	

APRIL

01 Sheffield Wednesday	(H)
08 Sheffield United	(A)
22 Nottingham Forest	(H)

All fixtures 11am,
subject to change.

FA WOMEN'S PREMIER LEAGUE
NORTHERN SECTION FIXTURES 2005-06

AUGUST

14 Curzon Ashton	(H)
21 Wolves	(A)
28 Newcastle United	(H)

SEPTEMBER

04 Lincoln City	(H)
07 Tranmere Rovers	(A)
18 Nottingham Forest	(H)
25 Stockport County	(A)

OCTOBER

02 Lincoln City	(A)
05 Tranmere Rovers	(H)
16 Middlesbrough	(A)
23 Aston Villa	(H)
30 Manchester City	(A)

NOVEMBER

13 Blackburn Rovers	(H)
20 Nottingham Forest	(A)
27 Stockport County	(H)

DECEMBER

11 Middlesbrough	(H)
18 Aston Villa	(A)

JANUARY

15 Manchester City	(H)
22 Blackburn Rovers	(A)
29 Curzon Ashton	(A)

FEBRUARY

05 Wolves	(H)
12 Newcastle United	(A)

Fixtures subject to change.

Play

10

Crisis? What crisis

Eeegor, Eeegor, Eeegor! Super Croat Igor Biscan rounds off the scoring, as the Reds hit back from two-down at half-time to win 4-2 at Fulham - their first away league win in 2004-05.

9

Happy Christmas

Stevie ignores the Boxing Day chill as the Reds hit five at West Bromwich Albion.

8 Rafa revealed

June 16, 2004. Alright, so this was before the season started but we had to mention the arrival of our new boss. Who knew back then what was to come. Ra-Ra-Rafa Benitez . . .

7

Derby delight

The skipper leads the way to open the scoring in the 2-1 win over Everton in March – sweet revenge for the defeat at Goodison Park.

Mellor shoots down Gunners

Neil Mellor's last-minute winner piles on the misery for the champions, as Arsenal's grip on the Premiership is loosened following Liverpool's 2-1 victory at Anfield.

Capital gain

Florent Sinama-Pongolle converts one of his two penalties (including in the shootout) as a youthful Reds side hold their nerve to knock Tottenham out of the Carling Cup quarter-final 4-3 on penalties.

4

Juve done it

From corners he will score some! Sami Hyypia wheels away after his goal stuns favourites Juventus in the Champions League.

3

Next stop Istanbul!

Is it over? No . . . yes . . . ! Luis Garcia shows his delight as his goal proves decisive in the Champions League semi-final with Chelsea at Anfield - as Claude Makelele ponders another appeal to the linesman.

2

You beauty!

Harry Kewell clings on after Steven Gerrard's superb strike keeps Liverpool's European dream alive against Olympiakos.

1

Turkish delight

The realisation of a dream, as Steven Gerrard holds aloft the European Cup following the dramatic penalty shootout victory over AC Milan in Istanbul. We've only won it five times!

Team line-ups

Grazer AK (4-5-1):

Kollmann

Pogatetz   Aufhauser   Muratovic
   Amerhauser   Skoro

Standfest   Tokic
   Ramusch   Ehmann

Schranz

Subs: Bazina (Skoro) 62, Sick (Aufhauser) 72, Dollinger (Amerhauser 81)
Subs not used: Almer, Majstorovic, Pirker Plassnegger

Liverpool (4-4-1-1):

Baros

Cisse

Kewell   Finnan
   Gerrard   Hamann

Riise   Josemi
   Hyypia   Carragher

Dudek

Subs: Diao (Baros) 73, Warnock (Gerrard) 80, Potter (Finnan) 85
Subs not used: Kirkland, Henchoz, Owen, Sinama-Pongolle

GRAZER AK 0
LIVERPOOL 2

**UEFA Champions League
Third Qualifying Round, 1st Leg.**
Tuesday, August 10 2004.
Attendance: 15,000

Goals: Gerrard (23, 79)
Bookings: Sick, Tokic (Grazer AK), Hamann (Liverpool)
Referee: Alain Sars (France)

Team line-ups

Liverpool (4-4-2):

Baros Cisse

Kewell Diao Gerrard Potter

Riise Hyypia Henchoz Carragher

Dudek

Subs: Warnock (Kewell) 59, Sinama-Pongolle (Cisse) 75, Hamann (Baros) 89
Subs not used: Harrison, Finnan, Biscan, Whitbread

Grazer AK (4-4-2):

Bazina Kollman

Amerhauser Plassnegger
Aufhauser Sick

Majstorovic Standfest
Pogatetz Tokic

Schranz

Subs: Muratovic (Plassnegger) 69, Dollinger (Majstorovic) 79,
Subs not used: Ramusch, Almer, Sencar, Hassler, Erkinger

LIVERPOOL 0
GRAZER AK 1

**UEFA Champions League
Third Qualifying Round, 2nd Leg,**
Tuesday, August 24 2004.
Attendance: 42,950

Goal: Tokic (55)
Bookings: Gerrard, Potter (Liverpool),
Aufhauser, Muratovic, Plassnegger, Pogatetz
(Grazer AK)
Referee: Luis Medina Cantalejo (Spain)

Team line-ups

Liverpool (4-4-1-1):

Cisse

Garcia

Kewell   Alonso   Gerrard   Finnan

Riise   Hyypia   Carragher   Josemi

Dudek

Subs: Baros (Cisse) 69, Warnock (Kewell) 76, Biscan (Garcia) 87
Subs not used: Kirkland, Diao, Hamann, Traore

Monaco (5-3-2):

Kallon   Adebayor

Farnerud   Perez   Squillaci

Evra   Maicon

Rodriguez   Zikos   Givet

Roma

Subs: Souleymane Camara (Evra) 46, El Fakiri (Givet) 80, Juan (Perez) 89
Subs not used: Audard, Modesto, Lacombe, Lescure

LIVERPOOL   2
MONACO   0

**UEFA Champions League,
Group A game 1,**
Wednesday, September 15, 2004.
Attendance: 33,517

Goals: Cisse (22), Baros (84)
Bookings: Gerrard (Liverpool), Givet, Zikos (Grazer AK)
Referee: Terje Hauge (Norway)

Team line-ups

Monaco (4-3-3):

Saviola

Chevanton   Nonda

Farnerud   Squillaci   Givet

Zikos   Evra
Maicon   Plasil

Roma

Subs: Perez (Chevanton) 67, Adebayor (Saviola) 73, Modesto (Farnerud) 79
Subs not used: Audard, Kallon, Oshadogan, El Fakiri

Liverpool (4-5-1):

Mellor

Riise   Garcia
Biscan   Gerrard

Hamann

Traore   Finnan
Hyypia   Carragher

Kirkland

Subs: Josemi (Garcia 4, Warnock 64), Kewell (Traore) 58
Subs not used: Dudek, Alonso, Diao, Sinama-Pongolle.

MONACO   1
LIVERPOOL   0

**UEFA Champions League,
Group A game 5,**
Tuesday, November 23, 2004.
Attendance: 15,000

Goal: Saviola (54)
Bookings: Traore, Hamann, Warnock (Liverpool)
Referee: Claus Bo Larsen (Denmark)

Team line-ups

Liverpool (4-4-2):

Baros Cisse

Riise
Alonso Hamann Garcia

Traore
Hyypia Carragher Josemi

Kirkland

Subs: Kewell (Riise) 66, Finnan (Cisse) 76, Sinama-Pongolle (Garcia) 84
Subs not used: Dudek, Diao, Biscan, Warnock

Deportivo (4-1-4-1):

Pandiani

Luque Valeron Duscher Mauro Silva

Victor

Capdevila Manuel Pablo
Andrade Cesar

Molina

Subs: Scaloni (Mauro Silva) 58, Romero (Pandiani) 82, Fran (Valeron) 86
Subs not used: Munua, Tristan, Munitis, Pablo Amo

LIVERPOOL 0
DEPORTIVO 0

**UEFA Champions League
Group A game 3,**
Tuesday 19 October 2004.
Attendance: 40,236

Bookings: Baros, Hamann (Liverpool), Andrade, Duscher, Luque, Victor (Deportivo)
Referee: Anders Frisk (Sweden)

Team line-ups

Deportivo (4-1-4-1):

Pandiani

Luque   Valeron   Duscher   Victor

Sergio Gonzalez

Hector   Romero
       Andrade   Cesar

Molina

Subs: Pablo Amo (Cesar) 45, Tristan (Pandiani) 59, Scaloni (Hector) 65
Subs not used: Munua, Fran, Munitis, Capdevila

Liverpool (4-4-1-1):

Baros

Kewell

Riise   Garcia
       Biscan   Hamann

Traore   Josemi
       Hyypia   Carragher

Kirkland

Subs: Finnan (Kewell) 58, Sinama-Pongolle (Baros) 84, Alonso (Garcia) 89
Subs not used: Dudek, Henchoz, Diao, Warnock

DEPORTIVO   0
LIVERPOOL   1

**UEFA Champions League
Group A game 4,**
Wednesday 3rd November 2004.
Attendance: 32,000

Goal: Jorge Andrade (og 14)
Bookings: Andrade, Cesar (Deportivo), Carragher, Hyypia (Liverpool)
Referee: Wolfgang Stark (Germany)

Team line-ups

Olympiakos (4-4-1-1)

Giovanni

Rivaldo

Georgatos Okkas

Stoltidis Kafes

Pantos Mavrogenidis

Schurrer Anatolakis

Nikopolidis

Subs: Venetidis (Mavrogenidis) 71, Georgiadis
(Giovanni) 71, Vallas (Georgatos) 84
Subs not used: Giannou, Castillo, Maric,
Kostoulas

Liverpool (4-4-1-1)

Baros

Garcia

Warnock Finnan

Alonso Hamann

Riise Josemi

Hyypia Carragher

Dudek

Subs: Kewell (Warnock) 46, Cisse (Josemi) 73,
Diao (Hamann) 82
Subs not used: Kirkland, Traore,
Sinama-Pongolle, Biscan

OLYMPIAKOS 1
LIVERPOOL 0

**UEFA Champions League,
Group A game 2,**
Tuesday, September 28, 2004.
Attendance: 33,000

Goals: Stoltidis (17)
Bookings: Anatolakis, Mavrogenidis, Schurrer,
Pantos (Olympiakos), Finnan, Warnock
(Liverpool)
Sent off: Pantos
Referee: Pierluigi Collina (Italy)

Team line-ups

Liverpool (4-4-1-1):

Baros

Kewell

Riise Nunez

Alonso Gerrard

Traore Finnan

Hyypia Carragher

Kirkland

Subs: Sinama-Pongolle (Traore) 46, Mellor (Baros) 78, Josemi (Finnan) 85
Subs not used: Dudek, Henchoz, Diao, Warnock

Olympiakos (4-4-1-1):

Giovanni

Rivaldo

Djordjevic

Stoltidis Georgiadis

Kafes

Venetidis Pantos

Schurrer Anatolakis

Nikopolidis

Subs: Rezic (Georgiadis) 70, Maric (Venetidis) 84, Okkas (Giovanni) 87
Subs not used: Giannou, Kouloucheris, Castillo, Vallas

LIVERPOOL 3
OLYMPIAKOS 1

**UEFA Champions League,
Group A game 6,**
Wednesday, December 8, 2004.
Attendance: 42,045

Goals: Rivaldo (26), Sinama-Pongolle (47) Mellor (81), Gerrard (86)
Bookings: Alonso, Carragher, Gerrard (Liverpool), Pantos, Schurrer, Anatolakis (Olympiakos)
Referee: Manuel Enrique Gonzalez (Spain)

LIVERPOOL 3
BAYER LEVERKUSEN 1

UEFA Champions League
last 16, first leg,
Tuesday, February 22, 2005.
Attendance: 40,942

Goals: Garcia (15), Riise (35), Hamann (90),
Franca (90)
Bookings: Dudek, Hamann (Liverpool), Freier,
Ponte (Bayer Leverkusen)
Referee: Kyros Vassaras (Greece)

Team line-ups

Liverpool (4-4-1-1):

Baros

Kewell

Riise · Garcia

Hamann · Biscan

Traore · Hyypia · Carragher · Finnan

Dudek

Subs: Le Tallec (Kewell) 77, Potter (Baros) 85, Smicer (Riise) 89
Subs not used: Carson, Nunez, Warnock, Welsh

Bayer Leverkusen (4-3-1-2):

Voronin · Berbatov

Krzynowek · Ponte · Freier

Ramelow

Placente · Callsen-Bracker · Schneider

Juan

Butt

Subs: Franca (Voronin) 68, Donovan (Ponte) 69, Bierofka (Freier) 83,
Subs not used: Starke, Fritz, Dum, Castro

Team line-ups

Bayer Leverkusen (4-3-1-2):

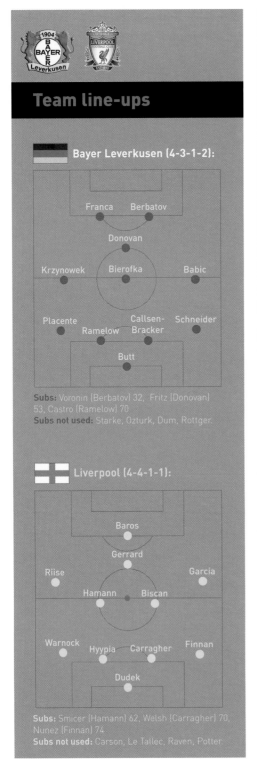

Franca Berbatov

Donovan

Krzynowek Bierofka Babic

Placente Callsen- Schneider
Ramelow Bracker

Butt

Subs: Voronin (Berbatov) 32, Fritz (Donovan) 53, Castro (Ramelow) 70
Subs not used: Starke, Ozturk, Dum, Rottger.

Liverpool (4-4-1-1):

Baros

Gerrard

Riise Garcia

Hamann Biscan

Warnock Finnan
Hyypia Carragher

Dudek

Subs: Smicer (Hamann) 62, Welsh (Carragher) 70, Nunez (Finnan) 74
Subs not used: Carson, Le Tallec, Raven, Potter.

BAYER LEVERKUSEN 1
LIVERPOOL 3

**UEFA Champions League
last 16, second leg,**
Wednesday, March 9, 2005.
Attendance: 23,000

Goals: Garcia (28, 32), Baros (67),
Krzynowek (88)
Booked: Bierofka (Bayer Leverkusen)
Referee: Alain Sars (France)

LIVERPOOL 2
JUVENTUS 1

**UEFA Champions League
quarter-final 1st leg,**
Tuesday, April 5, 2005.
Attendance: 41,216

Goals: Hyypia (10), Garcia (25), Cannavaro (63)
Bookings: None
Referee: Frank De Bleeckere (Belgium)

Team line-ups

Liverpool (4-4-1-1):

Baros

Le Tallec

Riise   Garcia

Biscan   Gerrard

Traore

Hyypia   Carragher   Finnan

Carson

Subs: Nunez (Baros) 66, Smicer (Le Tallec) 73
Subs not used: Dudek, Alonso, Warnock, Welsh, Potter

Juventus (4-4-2):

Ibrahimovic   Del Piero

Nedved   Emerson   Blasi   Camoranesi

Zambrotta   Zebina

Thuram   Cannavaro

Buffon

Subs: Pessotto (Blasi) 46, Trezeguet (Del Piero) 61, Montero (Zebina) 81
Subs not used: Chimenti, Appiah, Olivera, Zalayeta

67

Team line-ups

Juventus (4-4-2):

Del Piero Ibrahimovic

Nedved Emerson Olivera Camoranesi

Zambrotta Thuram

Montero Cannavaro

Buffon

Subs: Zalayeta (Olivera) 46, Pessotto (Montero) 83, Appiah (Camoranesi) 84
Subs not used: Chimenti, Birindelli, Blasi, Masiello

Liverpool (4-4-1-1):

Baros

Garcia

Riise Nunez

Biscan Alonso

Traore Finnan

Hyypia Carragher

Dudek

Subs: Smicer (Nunez) 58, Cisse (Baros) 75, Le Tallec (Garcia) 85
Subs not used: Carson, Warnock, Welsh, Potter

JUVENTUS 0
LIVERPOOL 0

**UEFA Champions League
quarter-final, 2nd leg,**
Wednesday, April 13, 2005.
Attendance: 55,464

Bookings: Emerson, Ibrahimovic, Montero,
Zambrotta (Juventus), Alonso, Finnan
(Liverpool)
Referee: Valentin Ivanov (Russia)

Team line-ups

Chelsea (4-3-3)

Drogba

Gudjohnsen   Cole

Tiago   Lampard
        Makelele

Gallas   Johnson
    Carvalho   Terry

        Cech

Subs: Robben (Tiago) 59, Kezman (Cole) 78
Subs not used: Cudicini, Smertin, Geremi,
Forssell, Huth

Liverpool (4-4-1-1):

Baros

Gerrard

Riise   Garcia
    Alonso   Biscan

Traore   Finnan
    Hyypia   Carragher

        Dudek

Subs: Cisse (Baros) 65, Kewell (Biscan) 86,
Smicer (Garcia) 90
Subs not used: Carson, Le Tallec, Nunez,
Warnock

CHELSEA   0
LIVERPOOL   0

**UEFA Champions League
semi-final, 1st leg,**
Wednesday, April 27, 2005.
Attendance: 40,497

Bookings: Cole, Kezman (Chelsea), Alonso,
Biscan (Liverpool)
Referee: Alain Sars (France)

LIVERPOOL 1
CHELSEA 0

**UEFA Champions League
semi-final 2nd leg,**
Tuesday, May 3, 2005.
Attendance: 42,529

Goal: Garcia (4)
Booking: Baros (Liverpool)
Referee: Lubos Michel (Slovakia)

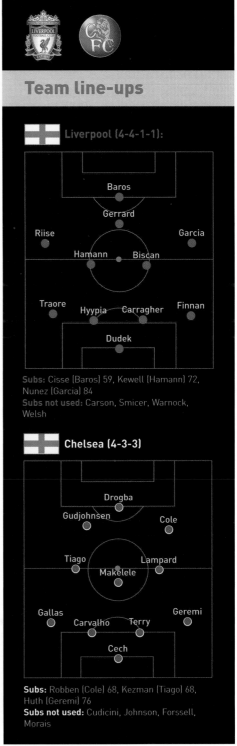

Team line-ups

Liverpool (4-4-1-1):

Baros

Gerrard

Riise   Garcia

Hamann   Biscan

Traore

Hyypia   Carragher   Finnan

Dudek

Subs: Cisse (Baros) 59, Kewell (Hamann) 72, Nunez (Garcia) 84
Subs not used: Carson, Smicer, Warnock, Welsh

Chelsea (4-3-3)

Drogba

Gudjohnsen

Cole

Tiago   Lampard

Makelele

Gallas   Geremi

Carvalho   Terry

Cech

Subs: Robben (Cole) 68, Kezman (Tiago) 68, Huth (Geremi) 76
Subs not used: Cudicini, Johnson, Forssell, Morais

Team line-ups

AC Milan (4-3-1-2):

Crespo Shevchenko
Kaka
Seedorf Pirlo Gattuso
Maldini Cafu
Nesta Stam
Dida

Subs: Tomasson (Crespo) 86, Serginho (Seedorf) 86, Costa (Gattuso) 111
Subs not used: Abbiati, Costacurta, Dhorasoo, Kaladze

Liverpool (4-4-1-1):

Baros
Kewell
Riise Garcia
Alonso Gerrard
Traore Finnan
Hyypia Carragher
Dudek

Subs: Smicer (Kewell) 23, Hamann (Finnan) 46, Cisse (Baros) 85
Subs not used: Carson, Biscan, Josemi, Nunez

AC MILAN   3
LIVERPOOL   3
(Liverpool win 3-2 on penalties)

UEFA Champions League Final, Istanbul
Wednesday, May 25, 2005.
Attendance: 65,000

Goals: Maldini (1), Crespo (39, 44), Gerrard (54), Smicer (56), Alonso (59)
Bookings: Baros, Carragher (Liverpool)
Referee: Manuel Enrique Mejuto Gonzalez (Spain)

EUROPEAN ROLL OF HONOUR

EUROPEAN CUP
WINNERS
1976-1977, 1977-1978, 1980-1981, 1983-1984, 2004-2005
RUNNERS-UP
1984-1985

UEFA CUP
WINNERS
1972-1973, 1975-1976, 2000-2001

EUROPEAN CUP WINNERS' CUP
RUNNERS-UP
1965-1966

WORLD CLUB CHAMPIONSHIP
RUNNERS-UP
1981, 1984

EUROPEAN SUPER CUP
WINNERS
1977, 2001
RUNNERS-UP
1978, 1985

EUROPEAN RESULTS

From Shankly's UEFA Cup in '73 to the magic of Rome '77 and Istanbul '05, Liverpool and Europe were destined to go together. With an unprecedented 10 major European trophies to our name, we remain the most successful British side in overseas competition. Apart from when English clubs were forced to sit out European competition, from the first participation in 1964-1965, the Reds have failed to qualify only three seasons since their first venture overseas.

Five European Cups, three UEFA Cups and two European Super Cup successes have been secured, while the unique atmosphere generated at Anfield during European nights has gone down in club folklore, from St Etienne during the 1976-1977 European Cup campaign to Olympiakos, Juventus and Chelsea last season.

The success in European competition has also brought about some notable scalps, as well as some impressive scorelines - including three matches where the Reds reached double figures. From the first taste of European Cup football under Bill Shankly, a 5-0 demolition of KR Reykjavik in August 1964, every result is listed in the following pages, including match details up to and including the memorable victory against AC Milan in Istanbul in May. All together now: 'We are the champions, champions of Europe!'

LIVERPOOL'S FULL LIST OF RESULTS IN EUROPE

Season	Round	Venue	Opponents	Opponent Country	Score	Scorers	Att
1964-65	EUROPEAN CUP						
17th Aug	1 Leg 1	(a)	Reykjavik	Ice	W 5-0	Wallace 2, Hunt 2, Chisnall	10,000
14th Sept	1 Leg 2	(h)	Reykjavik	"	W 6-1	Byrne, St John 2, Hunt, Graham, Stevenson	32,957
25th Nov	2 Leg 1	(h)	Anderlecht	Bel	W 3-0	St John, Hunt, Yeats	44,516
16th Dec	2 Leg 2	(a)	Anderlecht	"	W 1-0	Hunt	60,000
10th Feb	3 Leg 1	(a)	FC Cologne	W.Ger	D 0-0		40,000
17th Mar	3 Leg 2	(h)	FC Cologne	"	D 0-0		48,432
24th Mar	Replay	Rotterdam	FC Cologne	"	D 2-2	St John, Hunt	45,000
			(Liverpool won on toss of a coin)				
4th May	SF Leg 1	(h)	Inter Milan	Ita	W 3-1	Hunt, Callaghan, St John	54,082
12th May	SF Leg 1	(a)	Inter Milan	"	L 0-3		90,000
1965-66	EUROPEAN CUP WINNERS' CUP						
29th Sept	Pr Leg 1	(a)	Juventus	Ita	L 0-1		12,000
13th Oct	Pr Leg 2	(h)	Juventus	"	W 2-0	Lawler, Strong	51,055
1st Dec	1 Leg 1	(h)	Standard Liege	Bel	W 3-1	Lawler 2, Thompson	46,112
15th Dec	1 Leg 2	(a)	Standard Liege	"	W 2-1	Hunt, St John	35,000
1st Mar	2 Leg 1	(a)	Honved	Hun	D 0-0		20,000
8th Mar	2 Leg 2	(h)	Honved	"	W 2-0	Lawler, St John	54,631
14th Apr	SF Leg 1	(a)	Celtic	Sco	L 0-1		80,000
19th Apr	SF Leg 2	(h)	Celtic	"	W 2-0	Smith, Strong	54,208
5th May	Final	Glasgow	B. Dortmund	W.Ger	L 1-2 aet	Hunt	41,657
1966-67	EUROPEAN CUP						
28th Sept	Pr Leg 1	(h)	Petrolul Ploesti	Rom	W 2-0	St John, Callaghan	44,463
12th Oct	Pr Leg 2	(a)	Petrolul Ploesti	"	L 1-3	Hunt	20,000
19th Oct	Replay	Brussels	Petrolul Ploesti	"	W 2-0	St John, Thompson	15,000
7th Dec	1 Leg 1	(a)	Ajax Amsterdam	Hol	L 1-5	Lawler	65,000
14th Dec	1 Leg 2	(h)	Ajax Amsterdam	"	D 2-2	Hunt 2	53,846
1967-68	FAIRS CUP						
19th Sept	1 Leg 1	(a)	Malmo	Swe	W 2-0	Hateley 2	14,314
4th Oct	1 Leg 2	(h)	Malmo	"	W 2-1	Yeats, Hunt	39,795
7th Nov	2 Leg 1	(h)	TSV Munich 1860	W.Ger	W 8-0	St John, Hateley, Smith (pen) Hunt 2, Thompson, Callaghan 2	44,812
14th Nov	2 Leg 2	(a)	TSV Munich 1860	"	L 1-2	Callaghan	10,000
28th Nov	3 Leg 1	(a)	Ferencvaros	Hun	L 0-1		30,000
9th Jan	3 Leg 2	(h)	Ferencvaros	"	L 0-1		46,892
1968-69	FAIRS CUP						
18th Sept	1 Leg 1	(a)	Athletic Bilbao	Spa	L 1-2	Hunt	35,000
2nd Oct	1 Leg 2	(h)	Athletic Bilbao	"	W 2-1 aet	Lawler, Hughes	49,567
			(Liverpool lost on toss of coin)				
1969-70	FAIRS CUP						
16th Sept	1 Leg 1	(h)	Dundalk	Rep. Ire	W 10-0	Evans 2, Lawler, Smith 2, Graham 2, Lindsay, Thompson, Callaghan	32,562
30th Sept	1 Leg 2	(a)	Dundalk	"	W 4-0	Thompson 2, Graham, Callaghan	6,000
12th Nov	2 Leg 1	(a)	Vitoria Setubal	Por	L 0-1		16,000
26th Nov	2 Leg 2	(h)	Vitoria Setubal	"	W 3-2	Smith (pen), Evans, Hunt	41,633

Season	Round	Venue	Opponents	Opponent Country	Score	Scorers	Att
1970-71	FAIRS CUP						
15th Sept	1 Leg 1	(h)	Ferencvaros	Hun	W 1-0	Graham	37,531
29th Sept	1 Leg 2	(a)	Ferencvaros	"	D 1-1	Hughes	25,000
21st Oct	2 Leg 1	(h)	D. Bucharest	Rom	W 3-0	Lindsay, Lawler, Hughes	36,525
4th Nov	2 Leg 2	(a)	D. Bucharest	"	D 1-1	Boersma	45,000
9th Dec	3 Leg 1	(a)	Hibernian	Sco	W 1-0	Toshack	30,296
22nd Dec	3 Leg 2	(h)	Hibernian	"	W 2-0	Heighway, Boersma	37,815
10th Mar	4 Leg 1	(h)	Bayern Munich	W.Ger	W 3-0	Evans 3	45,616
24th Mar	4 Leg 2	(a)	Bayern Munich	"	D 1-1	Ross	23,000
14th Apr	SF Leg 1	(h)	Leeds United	Eng	L 0-1		52,577
28th Apr	SF Leg 2	(a)	Leeds United	"	D 0-0		40,462
1971-72	EUROPEAN CUP WINNERS' CUP						
15th Sept	1 Leg 1	(a)	Servette Geneva	Swi	L 1-2	Lawler	16,000
29th Sept	1 Leg 2	(h)	Servette Geneva	"	W 2-0	Hughes, Heighway	38,591
20th Oct	2 Leg 1	(h)	Bayern Munich	W.Ger	D 0-0		42,949
3rd Nov	2 Leg 2	(a)	Bayern Munich	"	L 1-3	Evans	40,000
1972-73	UEFA CUP						
12th Sept	1 Leg 1	(h)	E. Frankfurt	W.Ger	W 2-0	Keegan, Hughes	33,380
26th Sept	1 Leg 2	(a)	E. Frankfurt	"	D 0-0		20,000
24th Oct	2 Leg 1	(h)	AEK Athens	Gre	W 3-0	Boersma, Cormack, Smith (pen)	31,906
7th Nov	2 Leg 2	(a)	AEK Athens	"	W 3-1	Hughes 2, Boersma	25,000
29th Nov	3 Leg 1	(a)	Dynamo Berlin	E.Ger	D 0-0		19,000
13th Dec	3 Leg 2	(h)	Dynamo Berlin	"	W 3-1	Boersma, Heighway, Toshack	34,140
7th Mar	4 Leg 1	(h)	Dynamo Dresden	E.Ger	W 2-0	Hall, Boersma	33,270
21st Mar	4 Leg 2	(a)	Dynamo Dresden	"	W 1-0	Keegan	35,000
10th Apr	SF Leg 1	(h)	Tottenham H.	Eng	W 1-0	Lindsay	42,174
25th Apr	SF Leg 2	(a)	Tottenham H.	"	L 1-2	Heighway	46,919
10th May	F Leg 1	(h)	B. Moench'bach	W.Ger	W 3-0	Keegan 2, Lloyd	41,169
23rd May	F Leg 2	(a)	B. Moench'bach	"	L 0-2		35,000
1973-74	EUROPEAN CUP						
19th Sept	1 Leg 1	(a)	Jeunesse D'Esch	Lux	D 1-1	Hall	5,000
3rd Oct	1 Leg 2	(h)	Jeunesse D'Esch	"	W 2-0	Mond o.g., Toshack	28,714
24th Oct	2 Leg 1	(a)	R.S. Belgrade	Yug	L 1-2	Lawler	40,000
6th Nov	2 Leg 2	(h)	R.S. Belgrade"		L 1-2	Lawler	41,774
1974-75	EUROPEAN CUP WINNERS' CUP						
17th Sept	1 Leg 1	(h)	Stromsgodset	Nor	W 11-0	Lindsay (pen), Boersma 2, Thompson 2, Heighway, Cormack, Hughes, Smith Callaghan, Kennedy	24,743
1st Oct	1 Leg 2	(a)	Stromsgodset	"	W 1-0	Kennedy	17,000
23rd Oct	2 Leg 1	(h)	Ferencvaros	Hun	D 1-1	Keegan	35,027
5th Nov	2 Leg 2	(a)	Ferencvaros	"	D 0-0		30,000
1975-76	UEFA CUP						
17th Sept	1 Leg 1	(a)	Hibernian	Sco	L 0-1		19,219
30th Sept	1 Leg 2	(h)	Hibernian	"	W 3-1	Toshack 3	29,963
22nd Oct	2 Leg 1	(a)	Real Sociedad	Spa	W 3-1	Heighway, Callaghan, Thompson	20,000
4th Nov	2 Leg 2	(h)	Real Sociedad	"	W 6-0	Toshack, Kennedy 2, Fairclough Heighway, Neal	23,796

Season	Round	Venue	Opponents	Opponent Country	Score	Scorers	Att
1975-76	UEFA CUP (cont)						
26th Nov	3 Leg 1	(a)	Slask Wroclaw	Pol	W 2-1	Kennedy, Toshack	46,000
10th Dec	3 Leg 2	(h)	Slask Wroclaw	"	W 3-0	Case 3	17,886
3rd Mar	4 Leg 1	(a)	Dynamo Dresden	E.Ger	D 0-0		33,000
17th Mar	4 Leg 2	(h)	Dynamo Dresden	"	W 2-1	Case, Keegan	39,300
30th Mar	SF Leg 1	(a)	Barcelona	Spa	W 1-0	Toshack	70,000
14th Apr	SF Leg 2	(h)	Barcelona	"	D 1-1	Thompson	55,104
28th Apr	F Leg 1	(h)	FC Bruges	Bel	W 3-2	Kennedy, Case, Keegan (pen)	49,981
19th May	F Leg 2	(a)	FC Bruges	"	D 1-1	Keegan	33,000
1976-77	EUROPEAN CUP						
14th Sept	1 Leg 1	(h)	Crusaders	N.Ire	W 2-0	Neal (pen), Toshack	22,442
28th Sept	1 Leg 2	(a)	Crusaders	"	W 5-0	Keegan, Johnson 2, McDermott Heighway	10,500
20th Oct	2 Leg 1	(a)	Trabzonspor	Tur	L 0-1		25,000
3rd Nov	2 Leg 2	(h)	Trabzonspor	"	W 3-0	Heighway, Johnson, Keegan	42,275
2nd Mar	3 Leg 1	(a)	St Etienne	Fra	L 0-1		38,000
16th Mar	3 Leg 2	(h)	St Etienne	"	W 3-1	Keegan, Kennedy, Fairclough	55,043
6th Apr	SF Leg 1	(a)	FC Zurich	Swi	W 3-1	Neal 2 (1 pen), Heighway	30,500
20th Apr	SF Leg 2	(h)	FC Zurich	"	W 3-0	Case 2, Keegan	50,611
25th May	Final	Rome	B. Moench'bach	W.Ger	W 3-1	McDermott, Smith, Neal (pen)	57,000
1977-78	EUROPEAN CUP						
19th Oct	2 Leg 1	(h)	Dynamo Dresden	E.Ger	W 5-1	Hansen, Case 2, Neal (pen) Kennedy	39,835
2nd Nov	2 Leg 2	(a)	Dynamo Dresden	"	L 1-2	Heighway	33,000
1st Mar	3 Leg 1	(a)	Benfica	Por	W 2-1	Case, Hughes	70,000
15th Mar	3 Leg 2	(h)	Benfica	"	W 4-1	Callaghan, Dalglish, McDermott, Neal	48,364
29th Mar	SF Leg 1	(a)	B. Moench'bach	W.Ger	L 1-2	Johnson	66,000
12th Apr	SF Leg 2	(h)	B. Moench'bach	"	W 3-0	Kennedy, Dalglish, Case	51,500
10th May	Final	Wembley	FC Bruges	Bel	W 1-0	Dalglish	92,000
1977-78	EUROPEAN SUPER CUP						
22nd Nov	Leg 1	(a)	SV Hamburg	W.Ger	D 1-1	Fairclough	16,000
6th Dec	Leg 2	(h)	SV Hamburg	"	W 6-0	Thompson, Mc Dermott 3 Fairclough, Dalglish	34,931
1978-79	EUROPEAN CUP						
13th Sept	1 Leg 1	(a)	Nottingham Forest	Eng	L 0-2		38,316
27th Sept	1 Leg 2	(h)	Nottingham Forest	"	D 0-0		51,679
1978-79	EUROPEAN SUPER CUP						
4th Dec	1 Leg 1	(a)	Anderlecht	Bel	L 1-3	Case	35,000
19th Dec	1 Leg 2	(h)	Anderlecht	"	W 2-1	Hughes, Fairclough	23,598
1979-80	EUROPEAN CUP						
19th Sept	1 Leg 1	(h)	Dynamo Tblisi	Rus	W 2-1	Johnson, Case	35,270
3rd Oct	1 Leg 2	(a)	Dynamo Tblisi	"	L 0-3		80,000

Season	Round	Venue	Opponents	Opponent Country	Score	Scorers	Att
1980-81		EUROPEAN CUP					
17th Sept	1 Leg 1	(a)	Oulu Palloseura	Fin	D 1-1	McDermott	14,000
1st Oct	1 Leg 2	(h)	Oulu Palloseura	"	W 10-1	Souness 3 (1pen), McDermott 3, Lee, R.Kennedy, Fairclough 2	21,013
22nd Oct	2 Leg 1	(a)	Aberdeen	Sco	W 1-0	McDermott	24,000
5th Nov	2 Leg 2	(h)	Aberdeen	"	W 4-0	Miller o.g., Neal, Dalglish, Hansen	36,182
4th Mar	3 Leg 1	(h)	CSKA Sofia	Bul	W 5-1	Souness 3, Lee, McDermott	37,255
18th Mar	3 Leg 2	(a)	CSKA Sofia	"	W 1-0	Johnson	65,000
8th Apr	SF Leg 1	(h)	Bayern Munich	W.Ger	D 0-0		44,543
22nd Apr	SF Leg 2	(a)	Bayern Munich	"	D 1-1	R.Kennedy	77,600
27th May	Final	Paris	Real Madrid	Spa	W 1-0	A.Kennedy	48,360
1981-82		EUROPEAN CUP					
16th Sept	1 Leg 1	(a)	Oulu Palloseura	Fin	W 1-0	Dalglish	8,400
30th Sept	1 Leg 2	(h)	Oulu Palloseura	"	W 7-0	Dalglish, McDermott 2, R.Kennedy, Johnson, Rush, Lawrenson	20,789
21st Oct	2 Leg 1	(a)	AZ '67 Alkmaar	Hol	D 2-2	Johnson, Lee	15,000
4th Nov	2 Leg 2	(h)	AZ '67 Alkmaar	"	W 3-2	McDermott (pen), Rush, Hansen	29,703
3rd Mar	3 Leg 1	(h)	CSKA Sofia	Bul	W 1-0	Whelan	27,388
17th Mar	3 Leg 2	(a)	CSKA Sofia	"	L 0-2 aet		60,000
1982-83		EUROPEAN CUP					
14th Sept	1 Leg 1	(a)	Dundalk	Rep. Ire	W 4-1	Whelan 2, Rush, Hodgson	16,500
28th Sept	1 Leg 2	(h)	Dundalk	"	W 1-0	Whelan	12,021
19th Oct	2 Leg 1	(a)	JK Helsinki	Fin	L 0-1		5,722
2nd Nov	2 Leg 2	(h)	JK Helsinki	"	W 5-0	Dalglish, Johnson, Neal, A.Kennedy 2	16,434
2nd Mar	3 Leg 1	(a)	Widzew Lodz	Pol	L 0-2		45,531
16th Mar	3 Leg 2	(h)	Widzew Lodz	"	W 3-2	Neal (pen), Rush, Hodgson	44,494
1983-84		EUROPEAN CUP					
14th Sept	1 Leg 1	(a)	BK Odense	Den	W 1-0	Dalglish	30,000
28th Sept	1 Leg 2	(h)	BK Odense	"	W 5-0	Robinson 2, Dalglish 2, Clausen o.g.	14,985
19th Oct	2 Leg 1	(h)	Athletic Bilbao	Spa	D 0-0		33,063
2nd Nov	2 Leg 2	(a)	Athletic Bilbao	"	W 1-0	Rush	47,500
7th Mar	3 Leg 1	(h)	Benfica	Por	W 1-0	Rush	39,096
21st Mar	3 Leg 2	(a)	Benfica	"	W 4-1	Whelan 2, Johnston, Rush	70,000
11th Apr	SF Leg 1	(h)	D. Bucharest	Rom	W 1-0	Lee	36,941
25th Apr	SF Leg 2	(a)	D. Bucharest	"	W 2-1	Rush 2	60,000
30th May	Final	Rome	AS Roma	Ita	W 1-1 aet	Neal	69,693
		(Liverpool won 4-2 on penalties)					
1984-85		EUROPEAN CUP					
19th Sept	1 Leg 1	(a)	Lech Poznan	Pol	W 1-0	Wark	35,000
3rd Oct	1 Leg 2	(h)	Lech Poznan	"	W 4-0	Wark 3, Walsh	22,143
24th Oct	2 Leg 1	(h)	Benfica	Por	W 3-1	Rush 3	27,733
7th Nov	2 Leg 2	(a)	Benfica	"	L 0-1		50,000
6th Mar	3 Leg 1	(a)	Austria Vienna	Aut	D 1-1	Nicol	21,000
20th Mar	3 Leg 2	(h)	Austria Vienna	"	W 4-1	Walsh 2, Nicol, Obermayer o.g.	32,761

Season	Round	Venue	Opponents	Opponent Country	Score	Scorers	Att
1984-85	**EUROPEAN CUP (cont)**						
10th Apr	SF Leg 1 (h)		Panathinaikos	Gre	W 4-0	Wark, Rush 2, Beglin	39,488
24th Apr	SF Leg 2 (a)		Panathinaikos	"	W 1-0	Lawrenson	60,000
29th May	Final	Brussels	Juventus	Ita	L 0-1		60,000
1984-85	**EUROPEAN SUPER CUP**						
16th Jan		(a)	Juventus	Ita	L 0-2		60,000
1991-92	**UEFA CUP**						
18th Sept	1 Leg 1	(h)	Kuusysi Lahti	Fin	W 6-1	Saunders 4, Houghton 2	17,131
2nd Oct	1 Leg 2	(a)	Kuusysi Lahti	"	L 0-1		8,435
23rd Oct	2 Leg 1	(a)	Auxerre	Fra	L 0-2		16,500
6th Nov	2 Leg 2	(h)	Auxerre	"	W 3-0	Molby (pen), Marsh, Walters	23,094
27th Nov	3 Leg 1	(a)	Swarovski Tirol	Aut	W 2-0	Saunders 2	12,500
11th Dec	3 Leg 2	(h)	Swarovski Tirol	"	W 4-0	Saunders 3, Venison	16,007
4th Mar	4 Leg 1	(a)	Genoa	Ita	L 0-2		40,000
18th Mar	4 Leg 2	(h)	Genoa	"	L 1-2	Rush	38,840
1992-93	**EUROPEAN CUP WINNERS' CUP**						
16th Sept	1 Leg 1	(h)	Apollon Limassol	Cyp	W 6-1	Stewart 2, Rush 4	12,769
29th Sept	1 Leg 2	(a)	Apollon Limassol	"	W 2-1	Rush, Hutchison	8,000
22nd Oct	2 Leg 1	(a)	Spartak Moscow	Rus	L 2-4	Wright, McManaman	60,000
4th Nov	2 Leg 2	(h)	Spartak Moscow	"	L 0-2		37,993
1995-96	**UEFA CUP**						
12th Sept	1 Leg 1	(a)	S. Vladikavkaz	Rus	W 2-1	McManaman, Redknapp	43,000
26th Sept	1 Leg 2	(h)	S. Vladikavkaz	"	D 0-0		35,042
17th Oct	2 Leg 1	(a)	Brondby	Den	D 0-0		37,648
31st Oct	2 Leg 2	(h)	Brondby	"	L 0-1		35,878
1996-97	**EUROPEAN CUP WINNERS' CUP**						
12th Sept	1 Leg 1	(a)	MyPa 47	Fin	W 1-0	Bjornebye	5,500
26th Sept	1 Leg 2	(h)	MyPa 47	"	W 3-1	Berger, Collymore, Barnes	39,013
17th Oct	2 Leg 1	(a)	Sion	Swi	W 2-1	Fowler, Barnes	16,500
31st Oct	2 Leg 2	(h)	Sion	"	W 6-3	McManaman, Bjornebye Barnes, Fowler 2, Berger	38,514
6th Mar	3 Leg 1	(a)	Brann Bergen	Nor	D 1-1	Fowler	12,700
20th Mar	3 Leg 2	(h)	Brann Bergen	"	W 3-0	Fowler 2 (1 pen), Collymore	40,326
10th Apr	SF Leg 1	(a)	Paris St Germain	Fra	L 0-3		35,142
24th Apr	SF Leg 2	(h)	Paris St Germain	"	W 2-0	Fowler, Wright	38,984
1997-98	**UEFA CUP**						
16th Sept	1 Leg 1	(a)	Celtic	Sco	D 2-2	Owen, McManaman	48,526
30th Sept	1 Leg 2	(h)	Celtic	"	D 0-0		38,205
21st Oct	2 Leg 1	(a)	RC Strasbourg	Fra	L 0-3		18,813
4th Nov	2 Leg 2	(h)	RC Strasbourg	"	W 2-0	Fowler (pen), Riedle	32,426

Season	Round	Venue	Opponents	Opponent Country	Score	Scorers	Att
1998-99	**UEFA CUP**						
15th Sept	1 Leg 1 (a)		FC Kosice	Slovakia	W 3-0	Berger, Riedle, Owen	4,500
29th Sept	1 Leg 2 (h)		FC Kosice	"	W 5-0	Redknapp 2, Ince, Fowler 2	23,792
20th Oct	2 Leg 1 (h)		Valencia	Spa	D 0-0		36,004
3rd Nov	2 Leg 2 (a)		Valencia	"	D 2-2	McManaman, Berger	49,000
24th Nov	3 Leg 1 (a)		Celta Vigo	Spa	L 1-3	Owen	32,000
8th Dec	3 Leg 2 (h)		Celta Vigo	"	L 0-1		30,289
2000-01	**UEFA CUP**						
14th Sept	1 Leg 1 (a)		Rapid Bucharest	Rom	W 1-0	Barmby	12,000
28th Sept	1 Leg 2 (h)		Rapid Bucharest	"	D 0-0		37,954
26th Oct	2 Leg 1 (h)		Slovan Liberec	Cz Rep	W 1-0	Heskey	29,662
9th Nov	2 Leg 2 (a)		Slovan Liberec	"	W 3-2	Barmby, Heskey, Owen	6,808
23rd Nov	3 Leg 1 (a)		Olympiakos	Gre	D 2-2	Barmby, Gerrard	43,855
7th Dec	3 Leg 2 (h)		Olympiakos	"	W 2-0	Heskey, Barmby	35,484
15th Feb	4 Leg 1 (a)		AS Roma	Ita	W 2-0	Owen 2	59,718
22nd Feb	4 Leg 2 (h)		AS Roma	"	L 0-1		43,688
8th Mar	5 Leg 1 (a)		FC Porto	Por	D 0-0		21,150
15th Mar	5 Leg 2 (h)		FC Porto	"	W 2-0	Murphy, Owen	40,502
5th Apr	SF Leg 1 (a)		Barcelona	Spa	D 0-0		90,000
19th Apr	SF Leg 2 (h)		Barcelona	"	W 1-0	McAllister	44,203
16th May	Final	Dortmund	Alaves	Spa	W 5-4 aet	Babbel, Gerrard, McAllister (pen), Fowler, Geli o.g.	65,000
			(Liverpool won on golden goal)				
2001-02	**EUROPEAN CUP**						
8th Aug	Q. Leg 1 (a)		FC Haka	Fin	W 5-0	Heskey, Owen 3, Hyypia	33,217
21st Aug	Q. Leg 2 (h)		FC Haka	"	W 4-1	Fowler, Redknapp, Heskey, Wilson o.g.	31,602
			First Group Stage				
11th Sept	Group B (h)		Boavista	Por	D 1-1	Owen	30,015
19th Sept	Group B (a)		B. Dortmund	Ger	D 0-0		50,000
26th Sept	Group B (h)		Dynamo Kiev	Ukr	W 1-0	Litmanen	33,513
16th Oct	Group B (a)		Dynamo Kiev	"	W 2-1	Murphy, Gerrard	55,000
24th Oct	Group B (a)		Boavista	Por	D 1-1	Murphy	6,000
30th Oct	Group B (h)		B. Dortmund	Ger	W 2-0	Smicer, Wright	41,507
			Second Group Stage				
20th Nov	Group B (h)		Barcelona	Spa	L 1-3	Owen	41,521
5th Dec	Group B (a)		AS Roma	Ita	D 0-0		57,819
20th Feb	Group B (h)		Galatasaray	Tur	D 0-0		41,605
26th Feb	Group B (a)		Galatasaray	"	D 1-1	Heskey	22,100
13th Mar	Group B (a)		Barcelona	Spa	D 0-0		75,362
19th Mar	Group B (h)		AS Roma	Ita	W 2-0	Litmanen (pen), Heskey	41,794
3rd Apr	QF Leg 1 (h)		B. Leverkusen	Ger	W 1-0	Hyypia	42,454
9th Apr	QF Leg 2 (a)		B. Leverkusen	"	L 2-4	Xavier, Litmanen	22,500
2001-02	**EUROPEAN SUPER CUP**						
24th Aug		Monaco	Bayern Munich	Ger	W 3-2	Riise, Heskey, Owen	15,000

Season	Round	Venue	Opponents	Opponent Country	Score	Scorers	Att
2002-03	EUROPEAN CUP						
			First Group Stage				
17th Sept	Group B	(a)	Valencia	Spa	L 0-2		43,000
25th Sept	Group B	(h)	FC Basel	Swi	D 1-1	Baros	37,634
2nd Oct	Group B	(h)	Spartak Moscow	Rus	W 5-0	Heskey 2, Cheyrou, Hyypia, Diao	40,812
22nd Oct	Group B	(a)	Spartak Moscow	"	W 3-1	Owen 3	15,000
30th Oct	Group B	(h)	Valencia	Spa	L 0-1		41,831
12th Nov	Group B	(a)	FC Basel	Swi	D 3-3	Murphy, Smicer, Owen	35,000
2002-03	UEFA CUP						
28th Nov	3 Leg 1	(a)	Vitesse Arnhem	Hol	W 1-0	Owen	28,000
12th Dec	3 Leg 2	(h)	Vitesse Arnhem	"	W 1-0	Owen	23,576
20th Feb	4 Leg 1	(a)	Auxerre	Fra	W 1-0	Hyypia	20,452
27th Feb	4 Leg 2	(h)	Auxerre	"	W 2-0	Owen, Murphy	34,252
13th Mar	5 Leg 1	(a)	Celtic	Sco	D 1-1	Heskey	59,759
20th Mar	5 Leg 2	(h)	Celtic	"	L 0-2		44,238
2003-04	UEFA CUP						
24th Sept	1 Leg 1	(a)	Olimpija Ljubljana	Slovenia	D 1-1	Owen	10,000
15th Oct	1 Leg 2	(h)	Olimpija Ljubljana	"	W 3-0	LeTallec, Heskey, Kewell	42,880
6th Nov	2 Leg 1	(a)	Steaua Bucharest	Rom	D 1-1	Traore	25,000
27th Nov	2 Leg 2	(h)	Steaua Bucharest	"	W 1-0	Kewell	42,837
26th Feb	3 Leg 1	(h)	Levski Sofia	Bul	W 2-0	Gerrard, Kewell	39,149
3rd Mar	3 Leg 2	(a)	Levski Sofia	"	W 4-2	Gerrard, Owen, Hamann, Hyypia	40,281
11th Mar	4 Leg 1	(h)	O. Marseille	Fra	D 1-1	Baros	41,270
25th Mar	4 Leg 2	(a)	O. Marseille	"	L 1-2	Heskey	50,000
2004-05	EUROPEAN CUP						
10th Aug	Q. Leg 1	(a)	AK Graz	Aut	W 2-0	Gerrard 2	15,000
24th Aug	Q. Leg 2	(h)	AK Graz	"	L 0-1		42,950
			Group Stage				
15th Sept	Group A	(h)	AS Monaco	Fra	W 2-0	Cisse, Baros	33,517
28th Sept	Group A	(a)	Olympiakos	Gre	L 0-1		33,000
19th Oct	Group A	(h)	D. La Coruna	Spa	D 0-0		40,236
3rd Nov	Group A	(a)	D. La Coruna	"	W 1-0	Andrade o.g.	32,000
23rd Nov	Group A	(a)	AS Monaco	Fra	L 0-1		15,000
8th Dec	Group A	(h)	Olympiakos	Gre	W 3-1	Sinama-Pongolle, Mellor, Gerrard	42,045
22nd Feb	L. 16 L1	(h)	B. Leverkusen	Ger	W 3-1	Garcia, Riise, Hamann	40,942
9th Mar	L. 16 L2	(a)	B. Leverkusen	"	W 3-1	Garcia 2, Baros	23,000
5th Apr	QF Leg 1	(h)	Juventus	Ita	W 2-1	Hyypia, Garcia	41,216
13th Apr	QF Leg 1	(a)	Juventus	"	D 0-0		55,464
27th Apr	SF Leg 1	(a)	Chelsea	Eng	D 0-0		40,497
3rd May	SF Leg 1	(h)	Chelsea	"	W 1-0	Garcia	42,529
25th May	Final	Istanbul	AC Milan	Ita	W 3-3	Gerrard, Smicer, Alonso	65,000

(Liverpool won 3-2 on penalties)

LIVERPOOL'S EUROPEAN OPPONENTS

The break up of the former Soviet republics looms large in the opposition the Reds have yet to face in European competition. Nearly half of the countries Liverpool have yet to visit make up the number, although with their participation in the Champions League qualifiers, Wales (TNS) and Lithuania (FBK Kaunas) are two more countries crossed off the list.

The 19 countries the Reds have yet to visit in European competition are the following:

Albania, Andorra, Armenia, Azerbaijan, Belarus, Bosnia-Herzegovina, Croatia, Estonia, FYR Macedonia, Faroe Islands, Georgia, Israel, Kazakhstan, Latvia, Liechtenstein, Malta, Moldova, San Marino, Serbia and Montenegro.

In terms of most frequent opposition, Spanish (8), the former West German sides (7) and French clubs (6) are the most commonly visited, while Bayern Munich and Juventus are the most common opposition, having been faced four times each in competition (Bayern: 1970-71 Fairs Cup, 1971-72 European Cup Winners' Cup, 1980-81 European Cup, 2001-02 European Super Cup; Juventus: 1965-66 European Cup Winners' Cup, 1984-85 European Super Cup, 1984-85 European Cup, 2004-05 European Champions League). 'Big' clubs (in terms of competing in Europe on a regular basis) Liverpool have yet to face in European competition include: Manchester United, Arsenal, Lyon, PSV Eindhoven, Feyenoord, Lazio, Rosenborg, Sporting Lisbon, CSKA Moscow, Rangers and Fenerbahce.

Incidentally, the Champions League final against AC Milan in May 2005 saw Liverpool face the Italian side for the first time. The countries, and the clubs who Liverpool have faced (up to and including the 2005 Champions League final) are listed below and opposite:

AUSTRIA (3)
AK Graz, Austria Vienna, Swarovski Tirol.
BELGIUM (3)
FC Bruges, Anderlecht, Standard Liege.
BULGARIA (2)
CSKA Sofia, Levski Sofia.
CYPRUS (1)
Apollon Limassol.
CZECH REPUBLIC (1)
Slovan Liberec.
DENMARK (2)
Brondby, Odense.
ENGLAND (4)
Chelsea, Leeds United, Nottingham Forest, Tottenham Hotspur.
EAST GERMANY (2)
Dynamo Dresden, Dynamo Berlin.
FINLAND (5)
FC Haka , HJK Helsinki, Kuusysi Lahti, MyPa 47, Oulu Palloseura.
FRANCE (6)
Auxerre, Olimpique Marseille, Monaco, Paris St Germain, RC Strasbourg, St Etienne.
GERMANY (2)
Borussia Dortmund, Bayer Leverkusen.
GREECE (3)
AEK Athens, Olympiakos, Panathinaikos.
HOLLAND (3)
Ajax Amsterdam, AZ '67 Alkmaar, Vitesse Arnhem.
HUNGARY (2)
Ferencvaros, Honved.

LIVERPOOL'S EUROPEAN OPPONENTS

ICELAND (1)
Reykjavik.
ITALY (5)
Juventus, AS Roma, Genoa, Inter Milan, AC Milan.
LITHUANIA (1)
FBK Kaunas.
LUXEMBOURG (1)
Jeunesse D'Esch.
NORTHERN IRELAND (1)
Crusaders.
NORWAY (2)
Brann Bergen, Stromsgodset.
POLAND (3)
Lech Poznan, Slask Wroclaw, Widzew Lodz.
PORTUGAL (4)
Benfica, Boavista, FC Porto, Vitoria Setubal.
REPUBLIC OF IRELAND (1)
Dundalk.
ROMANIA (4)
Dinamo Bucharest, Petrolul Ploesti, Rapid Bucharest, Steaua Bucharest.
RUSSIA (3)
Dynamo Tblisi, Spartak Moscow, Spartak Vladikavkaz.
SCOTLAND (3)
Celtic, Hibernian, Aberdeen.
SLOVAKIA (1)
FC Kosice.
SLOVENIA (1)
Olimpija Ljubljana.
SPAIN (8)
Alaves, Atletico Bilbao, Barcelona, Celta Vigo, Deportivo La Coruna, Real Madrid, Real Sociedad, Valencia.
SWEDEN (1)
Malmo.
SWITZERLAND (4)
Servette Geneva, FC Sion, FC Zurich, FC Basel.
TURKEY (2)
Trabzonspor, Galatasaray.
WALES (1)
Total Network Solutions.
WEST GERMANY (7)
Bayern Munich, Borussia Moenchengladbach, Borussia Dortmund, FC Cologne, Eintracht Frankfurt, Hamburg, 1860 Munich.
UKRAINE (1)
Dynamo Kiev.
YUGOSLAVIA (1)
Red Star Belgrade.

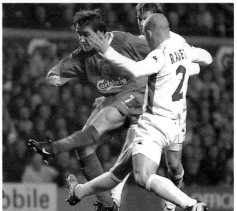

Liverpool in action against FC Haka, Auxerre and Valencia. The Reds have often faced Finnish, French and Spanish opposition

FROM TURF MOOR TO ISTANBUL . . .

From the instant the first ball was kicked to the moment Jerzy Dudek saved Andriy Shevchenko's penalty, the 2004/05 campaign was full of talking points. There were so many twists and turns over the course of a remarkable season. Each month in this section reflects the varying progress of the side in terms of league placing and results – with a Rafa soundbite thrown in for good measure. From the highs of Istanbul to the lows of Turf Moor, we take you back over the campaign – while the following list of off-field news may jog your memory. Did it really happen? Perhaps you'll believe now . . .

August
The 'will-he, won't he' saga dominates the press, concerning the future of Michael Owen at Liverpool. A non-playing substitute's role in the European Champions League qualifier at Graz AK indicates the desire of the club not to get the England striker cup-tied, and days later Michael leaves for the Bernabeu, with Antonio Nunez joining the Reds as part of the deal.
Incoming: Xabi Alonso (Real Sociedad), Antonio Nunez (Real Madrid)
Outgoing: Michael Owen (Real Madrid), Danny Murphy (Charlton Athletic)
Major injuries: Antonio Nunez (medial knee ligaments)

September
Xabi Alonso hails the "special atmosphere" of Liverpool following his Anfield move. Chris Kirkland claims that he would "play for free if it meant I could stay injury free." Rafa Benitez insists he is adapting well to the English climate, while Luis Garcia is delighted to be compared to Kenny Dalglish following an impressive display in the victory over West Bromwich Albion.
Major injuries: Steven Gerrard (broken metatarsal)

October
It is feared that summer signing Djibril Cisse will be out for the rest of the season after suffering a broken leg at Blackburn Rovers. Steven Gerrard and Milan Baros are in the top 35 players nominated for the FIFA World Player of the Year award, while former favourite David Fairclough believes the "future is very bright for Liverpool."
Major injuries: Djibril Cisse (broken leg)

November
Liverpool legend Emlyn Hughes passes away at the age of 57 from a brain tumour. The former Reds and England captain earned 62 caps, four league titles, two European Cups, two UEFA Cups and an FA Cup with the club during a distinguished career. Over 6,200 turn out at AFC Telford United's Bucks Head stadium to see Steven Gerrard make a winning comeback from injury for the reserves against Wolves.
Major injuries: Luis Garcia, Milan Baros (both hamstring)

December
Djibril Cisse reveals that he could have lost a leg, such was the seriousness of his injury suffered at Blackburn Rovers in October. Alan Hansen backs Rafa to be a big success, while the club confirm they are keen to keep Dietmar Hamann, the German midfielder's contract being due to expire in the summer. The 1-1 draw with Portsmouth prompts Rafa to demand more goals from his side, while Liverpool, along with the other Premiership clubs, donate £50,000 to the Tsunami Appeal.
Major injuries: Harry Kewell (pulled groin), Josemi (knee), Chris Kirkland (back)

January

The FA Cup third-round tie at Burnley is postponed less than an hour before kick-off due to the state of the Turf Moor pitch, a much-changed Reds side going out in the rearranged match. For now. Young midfielder John Welsh is rewarded with a contract extension until the summer of 2007.
Incoming: Fernando Morientes (Real Madrid), Scott Carson (Leeds United), Mauricio Pellegrino (Valencia), Anthony Le Tallec (recalled from loan at St Etienne)
Outgoing: Stephane Henchoz (Celtic), Salif Diao (Birmingham City, loan)
Major injuries: Xabi Alonso (broken ankle), Florent Sinama-Pongolle (anterior cruciate ligaments), Sami Hyypia (hip)

February

Chief executive Rick Parry insists any bid for Steven Gerrard - even of £50m - would be rejected in the summer. Gerrard plays for a European side who are beaten 6-3 by the Rest of the World in a Tsunami Charity match in Barcelona. Rafael Benitez hails new striker Fernando Morientes following his first goal for the club, against Fulham, while Anthony Le Tallec admits he made a mistake in requesting a loan move last summer. Young midfielder David Mannix signs a new two-and-a-half year deal and Jamie Carragher reveals his pride after being named Liverpool Echo Merseyside Sports Personality of the Year.

March

The Easter Sunday 'Tsunami Soccer Aid' match, which former Reds players Jason McAteer and David Johnson helped organise, proves a huge success with over 39,000 turning out at Anfield to see a Liverpool legends side - with Jan Molby on top form - see off a celebrity outfit. Meanwhile, Steven Gerrard pledges his future to the club in the wake of continued speculation linking the Reds captain with a move - while Rafa Benitez (who is pictured in a pub with fans the night before the European Cup clash with Bayer Leverkusen in Germany) doing likewise, dismissing speculation of a move to Madrid.
Major Injuries: Fernando Morientes (thigh), Dietmar Hamann (knee), Stephen Warnock (ankle), Neil Mellor (tendonitis)

April

Mrs Montse Benitez, Rafa's wife, has a premonition that Liverpool will win the European Cup. It's not to be taken lightly as it is revealed that Rafa's better half also had similar premonitions in the lead-up to her husband's La Liga and Uefa Cup triumphs when in charge of Valencia. The club and its fans are praised by Uefa for their handling of the first competitive meeting against Juventus since Heysel. Steven Gerrard is nominated for the PFA Player of the Year award and is selected in the PFA Team of the Year, while Djibril Cisse returns following his horrific injury suffered at Blackburn Rovers last October. The FA requests a fifth Champions League spot for English teams should Liverpool win the European Cup.
Major injuries: Steven Gerrard (groin)

May

Along with the small matter of Istanbul, Alan Hansen went on record as saying that he believes Jamie Carragher is 'ten times a better defender than I ever was'. The debate is started over a possible fifth European Cup spot for Liverpool with Everton clinching the final Champions League qualifying place in the league.
Outgoing: Vladimir Smicer (Bordeaux), Mauricio Pellegrino, Paul Harrison, Richie Partridge, Jon Otsemobor, Mark Smyth (all released)

AUGUST

THE GAMES

10	Grazer AK	A	2-0	(Gerrard 2)
14	Tottenham	A	1-1	(Cisse)
21	Man. City	H	2-1	(Baros, Gerrard)
24	Grazer AK	H	0-1	
29	Bolton	A	0-1	

WHERE THEY STOOD

9	Crystal Palace
10	Fulham
11	**Liverpool**
12	Manchester City
13	Norwich
14	Portsmouth
15	Tottenham

RAFA SAYS . . .

'Michael is not here anymore, it is better to talk about the players we do have'

SEPTEMBER

THE GAMES

11	West Brom	H	3-0	(Gerrard, Finnan, Garcia)
15	AS Monaco	H	2-0	(Cisse, Baros)
20	Man. Utd.	A	1-2	(O'Shea o.g.)
25	Norwich	H	3-0	(Baros, Garcia, Cisse)
28	Olympiakos	A	0-1	

WHERE THEY STOOD

9	Newcastle
10	Charlton
11	Manchester City
12	Liverpool
13	Portsmouth
14	Birmingham
15	Fulham

RAFA SAYS . . .

'We have made a step forward and there are a lot of bigger steps to go'

OCTOBER

THE GAMES

3	Chelsea	A	0-1	
16	Fulham	A	4-2	(Knight o.g., Baros, Alonso, Biscan)
19	**Deportivo**	**H**	**0-0**	
23	Charlton	H	2-0	(Riise, Garcia)
26	Millwall	A	3-0	(Diao, Baros 2)
30	Blackburn	A	2-2	(Riise, Baros)

WHERE THEY STOOD

1	Arsenal
2	Chelsea
3	Everton
4	Bolton
5	Middlesbrough
6	Manchester United
7	**Liverpool**

RAFA SAYS . . .

'I am pleased with the way we have kept possession and controlled the play against Fulham and Deportivo La Coruna'

NOVEMBER

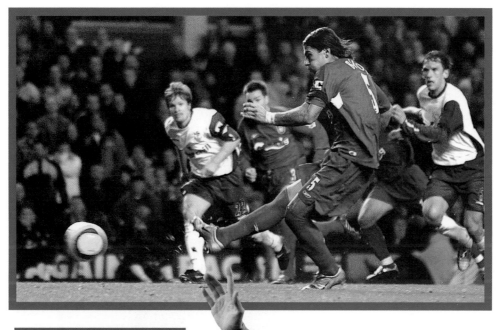

THE GAMES

3	**Deportivo**	**A**	**1-0**	(Andrade o.g.)
6	Birmingham	H	0-1	
10	M'boro	H	2-0	(Mellor 2)
13	Crystal P	H	3-2	(Baros 3)
20	M'boro	A	0-2	
23	**Monaco**	**A**	**0-1**	
28	Arsenal	H	2-1	(Alonso, Mellor)

WHERE THEY STOOD

1	Chelsea
2	Arsenal
3	Everton
4	Middlesbrough
5	Aston Villa
6	Manchester United
7	Bolton
8	**Liverpool**

RAFA SAYS . . .

'We seem to be losing strikers and wingers in each game at the moment'

DECEMBER

THE GAMES

1	Tottenham	A	1-1*aet	(S-Pongolle)
				*Liverpool win 4-3 on penalties
4	Aston Villa	A	1-1	(Kewell)
8	Olympiakos	H	3-1	(S-Pongolle, Mellor, Gerrard)
11	Everton	A	0-1	
14	Portsmouth	H	1-1	(Gerrard)
19	Newcastle	H	3-1	(Bramble o.g., Mellor, Baros)
26	West Brom	A	5-0	(Riise 2, S-Pongolle, Gerrard, Garcia)
28	Southampton	H	1-0	(S-Pongolle)

WHERE THEY STOOD

1	Chelsea
2	Arsenal
3	Everton
4	Manchester United
5	Middlesbrough
6	Liverpool
7	Charlton

RAFA SAYS . . .

'Where possible, I have tried to make use of the whole squad and that will be important at this time of year'

JANUARY

THE GAMES

1	Chelsea	H	0-1	
3	Norwich	A	2-1	(Garcia, Riise)
11	Watford	H	1-0	(Gerrard)
15	Man. Utd.	H	0-1	
18	Burnley	A	0-1	
22	Southampton	A	0-2	
25	Watford	A	1-0	(Gerrard)

WHERE THEY STOOD

1	Chelsea
2	Arsenal
3	Manchester United
4	Everton
5	**Liverpool**
6	Middlesbrough
7	Tottenham

RAFA SAYS . . .

'It is our idea to play as well as we did against Arsenal and Chelsea. These games are our reference'

FEBRUARY

THE GAMES

1	Charlton	A	2-1	(Morientes, Riise)
5	Fulham	H	3-1	(Morientes, Hyypia, Baros)
12	Birmingham	A	0-2	
22	**B.Leverkusen**	**H**	**3-1**	(Garcia, Riise, Hamann)
27	Chelsea	N	2-3	(Riise, Nunez)

WHERE THEY STOOD

1	Chelsea
2	Arsenal
3	Manchester United
4	Everton
5	**Liverpool**
6	Middlesbrough
7	Bolton

RAFA SAYS . . .

'I told the players that when I took on this job I took it as a challenge. I didn't come to earn money'

MARCH

THE GAMES

5	Newcastle	A	0-1	
9	**B.Leverkusen**	**A**	**3-1**	(Garcia 2, Baros)
16	Blackburn	H	0-0	
20	Everton	H	2-1	(Gerrard, Garcia)

WHERE THEY STOOD

1	Chelsea
2	Arsenal
3	Manchester United
4	Everton
5	**Liverpool**
6	Bolton
7	Middlesbrough

RAFA SAYS . . .

'This was a very satisfying win. We know how important the derby is ... once again our fans were magnificent'

APRIL

THE GAMES

2	Bolton	H	1-0	(Biscan)
5	Juventus	H	2-1	(Hyypia, Garcia)
9	Man. City	A	0-1	
13	Juventus	H	0-0	
16	Tottenham	H	2-2	(Garcia, Hyypia)
20	Portsmouth	A	2-1	(Morientes, Garcia)
23	C. Palace	A	0-1	
27	Chelsea	A	0-0	
30	M'boro	H	1-1	(Gerrard)

WHERE THEY STOOD

1	Chelsea
2	Arsenal
3	Manchester United
4	Everton
5	Liverpool
6	Bolton
7	Middlesbrough

RAFA SAYS . . .

'I always want to be positive but after the Palace game, I was frustrated by our inconsistency'

MAY

THE GAMES

3	Chelsea	H	1-0	(Garcia)
8	Arsenal	A	1-3	(Gerrard)
15	Aston Villa	H	2-1	(Cisse 2)
25	AC Milan	N	3-3*aet	(Gerrard, Smicer, Alonso)

*Liverpool win 3-2 on penalties

WHERE THEY FINISHED

1 Chelsea
2 Arsenal
3 Manchester United
4 Everton
5 **Liverpool**
6 Bolton
7 Middlesbrough

RAFA SAYS . . .

'I don't have words to express what I feel at the moment ... but the players believed and we won'

2004/05

■ Game played ▯ Goal scored
■ Substitute ■ Substituted player
■ Unused sub

Players (columns):
1 Jerzy Dudek · 3 Steve Finnan · 4 Sami Hyypia · 5 Milan Baros · 6 John Arne Riise · 7 Harry Kewell · 8 Steven Gerrard · 9 Djibril Cisse · 10 Luis Garcia · 11 Vladimir Smicer · 12 Mauricio Pellegrino · 13 Anthony Le Tallec · 14 Xabi Alonso · 16 Dietmar Hamann · 17 Josemi · 18 Antonio Nunez · 19 Fernando Morientes · 20 Scott Carson · 21 Djimi Traore · 22 Chris Kirkland · 23 Jamie Carragher · 24 Florent Sinama-Pongolle · 25 Igor Biscan · 26 Richie Partridge · 28 Stephen Warnock · 29 Patrice Luzi

DATE	OPPONENTS		RES	ATT
AUGUST				
10	Grazer AK (CLQ1)	A	2-0	15,000
14	Tottenham	A	1-1	35,105
21	**Man City**	H	**2-1**	42,831
24	Grazer AK (CLQ2)	H	0-1	42,950
29	Bolton	A	0-1	27,880
SEPTEMBER				
11	**West Brom**	H	**3-0**	42,947
15	AS Monaco (CL)	H	2-0	33,517
20	Man Utd	A	1-2*	67,857
25	**Norwich City**	H	**3-0**	43,152
28	Olympiakos (CL)	A	0-1	33,000
OCTOBER				
3	Chelsea	A	0-1	42,028
16	Fulham	A	4-2*	21,884
19	Deportivo (CL)	H	0-0	40,236
23	**Charlton**	H	**2-0**	41,625
26	Millwall (C Cup 3rd rd)	A	3-0	17,655
30	Blackburn	A	2-2	26,314
NOVEMBER				
3	Deportivo (CL)	A	1-0*	32,000
6	**Birmingham**	A	**0-1**	42,669
10	**M'Boro (C Cup 4th)**	H	**2-0**	28,176
13	**Crystal Palace**	H	**3-2**	42,862
20	Middlesbrough	A	0-2	34,752
23	Monaco (CL)	A	0-1	15,000
28	**Arsenal**	H	**2-1**	43,730
DECEMBER				
1	Tottenham (C Cup QF)	A	1-1†	36,100
4	Aston Villa	A	1-1	42,593
8	Olympiakos (CL)	H	3-1	42,045
11	Everton	A	0-1	40,552
14	**Portsmouth**	H	**1-1**	35,064
19	**Newcastle**	H	**3-1***	43,856
26	West Brom	A	5-0	27,533
28	**Southampton**	H	**1-0**	42,382
JANUARY				
1	**Chelsea**	H	**0-1**	43,886
3	Norwich	A	2-1	24,503
11	**Watford (C Cup sf 1st)**	H	**1-0**	35,739
15	**Man United**	H	**0-1**	44,183
18	Burnley (FAC3)	A	0-1	19,033
22	Southampton	A	0-2	32,017
25	Watford (C Cup sf 2nd)	A	1-0	19,797
FEBRUARY				
1	Charlton	A	2-1	27,102
5	**Fulham**	H	**3-1**	43,534
12	Birmingham	A	0-2	29,318
22	B Leverkusen (CL KO1)	H	3-1	40,942
27	Chelsea (C Cup Final)	N	2-3^	71,622
MARCH				
5	Newcastle	A	1-1	52,323
9	B Leverkusen (CL KO2)	A	3-1	23,000
16	**Blackburn**	H	**0-0**	37,763
20	**Everton**	H	**2-1**	44,224
APRIL				
2	**Bolton**	H	**1-0**	43,755
5	Juventus (CL QF 1st)	H	2-1	41,216
9	Man City	A	0-1	43,755
13	Juventus (CL QF 2nd)	A	0-0	59,400
16	**Tottenham**	H	**2-2**	44,029
20	Portsmouth	A	2-1	20,205
23	Crystal Palace	A	0-1	26,043
27	Chelsea (CL SF 1st)	H	0-0	40,497
30	**Middlesbrough**	H	**1-1**	43,250
MAY				
3	**Chelsea (CL SF 2nd)**	H	**1-0**	42,529
8	Arsenal	A	1-3	38,119
15	**Aston Villa**	H	**2-1**	43,406
25	AC Milan (CL final)	N	3-3+	65,000

* Own goals v Man Utd (O'Shea); v Fulham (Knight); v Deportivo (Andrade); v Newcastle (Bramble)
†aet (Liverpool win 4-3 on pens); ^aet; + aet (Liverpool win 3-2 on pens)

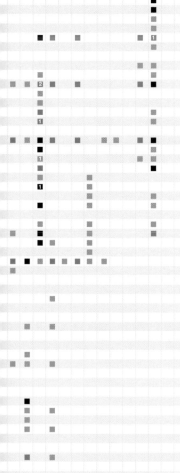

David Raven · John Welsh · Neil Mellor · Darren Potter · Jon Otsemobor · Zak Whitbread · Paul Harrison · Mark Smyth · Robbie Foy · Michael Owen · Stephane Henchoz · Salif Diao

31 32 33 34 36 37 40 41 42

FINAL TABLE

BARCLAYS PREMIERSHIP TABLE 2004/05

Team	Pd	HOME					AWAY					Pts	GD
		W	D	L	F	A	W	D	L	F	A		
1. Chelsea	38	14	5	0	35	6	15	3	1	37	9	95	+57
2. Arsenal	38	13	5	1	54	19	12	3	4	33	17	83	+51
3. Manchester Utd	38	12	6	1	31	12	10	5	4	27	14	77	+32
4. Everton	38	12	2	5	24	15	6	5	8	21	31	61	-1
5. Liverpool	38	12	4	3	31	15	5	3	11	21	26	58	+11
6. Bolton Wanderers	38	9	5	5	25	18	7	5	7	24	26	58	+5
7. Middlesbrough	38	9	6	4	29	19	5	7	7	24	27	55	+7
8. Manchester City	38	8	6	5	24	14	5	7	7	23	25	52	+8
9. Tottenham Hotspur	38	9	5	5	36	22	5	5	9	11	19	52	+6
10. Aston Villa	38	8	6	5	26	17	4	5	10	19	35	47	-7
11. Charlton Athletic	38	8	4	7	29	29	4	6	9	13	29	46	-16
12. Birmingham City	38	8	6	5	24	15	3	6	10	16	31	45	-6
13. Fulham	38	8	4	7	29	26	4	4	11	23	34	44	-8
14. Newcastle United	38	7	7	5	25	25	3	7	9	22	32	44	-10
15. Blackburn Rovers	38	5	8	6	21	22	4	7	8	11	21	42	-11
16. Portsmouth	38	8	4	7	30	26	2	5	12	13	32	39	-16
17. West Brom	38	5	8	6	17	24	1	8	10	19	37	34	-25
18. Crystal Palace	38	6	5	8	21	19	1	7	11	20	43	33	-21
19. Norwich City	38	7	5	7	29	32	0	7	12	13	45	33	-35
20. Southampton	38	5	9	5	30	30	1	5	13	15	36	32	-21

MINUTES ON PITCH 2004-2005

	LEAGUE	FA CUP	LEAGUE CUP	CHAMPS LEAGUE	TOTAL
DUDEK	2160	90	600	930	3780
HENCHOZ	0	0	300	90	390
FINNAN	2546	0	415	1054	4015
HYYPIA	2781	90	120	1380	4371
BAROS	1866	25	206	1054	3151
RIISE	2987	0	316	1355	4658
KEWELL	1399	0	56	596	2051
GERRARD	2465	0	300	920	3685
CISSE	931	0	0	432	1363
GARCIA	2344	0	212	1006	3562
SMICER	328	0	0	176	504
PELLEGRINO	911	0	90	0	1001
LE TALLEC	218	0	0	91	309
ALONSO	1809	0	0	661	2470
DIAO	415	0	277	115	807
HAMANN	2026	0	281	743	3050
JOSEMI	1125	0	90	499	1714
NUNEZ	902	87	224	194	1407
MORIENTES	1015	0	164	0	1179
CARSON	360	0	0	90	450
TRAORE	1767	65	426	854	3112
KIRKLAND	900	0	0	360	1260
CARRAGHER	3420	0	300	1360	5080
S-PONGOLLE	664	90	322	70	1146
BISCAN	728	90	463	719	2000
PARTRIDGE	0	0	30	0	30
WARNOCK	803	90	296	214	1403
LUZI	0	0	0	0	0
RAVEN	23	90	120	0	233
WELSH	175	76	82	20	353
MELLOR	478	14	260	102	854
POTTER	53	90	301	99	543
OTSEMOBOR	0	0	0	0	0
WHITBREAD	0	90	300	0	390
SMYTH	0	0	50	0	50
FOY	0	0	0	0	0

Up to and including 25th May 2005

PLAYER GOALS 2004-2005 SEASON

	ALL COMPETITIONS			
	UP TO AND INCLUDING: 25TH MAY 2005			
	1ST HALF	**2ND HALF**	**EXTRA-TIME**	**TOTAL**
BAROS	3	10	0	13
GARCIA	9	4	0	13
GERRARD	3	10	0	13
RIISE	4	4	0	8
CISSE	4	1	0	5
MELLOR	1	4	0	5
SINAMA-PONGOLLE	1	2	1	4
OWN GOALS	2	2	0	4
ALONSO	1	2	0	3
HYYPIA	1	2	0	3
MORIENTES	2	1	0	3
BISCAN	0	2	0	2
DIAO	1	0	0	1
FINNAN	1	0	0	1
HAMANN	0	1	0	1
KEWELL	1	0	0	1
NUNEZ	0	0	1	1
SMICER	0	1	0	1
TOTAL	**34**	**46**	**2**	**82**

Steven Gerrard's strike against Middlesbrough at Anfield was a contender for goal of the season

CURRENT APPEARANCES & GOALS FOR LIVERPOOL

UP TO AND INCLUDING 25TH MAY 2005

	LGE GMS	LGE GLS	FA GMS	FA GLS	L. CUP GMS	L. CUP GLS	EURO GMS (inc Spr Cup)	EURO GLS	OTHER GMS (inc C. Shield)	OTHER GLS	L'POOL GMS	L'POOL GLS
DUDEK	119	0	8	0	9	0	37	0	1	0	174	0
FINNAN	55	1	3	0	5	0	20	0	0	0	83	1
HYYPIA	216	17	18	0	15	1	62	6	2	0	313	24
BAROS	66	19	3	0	8	4	28	4	1	0	106	27
RIISE	140	19	6	0	11	1	45	2	2	0	204	22
KEWELL	54	8	3	0	3	1	20	3	0	0	80	12
GERRARD	200	27	13	1	15	4	54	9	1	0	283	41
CISSE	16	4	0	0	0	0	9	1	0	0	25	5
GARCIA	29	8	0	0	3	0	12	5	0	0	44	13
LE TALLEC	17	0	4	0	2	0	7	1	0	0	30	1
ALONSO	24	2	0	0	0	0	8	1	0	0	32	3
DIAO	37	1	2	0	8	1	14	1	0	0	61	3
HAMANN	174	8	14	1	11	0	50	2	2	0	251	11
JOSEMI	15	0	0	0	1	0	7	0	0	0	23	0
NUNEZ	18	0	1	0	3	1	5	0	0	0	27	1
MORIENTES	13	3	0	0	2	0	0	0	0	0	15	3
CARSON	4	0	0	0	0	0	1	0	0	0	5	0
TRAORE	73	0	3	0	13	0	27	1	1	0	117	1
KIRKLAND	25	0	3	0	6	0	11	0	0	0	45	0
CARRAGHER	254	2	18	0	22	0	65	0	1	0	360	2
S-P'GOLLE	31	4	4	0	7	1	7	1	0	0	49	6
BISCAN	72	2	7	0	15	1	23	0	1	0	118	3
VIGNAL	11	0	1	0	3	0	5	0	0	0	20	0
WARNOCK	19	0	1	0	4	0	6	0	0	0	30	0
LUZI	1	0	0	0	0	0	0	0	0	0	1	0
RAVEN	1	0	1	0	1	0	0	0	0	0	3	0
WELSH	4	0	1	0	3	0	2	0	0	0	10	0
MELLOR	12	2	2	0	6	3	2	1	0	0	22	6
POTTER	2	0	1	0	4	0	3	0	0	0	10	0
WHITBREAD	0	0	1	0	3	0	0	0	0	0	4	0
CHEYROU	31	2	6	2	2	0	8	1	1	0	48	5

MAN OF THE SEASON

We all dream of a team of Carraghers! Jamie Carragher was voted Redman of the Season in the club's official magazine LFC. The weekly publication awarded players points over the course of 2004/05 based on appearances, goals scored, key contributions to a goal, clean sheets, goals conceded and penalties saved (keepers) with bonus points dished out for men of the match and magic moments. Carra totted up 342 points, holding off second-placed Steven Gerrard (272 points) and John Arne Riise in third (270 points). Placed fourth was Luis Garcia (241) and fifth was Milan Baros (224). All together now: Number one is Carragher . . .

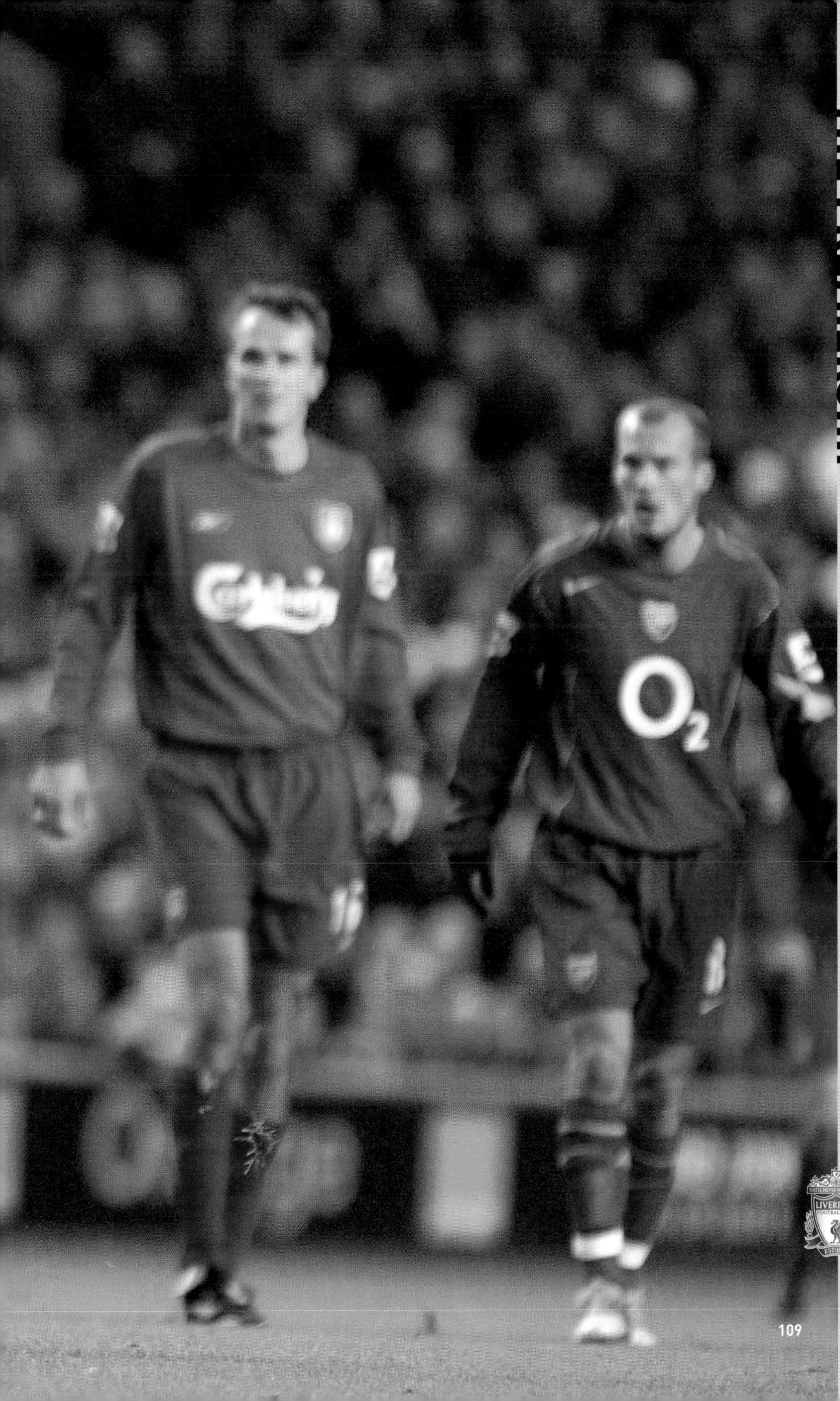

MOST POINTS WON BY TEAMS
IN PREMIER LEAGUE HISTORY

(up to end of 2004-2005 season)

		POINTS	HIGHEST POS	SEASONS IN PREMIERSHIP
1	MANCHESTER UNITED	1060	1st (8 times)	13
2	ARSENAL	946	1st (3 times)	13
3	LIVERPOOL	849	2nd (2001-2002)	13
4	CHELSEA	839	1st (2004-2005)	13
5	NEWCASTLE UNITED	728	2nd (2 times)	12
6	ASTON VILLA	725	2nd (1992-1993)	13
7	LEEDS UNITED	692	3rd (1999-2000)	12
8	TOTTENHAM HOTSPUR	663	7th (1994-1995)	13
9	BLACKBURN ROVERS	632	1st (1994-1995)	12
10	EVERTON	627	4th (2004-2005)	13
11	SOUTHAMPTON	587	8th (2002-2003)	13
12	WEST HAM UNITED	500	5th (1998-1999)	10
13	MIDDLESBROUGH	468	7th (2004-2005)	10
14	COVENTRY CITY	409	11th (2 times)	9
15	SHEFFIELD WEDNESDAY	392	7th (3 times)	8
16	WIMBLEDON (MK DONS)	391	6th (1993-1994)	8
17	MANCHESTER CITY	367	8th (2004-2005)	8
18	LEICESTER CITY	342	8th (1999-2000)	8
19	CHARLTON ATHLETIC	280	7th (2003-2004)	6
20	BOLTON WANDERERS	264	6th (2004-2005)	6
21	DERBY COUNTY	263	8th (1998-1999)	6
22	NOTTINGHAM FOREST	239	3rd (1994-1995)	5
23	IPSWICH TOWN	224	5th (2000-2001)	5
24	QUEENS PARK RANGERS	216	5th (1992-1993)	4
25	SUNDERLAND	214	7th (2 times)	5
26	NORWICH CITY	201	3rd (1992-1993)	4
27	FULHAM	188	9th (2003-2004)	4
28	CRYSTAL PALACE	160	18th (2004-2005)	4
29	BIRMINGHAM CITY	143	10th (2003-2004)	3
30	SHEFFIELD UNITED	94	14th (1992-1993)	2
31	OLDHAM ATHLETIC	89	19th (1992-1993)	2
32	PORTSMOUTH	84	13th (2003-2004)	2
33	BRADFORD CITY	62	17th (1999-2000)	2
34	WEST BROMWICH ALB	60	17th (2004-2005)	2
35	BARNSLEY	35	19th (1997-1998)	1
36	WOLVERHAMPTON W.	33	20th (2003-2004)	1
37	SWINDON TOWN	30	22nd (1994-1995)	1
38	WATFORD	24	20th (1999-2000)	1

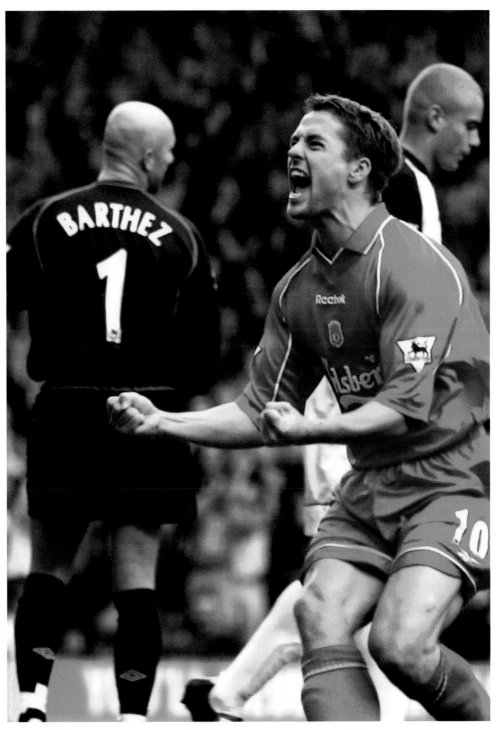

Michael Owen celebrates a goal in Liverpool's 3-1 win against Manchester United in November 2001. The Reds achieved their highest Premiership finish in 2001/2002

Liverpool have won more league games against Aston Villa than any other team

Liverpool have scored most Premiership goals against Leeds – and least against Wolves

PREMIERSHIP: CLUB BY CLUB

LIVERPOOL' S PREMIER LEAGUE RECORD - CLUB BY CLUB
(At end of 2004-05 season. Only teams in Premier League in 2004-05 included)

	PLAYED	WON	DREW	LOST	FOR	AGAINST
ARSENAL	162	66	40	56	230	204
ASTON VILLA	160	74	35	51	281	239
BIRMINGHAM CITY	92	46	18	28	154	129
BLACKBURN ROVERS	114	46	35	33	205	161
BOLTON WANDERERS	104	42	28	34	161	130
CHARLTON ATHLETIC	52	28	6	18	88	66
CHELSEA	124	57	26	41	199	175
CRYSTAL PALACE	26	15	6	5	57	17
EVERTON	172	63	54	55	232	207
FULHAM	36	20	11	5	69	37
MANCHESTER CITY	138	69	32	37	255	188
MANCHESTER UNITED	144	49	42	53	191	201
MIDDLESBROUGH	126	53	36	37	219	164
NEWCASTLE UNITED	140	64	37	39	237	180
NORWICH CITY	46	24	11	11	84	47
PORTSMOUTH	50	19	13	18	87	81
SOUTHAMPTON	74	35	18	21	112	86
TOTTENHAM HOTSPUR	124	57	32	35	198	143
WEST BROMWICH ALBION	112	51	33	28	173	127

LIVERPOOL GOALS v PREMIERSHIP OPPONENTS

	GAMES PLAYED	GOALS IN FIXTURE	AVE. PER GAME	LIVERPOOL GOALS	AVE.PER GAME
ARSENAL	26	58	2.23	35	1.35
ASTON VILLA	26	67	2.58	40	1.54
BARNSLEY	2	6	3	3	1.5
BIRMINGHAM CITY	6	17	2.83	9	1.5
BLACKBURN ROVERS	22	65	2.95	36	1.64
BOLTON WANDERERS	12	35	2.92	22	1.83
BRADFORD CITY	4	8	2	6	1.5
CHARLTON ATHLETIC	12	34	2.83	22	1.83
CHELSEA	26	65	2.5	31	1.19
COVENTRY CITY	18	44	2.44	27	1.5
CRYSTAL PALACE	8	26	3.25	20	2.5
DERBY COUNTY	12	30	2.5	22	1.83
EVERTON	26	55	2.12	29	1.12
FULHAM	8	22	2.75	15	1.88
IPSWICH TOWN	10	27	2.7	20	2
LEEDS UNITED	24	71	2.96	48	2
LEICESTER CITY	16	33	2.06	19	1.19
MANCHESTER CITY	16	48	3	30	1.88
MANCHESTER UNITED	26	71	2.73	31	1.19
MIDDLESBROUGH	20	48	2.4	30	1.5
NEWCASTLE UNITED	24	75	3.13	44	1.83
NORWICH CITY	8	24	3	17	2.13
NOTTINGHAM FOREST	10	29	2.9	18	1.8
OLDHAM ATHLETIC	4	12	3	8	2
PORTSMOUTH	4	9	2.25	6	1.5
QUEENS PARK RANGERS	8	20	2.5	13	1.62
SHEFFIELD UNITED	4	7	1.75	3	0.75
SHEFFIELD WEDNESDAY	16	43	2.69	27	1.69
SOUTHAMPTON	26	78	3	45	1.73
SUNDERLAND	10	16	1.6	10	1
SWINDON TOWN	2	9	4.5	7	3.5
TOTTENHAM HOTSPUR	26	77	2.96	45	1.73
WATFORD	2	6	3	3	1.5
WEST BROMWICH ALBION	4	16	4	16	4
WEST HAM UNITED	20	45	2.25	30	1.5
WIMBLEDON	16	39	2.44	22	1.37
WOLVERHAMPTON WANDERERS	2	3	1.5	2	1

(Up to and including end of 2004-05 season)

PREMIERSHIP NUMBERS GAME

SQUAD NUMBERS

Number Players (with Premiership appearances in brackets)

1	Grobbelaar (29),	James (171),	Westerveld (75),	Dudek (84)	
2	R.Jones (125),	Henchoz (135)			
3	Burrows (4),	Dicks (24),	Scales (3),	Kvarme (45),	Ziege (16),
	Xavier (14),	Finnan (55)			
4	Nicol (35),	McAteer (100),	Song (34),	Hyypia (143)	
5	M.Wright (104),	Staunton (44),	Baros (66)		
6	Hutchison (11),	Babb (128),	Babbel (42),	Riise (37)	
7	Clough (39),	McManaman (101),	Smicer (91),	Kewell (54)	
8	Stewart (8),	Collymore (61),	Leonhardsen (37),	Heskey (150),	Gerrard (30)
9	Rush (98),	Fowler (128),	Anelka (20),	Diouf (55),	Cisse (16)
10	Barnes (135),	Owen (178),	Garcia (29)		
11	Walters (35),	Redknapp (103),	Smicer (30)		
12	Whelan (23),	Scales (62),	Harkness (38),	Hyypia (73),	Dudek (35),
	P.Jones (2),	Pellegrino (12)			
13	James (14),	Riedle (60),	Murphy (130),	Le Tallec (4)	
14	Molby (25),	Ruddock (19),	Heggem (54),	Alonso (24)	
15	Redknapp (99),	Berger (148),	Diao (11)		
16	Thomas (99),	Dundee (3),	Hamann (174)		
17	McManaman (108),	Ince (65),	Gerrard (129),	Josemi (15)	
18	Rosenthal (3),	Owen (38),	Ferri (2),	Meijer (24),	Riise (103),
	Nunez (18)				
19	Piechnik (1),	Kennedy (16),	Friedel (14),	Arphexad (2),	Morientes (13)
20	Bjornebye (128),	Barmby (32),	Le Tallec (13),	Carson (4)	
21	Marsh (2),	Matteo (127),	McAllister (55),	Diao (26),	Traore (33)
22	Harkness (43),	Camara (33),	Kirkland (25)		
23	Fowler (108),	Carragher (254)			
24	L.Jones (3),	Murphy (40),	Diomede (2),	Sinama-Pongolle (31)	
25	Ruddock (96),	Thompson (48),	Biscan (72)		
27	Vignal (11)				
28	Gerrard (41),	Cheyrou (31),	Warnock (19)		
29	Friedel (11),	S.Wright (14),	Luzi (1)		
30	Traore (40)				
31	Raven (1)				
32	Newby (1),	Welsh (4)			
33	Mellor (12)				
34	Potter (2)				
36	Otsemobor (4)				
37	Litmanen (26)				

MOST APPEARANCES/GOALS IN PREMIER LEAGUE

Top 10 total appearances in Premier League		Top 10 goalscorers in Premier League	
Jamie Carragher	254	Robbie Fowler	120
Steve McManaman	240	Michael Owen	118
Robbie Fowler	236	Ian Rush	45
Jamie Redknapp	231	Steve McManaman	41
Sami Hyypia	216	Emile Heskey	39
Michael Owen	216	Jamie Redknapp	29
David James	214	Patrik Berger	28
Steven Gerrard	200	Steven Gerrard	27
Dietmar Hamann	174	Stan Collymore	26
Danny Murphy	170	Danny Murphy	25

Ian Rush, Emile Heskey, Jamie Redknapp and Danny Murphy feature in Liverpool's top 10 Premiership hitmen – behind Michael Owen and Robbie Fowler

Robbie Fowler (top) scores his 100th league goal in the 7-1 record thrashing of Southampton in 1999. Above: Milan Baros and Michael Owen share six against West Bromwich Albion in 2003

PREMIER LEAGUE FACTS & FIGURES

PREMIER LEAGUE RECORD

Season	P	W	D	L	F	A	Pts	Pos
1992-1993	42	16	11	15	62	55	59	6
1993-1994	42	17	9	16	59	55	60	8
1994-1995	42	21	11	10	65	37	74	4
1995-1996	38	20	11	7	70	34	71	3
1996-1997	38	19	11	8	62	37	68	4
1997-1998	38	18	11	9	68	42	65	3
1998-1999	38	15	9	14	68	49	54	7
1999-2000	38	19	10	9	51	30	67	4
2000-2001	38	20	9	9	71	39	69	3
2001-2002	38	24	8	6	67	30	80	2
2002-2003	38	18	10	10	61	41	64	5
2003-2004	38	16	12	10	55	37	60	4
2004-2005	38	17	7	14	52	41	58	5

BIGGEST PREMIERSHIP WINS (TOP FIVE)

Date	Opponents	Venue	Score	Scorers	Attendance
16th Jan 1999	Southampton	Home	Won 7-1	Fowler 3, Matteo, Carragher, Owen, Thompson	44,011
26th Apr 2003	West Bromwich	Away	Won 6-0	Owen 4, Baros 2	27,128
9th Feb 2002	Ipswich Town	Away	Won 6-0	Abel Xavier, Heskey 2, Hyypia, Owen 2	25,608
28th Oct 1995	Manchester City	Home	Won 6-0	Rush 2, Redknapp, Fowler 2, Ruddock	39,267
20th Aug 1994	Crystal Palace	Away	Won 6-1	Fowler, McManaman 2, Molby (pen), Rush 2	18,084

BIGGEST PREMIERSHIP DEFEATS (TOP FIVE)

Date	Opponents	Venue	Score	Scorers	Attendance
19th Dec 1992	Coventry City	Away	Lost 5-1	Redknapp	19,779
5th Apr 2003	Manchester United	Away	Lost 4-0		67,639
16th Dec 2001	Chelsea	Away	Lost 4-0		41,174
25th Apr 1998	Chelsea	Away	Lost 4-1	Riedle	34,639
3rd Apr 1992	Blackburn Rovers	Away	Lost 4-1	Rush	15,032

AVERAGE ATTENDANCES

Season	High	Low	Average
1992-1993	44,619	29,574	37,009
1993-1994	44,601	24,561	38,503
1994-1995	40,014	27,183	34,175
1995-1996	40,820	34,063	39,552
1996-1997	40,892	36,126	39,776
1997-1998	44,532	34,705	40,628
1998-1999	44,852	36,019	43,321
1999-2000	44,929	40,483	44,074
2000-2001	44,806	38,474	43,698
2001-2002	44,371	37,153	43,389
2002-2003	44,250	41,462	43,243
2003-2004	44,374	34,663	42,677
2004-2005	44,224	35,064	42,587

LIVERPOOL'S CHAMPIONSHIP-WINNING SEASONS

1900-01

Under the tutelage of Tom Watson, Liverpool won their first-ever League Championship. Watson had previously guided Sunderland's 'Team Of All The Talents' to the title on three occasions. Under the captaincy of Alex Raisbeck, the Championship was claimed in the final game of the campaign with the Reds winning 1-0 at West Bromwich Albion, with John Walker scoring the only goal of the game, and so added an English winners' medal to the one he'd gained with Hearts in Scotland.

It was the 1-0 win at Sunderland on February 23rd which was the catalyst for a run of 12 unbeaten games in which they won nine and drew three, conceding just four goals in the process.

	PLD	WON	DRAWN	LOST	GOALS FOR	GOALS AGAINST	POINTS
1 LIVERPOOL	**34**	**19**	**7**	**8**	**59**	**35**	**45**
2 SUNDERLAND	34	15	13	6	57	26	43

Appearances

Jack Cox	32	John 'Sailor' Hunter	8	Sam Raybould	31
John Davies	1	Jack Hunter	2	Jack Robertson	25
Billy Dunlop	33	Andy McGuigan	14	Tom Robertson	34
John Glover	10	Maurice Parry	8	Charlie Satterthwaite	21
Bill Goldie	34	Bill Perkins	34	John Walker	29
Raby Howell	2	Alex Raisbeck	31	Charlie Wilson	25

Goals: Raybould - 17, Cox - 10, T.Robertson - 9, Walker - 7, McGuigan - 5, Satterthwaite - 5, Sailor Hunter - 3, Goldie - 2, Raisbeck - 1, Wilson - 1.

1905-06

Just three years after their first success, Liverpool suffered relegation only to regain their top-flight status in 1904-05. They then became the first side to win Division Two and Division One in successive seasons. The club lost their opening three games and won only three of the first eight matches.

However, a tremendous run of nine wins and a draw in the next 10 engagements cemented their challenge. The Reds finished four points ahead of Preston North End. With prolific Jack Parkinson breaking his wrist in the first game Joe Hewitt emerged and top scored with 24 League goals. Another player came into the side - the legendary goalkeeper Sam Hardy, who was to enjoy a 13-year stint in the national side.

	PLD	WON	DRAWN	LOST	GOALS FOR	GOALS AGAINST	POINTS
1 LIVERPOOL	**38**	**23**	**5**	**10**	**79**	**46**	**51**
2 PRESTON NORTH END	38	17	13	8	54	39	47

Appearances

Jim Bradley	31	Jimmy Garside	4	David Murray	3
John Carlin	14	Arthur Goddard	38	Jack Parkinson	9
Tom Chorlton	6	Jimmy Gorman	1	Maurice Parry	36
Jack Cox	28	Harry Griffiths	1	Alex Raisbeck	36
Ted Doig	8	Sam Hardy	30	Sam Raybould	25
Billy Dunlop	31	Joe Hewitt	37	Robbie Robinson	34
George Fleming	4	George Lathom	5	Alf West	37

Goals: Hewitt - 24, Raybould - 10, Robinson - 10, Cox - 9, Parkinson - 7, Goddard - 6, Carlin - 6, West - 3, Chorlton - 1, Parry - 1, Raisbeck - 1, own goals - 1.

1921-22

Not noted for their scoring prowess - indeed six First Division sides scored more goals than them - their defence, with the outstanding Irish international Elisha Scott in goal and four international full-backs, conceded only 36. They were augmented by Jock McNab and Tom Bromilow, who also won full caps.

The Reds enjoyed a 30-match spell with just a single defeat. The club clinched the title with three games to play, wrapping it up with a 2-1 victory over the defending champions Burnley at Anfield.

1921-22 (cont)

	PLD	WON	DRAWN	LOST	GOALS		POINTS
					FOR	AGAINST	
1 LIVERPOOL	**42**	**26**	**8**	**8**	**70**	**31**	**60**
2 TOTTENHAM HOTSPUR	42	21	9	12	65	39	51

Appearances

Jack Bamber	8	Fred Hopkin	42	Frank Mitchell	3
Harry Beadles	11	Billy Lacey	39	Ted Parry	7
Tommy Bromilow	40	Harry Lewis	19	Elisha Scott	39
Harry Chambers	32	Eph Longworth	26	Danny Shone	15
Frank Checkland	5	Tommy Lucas	27	Harold Wadsworth	1
Willie Cunningham	1	Don Mackinlay	29	Walter Wadsworth	38
Dick Forshaw	42	Jock McNab	29		
Cyril Gilhespy	2	Bill Matthews	7		

Goals: Chambers - 19, Forshaw - 17, Beadles - 6, Shone - 6, Matthews - 4, Bromilow - 2, Lucas - 2, McNab - 2, Gilhespy - 1, Lacey - 1, Lewis - 1, Mackinlay - 1, own goals - 1.

1922-23

The title was successfully defended but manager David Ashworth resigned in mid-term, a forerunner of the shockwaves which the resignations of Bill Shankly and Kenny Dalglish was to cause latter-day Kopites.

The club had climbed to the top in January of the previous season and they remained at the summit for 16 months. On 21 occasions they kept a clean sheet, including a run of eight games in succession between December and March, accentuating the presence of the ever-present Elisha Scott in goal. Newcastle United was the only side to win at Anfield and the defence was breached only 31 times, a record for a 42-match season.

	PLD	WON	DRAWN	LOST	GOALS		POINTS
					FOR	AGAINST	
1 LIVERPOOL	**42**	**26**	**8**	**8**	**70**	**31**	**60**
2 SUNDERLAND	42	22	10	10	72	54	54

Appearances

Jack Bamber	4	Dick Johnson	37	Jack Sambrook	2
Harry Beadles	4	Billy Lacey	30	Elisha Scott	42
Tommy Bromilow	41	Eph Longworth	41	Danny Shone	1
Harry Chambers	39	Tommy Lucas	1	Harold Wadsworth	3
Dick Forshaw	42	Don Mackinlay	42	Walter Wadsworth	37
Cyril Gilhespy	10	Jock McNab	39		
Fred Hopkin	40	Dave Pratt	7		

Goals: Chambers - 22, Forshaw - 19, Johnson - 14, McKinlay - 5, Bromilow - 3, Gilhespy - 2, W.Wadsworth - 2, Hopkin - 1, Lacey - 1, McNab - 1.

1946-47

The season started on August 31st and ended on June 14th, the result of the severe winter that saw 146 League games postponed or abandoned. Liverpool visited long-time challengers Wolves on May 31st with Jack Balmer and Albert Stubbins putting the Reds into pole position at the top of the League. It meant that Stoke City could claim the Championship in their final game - some two weeks later on goal average, if they were to overcome Sheffield United. The 40-year old Jack Pickering, making his only League appearance of the season, wrote his name into Liverpool folklore by scoring the Yorkshiremen's winner and the first post-war title went to Merseyside.

Jack Balmer's hat-tricks in three successive League games and 15 in seven matches made national headlines, while two newcomers to the side were to become Anfield legends. Albert Stubbins, signed from Newcastle, scored 24 times and Billy Liddell made his first appearance. Elsewhere, the half-back line of Phil Taylor, Bill Jones and Laurie Hughes were all to play for England, while a former Amateur Cup winner with Bishop Auckland, Bob Paisley, made 33 appearances.

1946-47 (cont)

	PLD	WON	DRAWN	LOST	GOALS		POINTS
					FOR	AGAINST	
1 LIVERPOOL	42	25	7	10	84	52	57
2 MANCHESTER UNITED	42	22	12	8	95	54	56

Appearances

Charlie Ashcroft	2	Laurie Hughes	30	Stan Palk	6
Jack Balmer	39	Bill Jones	26	Bob Priday	9
Tom Bush	3	George Kaye	1	Barney Ramsden	23
Len Carney	2	Ray Lambert	36	Cyril Sidlow	34
Cyril Done	17	Billy Liddell	34	Eddie Spicer	10
John Easdale	2	Tommy McLeod	3	Albert Stubbins	36
Harry Eastham	19	Ray Minshull	6	Phil Taylor	35
Willie Fagan	18	Berry Nieuwenhuys	15	Billy Watkinson	6
Jim Harley	17	Bob Paisley	33		

Goals: Balmer - 24, Stubbins - 24, Done - 10, Fagan - 7, Liddell - 7, Nieuwenhuys - 5, Jones - 2, Priday - 2, Carney - 1, Taylor - 1, Watkinson - 1.

1963-64

Just two years after winning the Second Division title, Bill Shankly won his first League Championship by a margin of four points. The first three games at Anfield were lost but a 6-0 defeat of Wolves put the Reds back on track. On September 28th two Ian Callaghan goals saw off Everton, the start of five successive wins and a placing of third in the table. On November 23rd a Ron Yeats goal, his only one of the campaign, proved decisive at Old Trafford and sent the Reds to the head of the table.

Tottenham Hotspur, Manchester United and Everton contested the leadership with the Reds, but a 'double' over the Londoners and a 3-0 Anfield defeat of United meant a meeting with Arsenal on April 18th would bring the Championship trophy back to Anfield. Shankly's promise of delivery was duly observed with a 5-0 win. Roger Hunt signalled his emergence in the higher echelons of the goalscoring lists with 31 of the 92 goals the Reds registered - 60 of those coming in front of an adoring Kop.

	PLD	WON	DRAWN	LOST	GOALS		POINTS
					FOR	AGAINST	
1 LIVERPOOL	42	26	5	11	92	45	57
2 MANCHESTER UNITED	42	23	7	12	90	62	53

Appearances

Alf Arrowsmith	20	Chris Lawler	6	Willie Stevenson	38
Gerry Byrne	33	Tommy Lawrence	40	Peter Thompson	42
Ian Callaghan	42	Jimmy Melia	24	Bobby Thomson	2
Phil Ferns	18	Gordon Milne	42	Gordon Wallace	1
Jim Furnell	2	Ronnie Moran	35	Ron Yeats	36
Roger Hunt	41	Ian St John	40		

Goals: Hunt - 31, St John - 21, Arrowsmith - 15, Callaghan - 8, Thompson - 6, Melia - 4, Milne - 2, Moran - 2, Stevenson - 1, Yeats - 1, own goals - 1.

1965-66

League champions in 1963-64, FA Cup winners 1964-65, Bill Shankly's remarkable hat-trick was confirmed on April 30th with a 2-1 at Anfield against Chelsea. Their 7th Championship equalled Arsenal's record, and the 61 points accumulated was a comfortable six-point margin over runners-up Leeds United. More remarkable was the fact that the club only called on 14 players - including Alf Arrowsmith (five games) and Bobby Graham (just one appearance). Sunderland used 15 in 1891-92 in winning a Championship of just 26 matches.

The highlights of the season were the 5-0 hammering of Everton at Anfield, only 34 goals conceded - their best defensive record since 1922-3 - and the loss of just three of the last 29 games. Roger Hunt scored 29 goals in 37 appearances while Ian Callaghan was an ever-present, as he had been in the title-winning season of 1963-64.

1965-66 (cont)

	PLD	WON	DRAWN	LOST	GOALS		POINTS
					FOR	AGAINST	
1 LIVERPOOL	**42**	**26**	**9**	**7**	**79**	**34**	**61**
2 LEEDS UNITED	42	23	9	10	79	38	55

Appearances

Alf Arrowsmith	5	Chris Lawler	40	Willie Stevenson	41
Gerry Byrne	42	Tommy Lawrence	42	Geoff Strong	22
Ian Callaghan	42	Gordon Milne	28	Peter Thompson	40
Bobby Graham	1	Ian St John	41	Ron Yeats	42
Roger Hunt	37	Tommy Smith	42		

Goals: Hunt - 29, St John - 10, Milne - 7, Callaghan - 5, Lawler - 5, Stevenson - 5, Strong - 5, Thompson - 5, Smith - 3, Yeats - 2, Arrowsmith - 1, Byrne - 1, own goals - 1.

1972-73

For the first time, two major trophies were won by the club in the same season. The Reds used only 16 players in the League campaign with Ian Callaghan being an ever-present for the third Championship-winning season. Kevin Keegan and John Toshack scored 13 apiece but the strength came in the contributions of Cormack, Boersma, Hughes and Heighway.

The 2-0 defeat of Leeds United in the penultimate game of the season virtually wrapped up the title - Shankly's third - with only Arsenal winning at Anfield. The Reds failed to score in just four of the 42 matches.

The 3-2 aggregate defeat of Borussia Moenchengladbach in the UEFA Cup final capped a quite remarkable season with the promise of more to come from Shankly's slowly maturing side.

	PLD	WON	DRAWN	LOST	GOALS		POINTS
					FOR	AGAINST	
1 LIVERPOOL	**42**	**25**	**10**	**7**	**72**	**42**	**60**
2 ARSENAL	42	23	11	8	57	43	57

Appearances

Phil Boersma	19	Emlyn Hughes	41	Tommy Smith	33
Ian Callaghan	42	Kevin Keegan	41	Trevor Storton	4
Ray Clemence	41	Frank Lane	1	Phil Thompson	14
Peter Cormack	30	Chris Lawler	42	John Toshack	22
Brian Hall	21	Alec Lindsay	37		
Steve Heighway	38	Larry Lloyd	42		

Goals: Keegan - 13, Toshack - 13, Cormack - 8, Boersma - 7, Hughes - 7, Heighway - 6, Lindsay - 4, Callaghan - 3, Lawler - 3, Hall - 2, Lloyd - 2, Smith - 2, own goals - 2.

1975-76

The 1974-75 campaign was unusually barren in what was Bob Paisley's first in charge. However, he did introduce Ray Kennedy, Jimmy Case, Terry McDermott and Phil Neal into the side.

An indifferent start was followed by a run of 23 games with only one defeat, an Anfield reversal by Norwich City, before losing 1-0 at Highbury. Ipswich Town's challenge tailed off but Manchester United and QPR kept up the pressure. Following a 2-0 defeat at Anfield to Middlesbrough, the Reds embarked on a run of eight wins and a draw in the last nine games with newcomer David Fairclough scoring seven of the 17 scored by the champions-elect.

QPR wound up their season a point ahead of Liverpool with the Reds meeting Wolves at Molineux on May 4th. For Bob Paisley an amazing double was ahead. In 1946-47 he won a Championship medal in the last game of the season - at Molineux. History shows his first as a manager was also won at the famous old ground. After Wolves led through Steve Kindon, Keegan, Toshack and Ray Kennedy gave Liverpool their ninth title with Wolves suffering relegation. Only five games were lost - a First Division record at the time.

1975-76 (cont)

	PLD	WON	DRAWN	LOST	GOALS FOR	AGAINST	POINTS
1 LIVERPOOL	**42**	**23**	**14**	**5**	**66**	**31**	**60**
2 QPR	42	24	11	7	67	33	59

Appearances

Phil Boersma	3	Steve Heighway	39	Terry McDermott	9
Ian Callaghan	40	Emlyn Hughes	41	Phil Neal	42
Jimmy Case	27	Joey Jones	13	Tommy Smith	24
Ray Clemence	42	Kevin Keegan	41	Phil Thompson	41
Peter Cormack	17	Ray Kennedy	30	John Toshack	35
David Fairclough	14	Brian Kettle	1		
Brian Hall	13	Alec Lindsay	6		

Goals: Toshack - 16, Keegan - 12, Fairclough - 7, Case - 6, Kennedy - 6, Neal - 6, Heighway - 4, Callaghan - 3, Hall - 2, Hughes - 2, Cormack - 1, McDermott - 1.

1976-77

Liverpool's greatest season to date was based on a tremendous home record. They won 18 and drew three in the League and won seven and drew two Cup games. However, contrast this with just five wins on their travels in the League and only 15 goals scored. It was the first time the club had secured the Championship with an unbeaten home record.

Ipswich Town under Bobby Robson and Manchester City chased them but the goalless draw at home to West Ham United secured the first leg of what was a possible unprecedented treble. Manchester United prevented the Double a week later in the FA Cup final but the win in Rome within four days gave Paisley a record League/European Cup triumph in the same season. Kevin Keegan, in his final season top-scored with 12 goals while John Toshack, his co-striker in three Championship campaigns, moved to pastures new.

	PLD	WON	DRAWN	LOST	GOALS FOR	AGAINST	POINTS
1 LIVERPOOL	**42**	**23**	**11**	**8**	**62**	**33**	**57**
2 MANCHESTER CITY	42	21	14	7	60	34	56

Appearances

Ian Callaghan	33	David Johnson	26	Terry McDermott	26
Jimmy Case	27	Joey Jones	39	Phil Neal	42
Ray Clemence	42	Kevin Keegan	38	Tommy Smith	16
David Fairclough	20	Ray Kennedy	41	Phil Thompson	26
Steve Heighway	39	Brian Kettle	2	John Toshack	22
Emlyn Hughes	42	Alec Lindsay	1		

Goals: Keegan - 12, Toshack - 10, Heighway - 8, Kennedy - 7, Neal - 7, Johnson - 5, Fairclough - 3, Jones - 3, Thompson - 2, Callaghan - 1, Case - 1, Hughes - 1, McDermott - 1, own goals - 1.

1978-79

Liverpool's most impressive League campaign to date began with a run of ten wins and a draw in the opening 11 games, including the 7-0 demolition of Tottenham Hotspur. A Boxing Day 3-0 rout of Manchester United began a run of just one defeat in the final 22 games of the season.

Only 16 goals were conceded by Ray Clemence, just four at Anfield, and a new First Division record of 68 points was set. They won 19 and drew two of 21 at Anfield and the club's 30 League wins was a club record. Clemence kept a club record 28 clean sheets and only four sides managed to beat him at Anfield. The Reds' total of 85 goals earned the club a national newspaper prize of £50,000 for scoring an average of more than two goals per game.

	PLD	WON	DRAWN	LOST	GOALS FOR	AGAINST	POINTS
1 LIVERPOOL	**42**	**30**	**8**	**4**	**85**	**16**	**68**
2 NOTTINGHAM FOREST	42	21	18	3	61	26	60

Bringing it home. Bill Shankly and Bob Paisley celebrate Liverpool clinching the league championship on home soil. Paisley has won more titles than any other Reds boss

1978-79 (cont)

Appearances

Jimmy Case	37	Steve Heighway	28	Sammy Lee	2
Ray Clemence	42	Emlyn Hughes	16	Terry McDermott	37
Kenny Dalglish	42	David Johnson	30	Phil Neal	42
David Fairclough	4	Alan Kennedy	37	Graeme Souness	41
Alan Hansen	34	Ray Kennedy	42	Phil Thompson	39

Goals: Dalglish - 21, Johnson - 16, R.Kennedy - 10, McDermott - 8, Souness - 8, Case - 7, Neal - 5, Heighway - 4, A.Kennedy - 3, Fairclough - 2, Hansen - 1.

1979-80

The Reds retained the title once more and remained unbeaten at home again, conceding only eight goals and extending their record to 12 Championships. David Johnson succeeded strike partner Kenny Dalglish as the top scorer with 21 goals and rather amazingly the club met Aston Villa on May 3rd, with victory ensuring the title would be gained over underachievers Manchester United.

The previous season the title was won at Anfield against Villa! A 4-1 victory ensured that the trophy was once again on its way to Merseyside. During the campaign the club signed youngsters Ronnie Whelan and Ian Rush, as well as Newcastle United full-back Alan Kennedy.

	PLD	WON	DRAWN	LOST	GOALS FOR	AGAINST	POINTS
1 LIVERPOOL	**42**	**25**	**10**	**7**	**81**	**30**	**60**
2 MANCHESTER UNITED	42	24	10	8	65	35	58

Appearances

Jimmy Case	37	Steve Heighway	9	Terry McDermott	37
Ray Clemence	41	Colin Irwin	8	Phil Neal	42
Avi Cohen	4	David Johnson	37	Steve Ogrizovic	1
Kenny Dalglish	42	Alan Kennedy	37	Graeme Souness	41
David Fairclough	14	Ray Kennedy	40	Phil Thompson	42
Alan Hansen	38	Sammy Lee	7		

Goals: Johnson - 21, Dalglish - 16, McDermott - 11, R.Kennedy - 9, Fairclough - 5, Hansen - 4, Case - 3, Irwin - 2, Cohen - 1, A.Kennedy - 1, Neal - 1, Souness - 1, own goals - 6.

1981-82

Liverpool won only six matches out of 17 by Boxing Day - a run which also coincided with the death of Bill Shankly on September 29th at the age of 67. After the defeat at Anfield the day after Christmas, a lambasting by coach Joe Fagan had the desired effect. The club was in the bottom half of the table at the turn of the year but 20 wins, two losses and three draws, including a run of 11 wins in a row, took them to their fifth title in seven seasons.

The Reds won by four points from Ipswich Town. The visit of Tottenham Hotspur in the penultimate game of the season saw a title success that Bob Paisley called "the best Championship win of the lot" due to the ground the side had to make up. Of the 129 goals scored in all competitions, Dalglish and Rush netted 52 between them, Rush the top club scorer for the first time.

	PLD	WON	DRAWN	LOST	GOALS FOR	AGAINST	POINTS
1 LIVERPOOL	**42**	**26**	**9**	**7**	**80**	**32**	**87**
2 IPSWICH TOWN	42	26	5	11	75	53	83

Appearances

Kenny Dalglish	42	Ray Kennedy	15	Kevin Sheedy	2
Bruce Grobbelaar	42	Mark Lawrenson	39	Graeme Souness	35
Alan Hansen	35	Sammy Lee	35	Phil Thompson	34
David Johnson	15	Terry McDermott	29	Ronnie Whelan	32
Craig Johnston	18	Phil Neal	42		
Alan Kennedy	34	Ian Rush	32		

Goals: Rush - 17, McDermott - 14, Dalglish - 13, Whelan - 10, Johnston - 6, Souness - 5, A.Kennedy - 3, Lee - 3, Johnson - 2, R.Kennedy - 2, Lawrenson - 2, Neal - 2, own goals - 1.

1982-83

The season started with Bob Paisley already stating it was to be his last in charge. The team responded by losing just three of the first 35 games with only a minor stutter in October, when they gained just two points from four matches, causing any consternation.

A crushing 5-0 defeat of Everton - with Ian Rush netting four goals - and five goals in games against Notts County, Southampton, Manchester City and Stoke City meant that the Reds had a 16-point lead over nearest challengers Watford.

The final seven games saw the side draw two and lose five of Paisley's last campaign but the most successful manager of all-time signed off with six Championships, three European Cups, three League Cups and a UEFA Cup in his nine seasons at the helm.

The club had led the table from October 30th, and had an 11-point lead over Watford at the end of the season.

	PLD	WON	DRAWN	LOST	GOALS FOR	AGAINST	POINTS
1 LIVERPOOL	42	24	10	8	87	37	82
2 WATFORD	42	22	5	15	74	57	71

Appearances

Kenny Dalglish	42	Alan Kennedy	42	Ian Rush	34
David Fairclough	8	Mark Lawrenson	40	Graeme Souness	41
Bruce Grobbelaar	42	Sammy Lee	40	Phil Thompson	24
Alan Hansen	34	Terry McDermott	2	Ronnie Whelan	28
David Hodgson	23	Phil Neal	42		
Craig Johnston	33	Steve Nicol	4		

Goals: Rush - 24, Dalglish - 18, Souness - 9, Neal - 8, Johnston - 7, Lawrenson - 5, Hodgson - 4, Fairclough - 3, Kennedy - 3, Lee - 3, Whelan - 2, own goal - 1.

1983-84

At the age of 62 Joe Fagan, the last of the great triumvirate of boot room managers, took over the reins. After just four wins from the opening eight matches, the club got into gear and six victories from the next unbeaten eight games included a 6-0 demolition of Luton Town, where Ian Rush equalled the club record of scoring five times. Only 15 players made League appearances with Rush's 32 goals the best return for the club since Roger Hunt's club record in the old Second Division in 1961-62. It was the best by a player in a Championship-winning season.

By the time they travelled to Notts County in the penultimate game of the season, they only needed a draw for a third successive title to emulate Huddersfield Town in the 'Twenties' and Arsenal in the 'Thirties'.

Joe Fagan's career in management gave him English football's first 'treble' with League Cup success and the penalty shoot-out win in the European Cup final in Rome.

	PLD	WON	DRAWN	LOST	GOALS FOR	AGAINST	POINTS
1 LIVERPOOL	42	22	14	6	73	32	80
2 SOUTHAMPTON	42	22	11	9	66	38	77

Appearances

Kenny Dalglish	33	Alan Kennedy	42	Michael Robinson	24
Bruce Grobbelaar	42	Mark Lawrenson	42	Ian Rush	41
Alan Hansen	42	Sammy Lee	42	Graeme Souness	37
David Hodgson	5	Phil Neal	41	John Wark	9
Craig Johnston	29	Steve Nicol	23	Ronnie Whelan	23

Goals: Rush - 32, Dalglish - 7, Souness - 7, Robinson - 6, Nicol - 5, Whelan - 4, Johnston - 2, Kennedy - 2, Lee - 2, Wark - 2, Hansen - 1, Neal - 1, own goals - 2.

1985-86

Kenny Dalglish's first season in charge emulated that of his predecessor Joe Fagan, by annexing the title from local rivals Everton. A reasonable start only by Liverpool's standards saw them ten points behind Manchester United by the Autumn, who had won their first ten games. Then Everton emerged as favourites opening up an 11-point lead in the New Year.

With Dalglish returning to the side the club won 11 and drew one of their remaining 12 games. Everton were the only visiting team to win at Anfield, but that became the catalyst for the Reds' fine finish to the season.

Quite fittingly it was Dalglish's goal at Stamford Bridge in the final game that clinched the Championship one week before the FA Cup final success against Everton.

	PLD	WON	DRAWN	LOST	GOALS FOR	GOALS AGAINST	POINTS
1 LIVERPOOL	**42**	**26**	**10**	**6**	**89**	**37**	**88**
2 EVERTON	42	26	8	8	87	41	86

Appearances

Jim Beglin	34	Alan Kennedy	8	Phil Neal	13
Kenny Dalglish	21	Mark Lawrenson	38	Steve Nicol	34
Gary Gillespie	14	Sammy Lee	15	Ian Rush	40
Bruce Grobbelaar	42	Kevin MacDonald	17	Paul Walsh	20
Alan Hansen	41	Steve McMahon	23	John Wark	9
Craig Johnston	41	Jan Molby	39	Ronnie Whelan	39

Goals: Rush - 22, Molby - 14, Walsh - 11, Whelan - 10, Johnston - 7, McMahon - 6, Nicol - 4, Dalglish - 3, Gillespie - 3, Lawrenson - 3, Wark - 3, Beglin - 1, MacDonald - 1, Neal - 1.

1987-88

With Ian Rush moving to Italy, Kenny Dalglish strengthened his squad, spending wisely on John Barnes, Peter Beardsley and the prolific John Aldridge.

Their attacking football astounded the watching millions and they lost only two games all season, scoring 87 times in 40 games. They amassed a club record 90 points and by Christmas were already ten points clear of their nearest challengers Nottingham Forest.

Aldridge scored in the first nine games of the campaign and the club equalled Leeds United's record by remaining unbeaten in 29 games from the start of the season, until Wayne Clarke's 'inevitable' winner at Goodison Park. Beardsley's goal against Tottenham Hotspur on April 23rd clinched a 17th Championship.

	PLD	WON	DRAWN	LOST	GOALS FOR	GOALS AGAINST	POINTS
1 LIVERPOOL	**40**	**26**	**12**	**2**	**87**	**24**	**90**
2 MANCHESTER UNITED	40	23	12	5	71	38	81

Appearances

Gary Ablett	17	Mike Hooper	2	Steve Nicol	40
John Aldridge	36	Ray Houghton	28	Nigel Spackman	27
John Barnes	38	Craig Johnston	30	Barry Venison	18
Peter Beardsley	38	Mark Lawrenson	14	Paul Walsh	8
Kenny Dalglish	2	Kevin MacDonald	1	John Wark	1
Gary Gillespie	35	Steve McMahon	40	Alex Watson	2
Bruce Grobbelaar	38	Jan Molby	7	Ronnie Whelan	28
Alan Hansen	39				

Goals: Aldridge - 26, Barnes - 15, Beardsley - 15, McMahon - 9, Nicol - 6, Houghton - 5, Johnston - 5, Gillespie - 4, Hansen - 1, Whelan - 1.

1989-90

With Ian Rush now back in business, John Aldridge was allowed to move to Spain, but not before he 'celebrated' his transfer with a penalty in the 9-0 thrashing of Crystal Palace in September. Eight outfield players scored in the game - an English record. Ironic that it was Palace who ended hopes of another 'Double' in the FA Cup semi-finals. After a 2-0 defeat at Sheffield Wednesday in November, the Reds lost only once in the remaining 23 games. After clinching the title, Kenny Dalglish came on as a substitute in the final minutes of the last home game against Derby County - his last in the League at Anfield.

The Kop had a new hero in loan signing Ronny Rosenthal, who scored seven times in just eight appearances at the end of the season while Bruce Grobbelaar was an ever-present, as he had been in the four previous title-winning campaigns. For the only time in his career John Barnes top-scored with 22 League goals thanks to a last day hat-trick against Coventry City.

	PLD	WON	DRAWN	LOST	GOALS FOR	AGAINST	POINTS
1 LIVERPOOL	**38**	**23**	**10**	**5**	**78**	**37**	**79**
2 ASTON VILLA	38	21	7	10	57	38	70

Appearances

Gary Ablett	15	Bruce Grobbelaar	38	Steve Nicol	23
John Aldridge	2	Alan Hansen	31	Ronny Rosenthal	8
John Barnes	34	Ray Houghton	19	Ian Rush	36
Peter Beardsley	29	Glenn Hysen	35	Steve Staunton	20
David Burrows	26	Steve McMahon	38	Nick Tanner	4
Kenny Dalglish	1	Mike Marsh	2	Barry Venison	25
Gary Gillespie	13	Jan Molby	17	Ronnie Whelan	34

Goals: Barnes - 22, Rush - 18, Beardsley - 10, Rosenthal - 7, Nicol - 6, McMahon - 5, Gillespie - 4, Aldridge - 1, Houghton - 1, Hysen - 1, Molby - 1, Whelan - 1, own goal - 1.

King Barnesie: John Barnes and the Liverpool team celebrate their 1988 league triumph

THE LEAGUE FINISHES

DIVISION ONE/PREMIERSHIP - 90 SEASONS	
Number of times	
First	18
Second	11
Third	5
Fourth	7
Fifth	9
Sixth	2
Seventh	4
Eighth	4
Ninth	4
Tenth	2
Eleventh	5
Twelfth	4
Thirteenth	2
Fourteenth	1
Fifteenth	1
Sixteenth	4
Seventeenth	3
Eighteenth	2
Nineteenth	1
Twentieth	0
Twenty-first	0
Twenty-second	1

DIVISION TWO - 11 SEASONS	
Number of times	
First	4
Third	4
Fourth	2
Eleventh	1

THE LEAGUE RECORDS

GENERAL

10-1	Biggest league win at Anfield:	v Rotherham 18/2/1896
7-0	Biggest league win away: Crewe 28/3/1896	v Burton Swifts 29/2/1896 and v
31	Most players played in a season:	1953/54
14	Fewest number:	1965/66
85	Record number of games (including cup fixtures) unbeaten at home between February 1978 and January 1981	
63	Record number of games unbeaten at home (league only)	
31	Record number of games unbeaten (league only)	

THE LEAGUE RECORDS

POINTS

90	Highest-ever points total (3 points for a win):	1987/88
98	If three points for a win:	1978/79

HOME RECORD

9	Number of seasons Liverpool have gone through a league campaign unbeaten (last season was 1987/88)	
19	Most wins:	1978/79
7	Fewest wins:	1894/95
11	Most draws:	1951/52
0	Fewest draws:	1893/94 & 1963/64
8	Most defeats:	1906/07

AWAY RECORD

1	No. of seasons Liverpool unbeaten away in a league campaign (14 games, 1893-94)	
13	Most wins:	1904/05
1	Fewest wins:	1894/95
12	Most draws:	1980/81
1	Fewest draws:	1895/96, 1899/1900, 1902/03, 1904/05 & 1908/09
17	Most defeats:	1953/54

OVERALL

30	Most wins in a season:	1978/79
19	Most draws in a season:	1951/52
23	Most defeats in a season:	1953/54

GOALS

4	Fewest goals conceded at Anfield in a season:	1978/79
38	Most goals conceded at Anfield in a season:	1931/32 and 1953/54
12	Fewest goals scored away:	1970/71
42	Most goals scored away:	1946/47
10	Fewest goals conceded away:	1975/76
59	Most goals conceded away:	1934/35, 1953/54 & 1954/55
68	Most goals scored at Anfield:	1961/62
24	Fewest goals scored at home:	1903/04
106	Most league goals:	1895/96

SEQUENCES

12	Longest sequence of league wins, 21/04/1990-06/10/1990
21	Longest sequence of league wins at home, 29/01/72-20/01/73
9	Longest sequence of league defeats, 29/04/1899-14/10/1899
6	Longest sequence of league draws, 19/02/1975-19/03/1975
31	Longest sequence of unbeaten league matches, 04/05/1987-16/03/1988
14	Longest sequence without a league win, 12/12/1953-20/03/1954
9	Longest sequence of successive defeats, 29/04/1899-14/10/1899
29	Successive scoring runs, from 27/04/1957
5	Successive non-scoring runs, from 22/12/1906, 03/01/1947, 18/12/1971, 01/09/1993, 21/04/1999

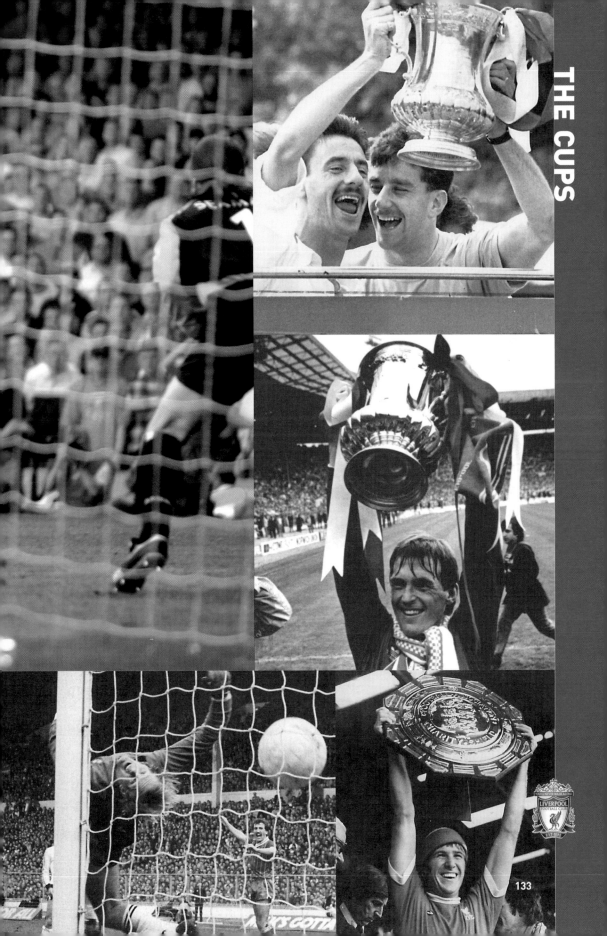

THE FA CUP RECORD

Date	Round	Venue	Opponents	Opponent Division	Score	Scorers	Att
1892-93							
15th Oct	1st Qual	(a)	Nantwich	Non Lge	W 4-0	Miller 3, Wyllie	700
29th Oct	2nd Qual	(h)	Newtown	Non Lge	W 9-0	Wyllie 3, McVean 2, McCartney H.McQueen, Cameron, Townsend o.g.	4,000
19th Nov	3rd Qual	(a)	Northwich Victoria	Non Lge	L 1-2	Wyllie	1,000
1893-94							
27th Jan	1	(h)	Grimsby Town	2	W 3-0	Bradshaw (2), McQue	8,000
10th Feb	2	(h)	Preston North End	1	W 3-2	Henderson (2), McVean	18,000
24th Feb	3	(a)	Bolton Wanderers	1	L 0-3		20,000
1894-95							
2nd Feb	1	(a)	Barnsley St Peters	Non Lge	*D 2-1	Mc Vean, Ross	4,000
11th Feb	1 Rep.	(h)	Barnsley St Peters	Non Lge	W 4-0	Bradshaw, Drummond, McVean, H.McQueen	4,000
16th Feb	2	(h)	Nottingham Forest	1	L 0-2		5,000
1895-96							
1st Feb	1	(h)	Millwall	Non Lge	W 4-1	Ross, Becton, Allan, Bradshaw	10,000
15th Feb	2	(a)	Wolverhampton W.	1	L 0-2		15,000
1896-97							
30th Jan	1	(h)	Burton Swifts	2	W 4-3	Hannah, Allan, Cleghorn, Ross	4,000
13th Feb	2	(a)	West Bromwich Alb.	1	W 2-1	McVean, Neill	16,000
27th Feb	3	(h)	Nottingham Forest	1	D 1-1	Becton	15,000
3rd Mar	3 Rep.	(a)	Nottingham Forest	1	W 1-0	Allan	10,000
20th Mar	S.F.	Bramall La.	Aston Villa	1	L 0-3		30,000
1897-98							
29th Jan	1	(h)	Hucknall St John's	Non Lge	W 2-0	Becton, McQue	8,000
12th Feb	2	(a)	Newton Heath	2	D 0-0		12,000
16th Feb	2 Rep	(h)	Newton Heath	2	W 2-1	Wilkie, Cunliffe	6,000
25th Feb	3	(a)	Derby County	1	D 1-1	Bradshaw	20,000
2nd Mar	3 Rep	(h)	Derby County	1	L 1-5	Becton (pen)	15,000
1898-99							
28th Jan	1	(h)	Blackburn Rovers	1	W 2-0	Cox, Allan	14,000
11th Feb	2	(h)	Newcastle United	1	W 3-1	Morgan, Raisbeck, Higgins o.g.	7,000
25th Feb	3	(a)	West Bromwich Alb.	1	W 2-0	Morgan, Robertson	17,124
18th Mar	S.F.	Nottingham	Sheffield United	1	D 2-2	Allan, Morgan	35,000
23rd Mar	S.F. Rep	Bolton	Sheffield United	1	D 4-4	Walker, Allan, Boyle o.g., Cox	20,000
30th Mar	S.F.Rep (2)	Derby	Sheffield United	1	L 0-1		20,000
1899-1900							
27th Jan	1	(a)	Stoke City.	1	D 0-0		8,000
1st Feb	1 Rep	(h)	Stoke City	1	W 1-0	Hunter	10,000
17th Feb	2	(h)	West Bromwich Alb.	1	D 1-1	Cox	15,000
21st Feb	2 Rep	(a)	West Bromwich Alb.	1	L 1-2	Robertson	13,000
1900-01							
5th Jan	Qual	(a)	West Ham United	Non Lge	W 1-0	Raybould	6,000
9th Feb	1	(a)	Notts County	1	L 0-2		15,000

* (Match counted as a draw after Barnsley protest)

Date	Round	Venue	Opponents	Opponent Division	Score	Scorers	Att
1901-02							
25th Jan	1	(h)	Everton	1	D 2-2	T.Robertson (pen), Hunter	25,000
30th Jan	1 Rep	(a)	Everton	1	W 2-0	Raisbeck, Hunter	20,000
8th Feb	2	(a)	Southampton	Non Lge	L 1-4	Fleming	20,000
1902-03							
7th Feb	1	(a)	Manchester United	2	L 1-2	Raybould	15,000
1903-04							
6th Feb	1	(a)	Blackburn Rovers	1	L 1-3	Raybould	10,000
1904-05							
4th Feb	1	(h)	Everton	1	D 1-1	Parkinson	28,000
8th Feb	1 Rep	(a)	Everton	1	L 1-2	Goddard	40,000
1905-06							
13th Jan	1	(h)	Leicester Fosse	2	W 2-1	Raybould, Goddard	12,000
3rd Feb	2	(h)	Barnsley	2	W 1-0	West	10,000
24th Feb	3	(h)	Brentford	Non Lge	W 2-0	Hewitt, Goddard	20,000
10th Mar	4	(h)	Southampton	Non Lge	W 3-0	Raybould 3	20,000
31st Mar	S.F.	Villa Park	Everton	1	L 0-2		37,000
1906-07							
12th Jan	1	(h)	Birmingham City	1	W 2-1	Raybould 2	20,000
2nd Feb	2	(a)	Oldham Athletic	Non Lge	W 1-0	McPherson	21,500
23rd Feb	3	(h)	Bradford City	2	W 1-0	Cox	18,000
9th Mar	4	(a)	Sheffield Wed.	1	L 0-1		30,000
1907-08							
11th Jan	1	(h)	Derby County	2	W 4-2	Cox, Gorman, Bradley, Parkinson	15,000
1st Feb	2	(h)	Brighton	Non Lge	D 1-1	Cox	36,000
5th Feb	2 Rep	(a)	Brighton	Non Lge	W 3-0	Bradley 2, Cox	10,000
22nd Feb	3	(a)	Newcastle United	1	L 1-3	Saul	45,987
1908-09							
16th Jan	1	(h)	Lincoln City	Non Lge	W 5-1	Orr 3, Hewitt, Parkinson	8,000
6th Feb	2	(h)	Norwich City	Non Lge	L 2-3	Cox, Robinson	25,000
1909-10							
15th Jan	1	(a)	Bristol City	1	L 0-2		10,000
1910-11							
14th Jan	1	(h)	Gainsborough Trin.	2	W 3-2	Bowyer 2, Goddard	15,000
4th Feb	2	(a)	Everton	1	L 1-2	Parkinson	50,000
1911-12							
13th Jan	1	(h)	Leyton	Non Lge	W 1-0	Parkinson	33,000
3rd Feb	2	(a)	Fulham	2	L 0-3		30,000

Date	Round	Venue	Opponents	Opponent Division	Score	Scorers	Att
1912-13							
15th Jan	1	(h)	Bristol City	2	W 3-0	Goddard (pen), Peake, Lacey	15,000
1st Feb	2	(a)	Arsenal	1	W 4-1	Metcalf 3, Lacey	8,653
22nd Feb	3	(h)	Newcastle United	1	D 1-1	Lacey	37,903
26th Feb	3 Rep	(a)	Newcastle United	1	L 0-1		45,000
1913-14							
10th Jan	1	(h)	Barnsley	2	D 1-1	Lacey	33,000
15th Jan	1 Rep	(a)	Barnsley	2	W 1-0	Lacey	23,999
31st Jan	2	(h)	Gillingham	Non Lge	W 2-0	Lacey, Ferguson	42,045
21st Feb	3	(a)	West Ham United	Non Lge	D 1-1	Miller	15,000
25th Feb	3 Rep	(h)	West Ham United	Non Lge	W 5-1	Lacey 2, Miller 2, Metcalf	43,729
7th Mar	4	(h)	QPR	Non Lge	W 2-1	Sheldon, Miller	43,000
28th Mar	S.F.	Tottenham	Aston Villa	1	W 2-0	Nicholl 2	27,474
25th Apr	Final	Crystal Pal.	Burnley	1	L 0-1		72,778
1914-15							
9th Jan	1	(h)	Stockport County	2	W 3-0	Pagnam 2, Metcalf	10,000
30th Jan	2	(a)	Sheffield United	1	L 0-1		25,000
1919-20							
10th Jan	1	(a)	South Shields	2	D 1-1	Lewis	10,000
14th Jan	1 Rep	(h)	South Shields	2	W 2-0	Lewis, Sheldon	40,000
31st Jan	2	(a)	Luton Town	Non Lge	W 2-0	Lacey 2	12,640
23rd Feb	3	(h)	Birmingham City	2	W 2-0	Sheldon, T.Miller	50,000
6th Mar	4	(a)	Huddersfield Town	2	L 1-2	T.Miller	44,248
1920-21							
8th Jan	1	(h)	Manchester United	1	D 1-1	Chambers	36,000
12th Jan	1 Rep	(a)	Manchester United	1	W 2-1	Lacey, Chambers	29,189
29th Jan	2	(a)	Newcastle United	1	L 0-1		61,400
1921-22							
7th Jan	1	(a)	Sunderland	1	D 1-1	Forshaw	30,000
11th Jan	1 Rep	(h)	Sunderland	1	W 5-0	Forshaw 2, Chambers 2, W.Wadsworth	46,000
28th Jan	2	(h)	West Bromwich Alb.	1	L 0-1		50,000
1922-23							
13th Jan	1	(h)	Arsenal	1	D 0-0		37,000
17th Jan	1 Rep	(a)	Arsenal	1	W 4-1	Chambers 2, Johnson, McKinlay (pen)	40,000
3rd Feb	2	(a)	Wolverhampton W.	2	W 2-0	Johnson, Forshaw	40,079
24th Feb	3	(h)	Sheffield United	1	L 1-2	Chambers	51,859
1923-24							
12th Jan	1	(h)	Bradford City	2	W 2-1	Chambers 2	25,000
2nd Feb	2	(a)	Bolton Wanderers	1	W 4-1	Walsh 3, Chambers	51,596
23rd Feb	3	(a)	Southampton	2	D 0-0		18,671
27th Feb	3 Rep	(h)	Southampton	2	W 2-0	Chambers, Forshaw	49,000
8th Mar	4	(a)	Newcastle United	1	L 0-1		56,595

Date	Round	Venue	Opponents	Opponent Division	Score	Scorers	Att
1924-25							
10th Jan	1	(h)	Leeds United	1	W 3-0	Shone 2, Hopkin	39,000
31st Jan	2	(a)	Bristol City	3 Sth	W 1-0	Rawlings	29,362
21st Feb	3	(h)	Birmingham City	1	W 2-1	Rawlings, Shone	44,000
7th Mar	4	(a)	Southampton	2	L 0-1		21,501
1925-26							
9th Jan	3	(a)	Southampton	2	D 0-0		18,031
13th Jan	3 Rep	(h)	Southampton	2	W 1-0	Forshaw	42,000
30th Jan	4	(a)	Fulham	2	L 1-3	Forshaw	36,381
1926-27							
8th Jan	3	(a)	Bournemouth	3 Sth	D 1-1	Hodgson	13,243
12th Jan	3 Rep	(h)	Bournemouth	3 Sth	W 4-1	Hopkin, Chambers 3	36,800
29th Jan	4	(h)	Southport	3 Nth	W 3-1	Hodgson, Chambers, Edmed	51,600
19th Feb	5	(a)	Arsenal	1	L 0-2		43,000
1927-28							
14th Jan	3	(h)	Darlington	3 Nth	W 1-0	Chambers	28,500
28th Jan	4	(a)	Cardiff City	1	L 1-2	Edmed (pen)	20,000
1928-29							
12th Jan	3	(a)	Bristol City	2	W 2-0	Salisbury, Hodgson	28,500
26th Jan	4	(h)	Bolton Wanderers	1	D 0-0		55,055
30th Jan	4 Rep	(a)	Bolton Wanderers	1	L 2-5 aet	Lindsay, Hodgson	41,808
1929-30							
11th Jan	3	(h)	Cardiff City	2	L 1-2	McPherson	50,141
1930-31							
10th Jan	3	(h)	Birmingham City	1	L 0-2		40,500
1931-32							
9th Jan	3	(a)	Everton	1	W 2-1	Gunson, Hodgson	57,090
23rd Jan	4	(a)	Chesterfield	2	W 4-2	Barton 4	28,393
13th Feb	5	(h)	Grimsby Town	1	W 1-0	Gunson	49,479
27th Feb	6	(h)	Chelsea	1	L 0-2		57,804
1932-33							
14th Jan	3	(a)	West Bromwich Alb.	1	L 0-2		29,170
1933-34							
13th Jan	3	(h)	Fulham	2	D 1-1	Hodgson	45,619
17th Jan	3 Rep	(a)	Fulham	2	W 3-2 aet	Hanson, Bradshaw, S.Roberts	28,319
27th Jan	4	(h)	Tranmere Rovers (match played at Anfield)	3 Nth	W 3-1	English 2, Nieuwenhuys	61,036
17th Feb	5	(h)	Bolton Wanderers	2	L 0-3		54,912
1934-35							
12th Jan	3	(a)	Yeovil & Petters	Non Lge	W 6-2	Nieuwenhuys, Wright, Hodgson 2, Roberts 2	13,000
26th Jan	4	(a)	Blackburn Rovers	1	L 0-1		49,546

Date	Round	Venue	Opponents	Opponent Division	Score	Scorers	Att
1935-36							
11th Jan	3	(h)	Swansea Town	2	W 1-0	Wright	33,494
25th Jan	4	(h)	Arsenal	1	L 0-2		53,720
1936-37							
16th Jan	3	(a)	Norwich City	2	L 0-3		26,800
1937-38							
8th Jan	3	(a)	Crystal Palace	3 Sth	D 0-0		33,000
12th Jan	3 Rep	(h)	Crystal Palace	3 Sth	W 3-1 aet	Shafto, Collins o.g., Fagan (pen)	35,919
22nd Jan	4	(a)	Sheffield United	2	D 1-1	Hanson	50,264
26th Jan	4 Rep	(h)	Sheffield United	2	W 1-0	Johnson o.g.	48,297
12th Feb	5	(h)	Huddersfield Town	1	L 0-1		57,682
1938-39							
7th Jan	3	(h)	Luton Town	2	W 3-0	Balmer 2, Paterson	40,431
21st Jan	4	(h)	Stockport County	3 Nth	W 5-1	Nieuwenhuys 2, Eastham, Balmer 2	39,407
11th Feb	5	(a)	Wolverhampton W.	1	L 1-4	Fagan (pen)	61,315
1945-46							
5th Jan	3 Leg 1	(a)	Chester	3 Nth	W 2-0	Liddell, Fagan	12,000
9th Jan	3 Leg 2	(h)	Chester	3 Nth	W 2-1	Fagan 2	11,207
26th Jan	4 Leg 1	(a)	Bolton Wanderers	1	L 0-5		39,692
30th Jan	4 Leg 2	(h)	Bolton Wanderers	1	W 2-0	Balmer, Nieuwenhuys	35,247
1946-47							
11th Jan	3	(a)	Walsall	3 Sth	W 5-2	Foulkes o.g., Done, Liddell, Balmer 2	18,379
25th Jan	4	(h)	Grimsby Town	1	W 2-0	Stubbins, Done	42,265
8th Feb	5	(h)	Derby County	1	W 1-0	Balmer	44,493
1st Mar	6	(h)	Birmingham City	2	W 4-1	Stubbins 3, Balmer	51,911
29th Mar	S.F.	Ewood Pk	Burnley	2	D 0-0 aet		52,570
12th Apr	S.F. Rep	Maine Rd	Burnley	2	L 0-1		72,000
1947-48							
10th Jan	3	(h)	Nottingham Forest	2	W 4-1	Priday, Stubbins 2, Liddell	48,569
24th Jan	4	(a)	Manchester United	1	L 0-3		74,721
			(match played at Goodison Park due to bomb damage)				
1948-49							
8th Jan	3	(a)	Nottingham Forest	2	D 2-2 aet	Fagan, Done	35,000
15th Jan	3 Rep	(h)	Nottingham Forest	2	W 4-0	Payne, Balmer 2, Stubbins	52,218
29th Jan	4	(h)	Notts County	3 Sth	W 1-0	Liddell	61,003
12th Feb	5	(a)	Wolverhampton W.	1	L 1-3	Done	54,983
1949-50							
7th Jan	3	(a)	Blackburn Rovers	2	D 0-0		52,468
11th Jan	3 Rep	(h)	Blackburn Rovers	2	W 2-1	Payne, Fagan	52,221
28th Jan	4	(h)	Exeter City	3 Sth	W 3-1	Baron, Fagan, Payne	45,209
11th Feb	5	(a)	Stockport County	3 Nth	W 2-1	Fagan, Stubbins	27,833
4th Mar	6	(h)	Blackpool	1	W 2-1	Fagan, Liddell	53,973
25th Mar	S.F.	Maine Rd	Everton	1	W 2-0	Paisley, Liddell	72,000
29th Apr	Final	Wembley	Arsenal	1	L 0-2		98,249

Date	Round	Venue	Opponents	Opponent Division	Score	Scorers	Att
1950-51							
6th Jan	3	(a)	Norwich City	3 Sth	L 1-3	Balmer	34,641
1951-52							
12th Jan	3	(h)	Workington Town	3 Nth	W 1-0	Payne	52,581
2nd Feb	4	(h)	Wolverhampton W.	1	W 2-1	Paisley, Done	61,905
23rd Feb	5	(a)	Burnley	1	L 0-2		52,070
1952-53							
10th Jan	3	(a)	Gateshead	3 Nth	L 0-1		15,193
1953-54							
9th Jan	3	(a)	Bolton Wanderers	1	L 0-1		45,341
1954-55							
8th Jan	3	(a)	Lincoln City	2	D 1-1	Evans	15,399
12th Jan	3 Rep	(h)	Lincoln City	2	W 1-0 aet	Evans	32,179
29th Jan	4	(a)	Everton	1	W 4-0	Liddell, A'Court, Evans 2	72,000
19th Feb	5	(h)	Huddersfield Town	1	L 0-2		57,115
1955-56							
7th Jan	3	(h)	Accrington Stanley	3 Nth	W 2-0	Liddell 2	48,385
28th Jan	4	(h)	Scunthorpe United	3 Nth	D 3-3	Liddell 2, Payne	53,393
6th Feb	4 Rep	(a)	Scunthorpe United	3 Nth	W 2-1 aet	Liddell, Arnell	19,500
18th Feb	5	(a)	Manchester City	1	D 0-0		70,640
22nd Feb	5 Rep	(h)	Manchester City	1	L 1-2	Arnell	57,528
1956-57							
5th Jan	3	(a)	Southend United	3 Sth	L 1-2	Wheeler	18,253
1957-58							
4th Jan	3	(h)	Southend United	3 Sth	D 1-1	Smith o.g.	43,454
8th Jan	3 Rep	(a)	Southend United	3 Sth	W 3-2	Molyneux, White, Rowley	20,000
25th Jan	4	(h)	Northampton Town	3 Sth	W 3-1	Liddell, Collins o.g., Bimpson	56,939
15th Feb	5	(a)	Scunthorpe United	3 Nth	W 1-0	Murdoch	23,000
1st Mar	6	(a)	Blackburn Rovers	2	L 1-2	Murdoch	51,000
1958-59							
15th Jan	3	(a)	Worcester City	Non Lge	L 1-2	Twentyman (pen)	15,011
1959-60							
9th Jan	3	(h)	Leyton Orient	2	W 2-1	Hunt 2	40,343
30th Jan	4	(h)	Manchester United	1	L 1-3	Wheeler	56,736
1960-61							
7th Jan	3	(h)	Coventry City	3	W 3-2	Hunt, Lewis, Harrower	50,909
28th Jan	4	(h)	Sunderland	2	L 0-2		46,185
1st Feb	4 Rep	(h)	Burnley	1	W 2-1 aet	St John, Moran (pen)	57,906
16th Mar	5	(a)	Arsenal	1	W 2-1	Melia, Moran (pen)	55,245
30th Mar	6	(h)	West Ham United	1	W 1-0	Hunt	49,036
27th Apr	S.F.	H'borough	Leicester City	1	L 0-1		65,000

The cup that cheers – goalscoring hero Ian St John helps Liverpool to beat Leeds in 1965 (top) and Steve Heighway jumps for joy after scoring in the 1974 Wembley triumph

Date	Round	Venue	Opponents	Opponent Division	Score	Scorers	Att
1961-62							
6th Jan	3	(h)	Chelsea	1	W 4-3	St John 2, Hunt, A'Court	48,455
27th Jan	4	(a)	Oldham Athletic	4	W 2-1	St John 2	42,000
17th Feb	5	(h)	Preston North End	2	D 0-0		54,967
20th Feb	5 Rep	(a)	Preston North End	2	D 0-0 aet		37,831
26th Feb	5 Rep (2)	Old Trafford	Preston North End	2	L 0-1		43,944
1962-63							
9th Jan	3	(a)	Wrexham	3	W 3-0	Hunt, Lewis, Melia	29,992
26th Jan	4	(a)	Burnley	1	D 1-1	Lewis	49,885
21st Feb	4 Rep	(h)	Burnley	1	W 2-1 aet	St John, Moran (pen)	57,906
16th Mar	5	(a)	Arsenal	1	W 2-1	Melia, Moran (pen)	55,245
30th Mar	6	(h)	West Ham United	1	W 1-0	Hunt	49,036
27th Apr	S.F.	Hillsborough	Leicester City	1	L 0-1		65,000
1963-64							
4th Jan	3	(h)	Derby County	2	W 5-0	Arrowsmith 4, Hunt	46,460
25th Jan	4	(h)	Port Vale	3	D 0-0		52,327
27th Jan	4 Rep	(a)	Port Vale	3	W 2-1 aet	Hunt, Thompson	42,179
15th Feb	5	(a)	Arsenal	1	W 1-0	St John	61,295
29th Feb	6	(h)	Swansea Town	2	L 1-2	Thompson	52,608
1964-65							
9th Jan	3	(a)	West Bromwich Alb.	1	W 2-1	Hunt, St John	28,360
30th Jan	4	(h)	Stockport County	4	D 1-1	Milne	51,587
3rd Feb	4 Rep	(a)	Stockport County	4	W 2-0	Hunt 2	24,080
20th Feb	5	(a)	Bolton Wanderers	2	W 1-0	Callaghan	52,207
6th Mar	6	(a)	Leicester City	1	D 0-0		39,356
10th Mar	6 Rep	(h)	Leicester City	1	W 1-0	Hunt	53,324
27th Mar	S.F.	Villa Park	Chelsea	1	W 2-0	Thompson, Stevenson (pen)	67,686
1st May	Final	Wembley	Leeds United	1	W 2-1aet	Hunt, St John	100,000
1965-66							
22nd Jan	3	(h)	Chelsea	1	L 1-2	Hunt	54,097
1966-67							
28th Jan	3	(a)	Watford	3	D 0-0		33,000
1st Feb	3 Rep	(h)	Watford	3	W 3-1	St John, Hunt, Lawler	54,451
18th Feb	4	(h)	Aston Villa	1	W 1-0	St John	52,447
11th Mar	5	(a)	Everton	1	L 0-1		64,851
			(a further 40,149 watched on closed-circuit TV at Anfield)				
1967-68							
27th Jan	3	(a)	Bournemouth	3	D 0-0		24,388
30th Jan	3 Rep	(h)	Bournemouth	3	W 4-1	Hateley, Thompson, Hunt Lawler	54,075
17th Feb	4	(a)	Walsall	3	D 0-0		21,066
19th Feb	4 Rep	(h)	Walsall	3	W 5-2	Hateley 4, Strong	39,113
9th Mar	5	(a)	Tottenham Hotspur	1	D 1-1	Hateley	54,005
12th Mar	5 Rep	(h)	Tottenham Hotspur	1	W 2-1	Hunt, Smith (pen)	53,658
30th Mar	6	(a)	West Bromwich Alb.	1	D 0-0		53,062
8th Apr	6 Rep	(h)	West Bromwich Alb.	1	D 1-1aet	Hateley	54,273
18th Apr	6 Rep (2)	Maine Rd	West Bromwich Alb.	1	L 1-2	Hateley	56,000

Date	Round	Venue	Opponents	Opponent Division	Score	Scorers	Att
1968-69							
4th Jan	3	(h)	Doncaster Rovers	4	W 2-0	Hunt, Callaghan	48,330
25th Jan	4	(h)	Burnley	1	W 2-1	Smith (pen), Hughes	53,677
1st Mar	5	(a)	Leicester City	1	D 0-0		42,002
3rd Mar	5 Rep	(h)	Leicester City	1	L 0-1		54,666
1969-70							
7th Jan	3	(a)	Coventry City	1	D 1-1	Graham	33,688
12th Jan	3 Rep	(h)	Coventry City	1	W 3-0	Ross, Thompson, Graham	51,261
24th Jan	4	(h)	Wrexham	4	W 3-1	Graham 2, St John	54,096
7th Feb	5	(h)	Leicester City	2	D 0-0		53,785
11th Feb	5 Rep	(a)	Leicester City	2	W 2-0	Evans 2	42,100
21st Feb	6	(a)	Watford	2	L 0-1		34,047
1970-71							
2nd Jan	3	(h)	Aldershot	4	W 1-0	McLaughlin	45,500
23rd Jan	4	(h)	Swansea Town	3	W 3-0	Toshack, St John, Lawler	47,229
13th Feb	5	(h)	Southampton	1	W 1-0	Lawler	50,226
6th Mar	6	(h)	Tottenham Hotspur	1	D 0-0		54,731
16th Mar	6 Rep	(a)	Tottenham Hotspur	1	W 1-0	Heighway	56,283
27th Mar	S.F.	Old Trafford	Everton	1	W 2-1	Evans, Hall	62,144
8th May	Final	Wembley	Arsenal	1	L 1-2 aet	Heighway	100,000
1971-72							
15th Jan	3	(a)	Oxford United	2	W 3-0	Keegan 2, Lindsay	18,000
5th Feb	4	(h)	Leeds United	1	D 0-0		56,300
9th Feb	4 Rep	(a)	Leeds United	1	L 0-2		45,821
1972-73							
13th Jan	3	(a)	Burnley	2	D 0-0		35,730
16th Jan	3 Rep	(h)	Burnley	2	W 3-0	Toshack 2, Cormack	56,124
3rd Feb	4	(h)	Manchester City	1	D 0-0		56,296
7th Feb	4 Rep	(a)	Manchester City	1	L 0-2		49,572
1973-74							
5th Jan	3	(h)	Doncaster Rovers	4	D 2-2	Keegan 2	31,483
8th Jan	3 Rep	(a)	Doncaster Rovers	4	W 2-0	Heighway, Cormack	22,499
26th Jan	4	(h)	Carlisle United	2	D 0-0		47,211
29th Jan	4 Rep	(a)	Carlisle United	2	W 2-0	Boersma, Toshack	21,262
16th Feb	5	(h)	Ipswich Town	1	W 2-0	Hall, Keegan	45,340
9th Mar	6	(a)	Bristol City	2	W 1-0	Toshack	37,671
30th Mar	S.F.	Old Trafford	Leicester City	1	D 0-0		60,000
3rd Apr	S.F. Rep	Villa Park	Leicester City	1	W 3-1	Hall, Keegan, Toshack	55,619
4th May	Final	Wembley	Newcastle United	1	W 3-0	Keegan 2, Heighway	100,000
1974-75							
4th Jan	3	(h)	Stoke City	1	W 2-0	Heighway, Keegan	48,723
25th Jan	4	(a)	Ipswich Town	1	L 0-1		34,708
1975-76							
3rd Jan	3	(a)	West Ham United	1	W 2-0	Keegan, Toshack	32,363
24th Jan	4	(a)	Derby County	1	L 0-1		38,200

Date	Round	Venue	Opponents	Opponent Division	Score	Scorers	Att

1976-77

Date	Round	Venue	Opponents	Opponent Division	Score	Scorers	Att
8th Jan	3	(h)	Crystal Palace	3	D 0-0		44,730
11th Jan	3 Rep	(a)	Crystal Palace	3	W 3-2	Keegan, Heighway 2	42,644
29th Jan	4	(h)	Carlisle United	2	W 3-0	Keegan, Toshack, Heighway	45,358
26th Feb	5	(h)	Oldham Athletic	2	W 3-1	Keegan, Case, Neal (pen)	52,455
19th Mar	6	(h)	Middlesbrough	1	W 2-0	Fairclough, Keegan	55,881
23rd Apr	S.F.	Maine Rd	Everton	1	D 2-2	McDermott, Case	52,637
27th Apr	S.F. Rep	Maine Rd	Everton	1	W 3-0	Neal (pen), Case, Kennedy	52,579
21st May	Final	Wembley	Manchester United	1	L 1-2	Case	100,000

1977-78

Date	Round	Venue	Opponents	Opponent Division	Score	Scorers	Att
7th Jan	3	(a)	Chelsea	1	L 2-4	Johnson, Dalglish	45,449

1978-79

Date	Round	Venue	Opponents	Opponent Division	Score	Scorers	Att
10th Jan	3	(a)	Southend United	3	D 0-0		31,033
17th Jan	3 Rep	(h)	Southend United	3	W 3-0	Case, Dalglish, R.Kennedy	37,797
30th Jan	4	(h)	Blackburn Rovers	2	W 1-0	Dalglish	43,432
28th Feb	5	(h)	Burnley	2	W 3-0	Johnson 2, Souness	47,161
10th Mar	6	(a)	Ipswich Town	1	W 1-0	Dalglish	31,322
31st Mar	S.F.	Maine Rd	Manchester United	1	D 2-2	Dalglish, Hansen	52,584
4th Apr	S.F. Rep	Goodison	Manchester United	1	L 0-1		53,069

1979-80

Date	Round	Venue	Opponents	Opponent Division	Score	Scorers	Att
5th Jan	3	(h)	Grimsby Town	3	W 5-0	Souness, Johnson 3, Case	49,706
26th Jan	4	(a)	Nottingham Forest	1	W 2-0	Dalglish, McDermott (pen)	33,277
16th Feb	5	(h)	Bury	3	W 2-0	Fairclough 2	43,769
8th Mar	6	(a)	Tottenham Hotspur	1	W 1-0	Mc Dermott	48,033
12th Apr	S.F.	Hillsborough	Arsenal	1	D 0-0		50,174
16th Apr	S.F. Rep	Villa Park	Arsenal	1	D 1-1 aet	Fairclough	40,679
28th Apr	S.F.Rep (2)	Villa Park	Arsenal	1	D 1-1 aet	Dalglish	42,975
1st May	S.F.Rep (3)	Highfield Rd	Arsenal	1	L 0-1		35,335

1980-81

Date	Round	Venue	Opponents	Opponent Division	Score	Scorers	Att
3rd Jan	3	(h)	Altrincham	Non Lge	W 4-1	McDermott, Dalglish 2, R.Kennedy	37,170
24th Jan	4	(a)	Everton	1	L 1-2	Case	53,804

1981-82

Date	Round	Venue	Opponents	Opponent Division	Score	Scorers	Att
2nd Jan	3	(a)	Swansea City	1	W 4-0	Hansen, Rush 2, Lawrenson	24,179
23rd Jan	4	(a)	Sunderland	1	W 3-0	Dalglish 2, Rush	28,582
13th Feb	5	(a)	Chelsea	2	L 0-2		41,422

1982-83

Date	Round	Venue	Opponents	Opponent Division	Score	Scorers	Att
8th Jan	3	(a)	Blackburn Rovers	2	W 2-1	Hodgson, Rush	21,967
29th Jan	4	(h)	Stoke City	1	W 2-0	Dalglish, Rush	36,666
20th Feb	5	(h)	Brighton	1	L 1-2	Johnston	44,868

1983-84

Date	Round	Venue	Opponents	Opponent Division	Score	Scorers	Att
6th Jan	3	(h)	Newcastle United	2	W 4-0	Robinson, Rush 2, Johnston	33,566
29th Jan	4	(a)	Brighton	2	L 0-2		19,057

Date	Round	Venue	Opponents	Opponent Division	Score	Scorers	Att
1984-85							
5th Jan	3	(h)	Aston Villa	1	W 3-0	Rush 2, Wark	36,877
27th Jan	4	(h)	Tottenham Hotspur	1	W 1-0	Rush	27,905
16th Feb	5	(a)	York City	3	D 1-1	Rush	13,485
20th Feb	5 Rep	(h)	York City	3	W 7-0	Whelan 2, Wark 3, Neal, Walsh	43,010
10th Mar	6	(a)	Barnsley	2	W 4-0	Rush 3, Whelan	19,838
13th Apr	S.F.	Goodison	Manchester United	1	D 2-2 aet	Whelan, Walsh	51,690
17th Apr	S.F. Rep	Maine Rd	Manchester United	1	L 1-2	McGrath o.g.	45,775
1985-86							
4th Jan	3	(h)	Norwich City	2	W 5-0	MacDonald, Walsh, McMahon Whelan, Wark	29,082
26th Jan	4	(a)	Chelsea	1	W 2-1	Rush, Lawrenson	33,625
15th Feb	5	(a)	York City	3	D 1-1	Molby (pen)	12,443
18th Feb	5 Rep	(h)	York City	3	W 3-1 aet	Wark, Molby, Dalglish	29,362
11th Mar	6	(h)	Watford	1	D 0-0		36,775
17th Mar	6 Rep	(a)	Watford	1	W 2-1 aet	Molby (pen), Rush	28,097
5th Apr	S.F.	Tottenham	Southampton	1	W 2-0 aet	Rush 2	44,605
10th May	Final	Wembley	Everton	1	W 3-1	Rush 2, Johnston	98,000
1986-87							
11th Jan	3	(a)	Luton Town	1	D 0-0		11,085
26th Jan	3 Rep	(h)	Luton Town	1	D 0-0 aet		34,822
28th Jan	3 Rep (2)	(a)	Luton Town	1	L 0-3		14,687
1987-88							
9th Jan	3	(a)	Stoke City	2	D 0-0		31,979
12th Jan	3 Rep	(h)	Stoke City	2	W 1-0	Beardsley	39,147
31st Jan	4	(a)	Aston Villa	2	W 2-0	Barnes, Beardsley	46,324
21st Feb	5	(a)	Everton	1	W 1-0	Houghton	48,270
13th Mar	6	(a)	Manchester City	2	W 4-0	Houghton, Beardsley (pen) Johnston, Barnes	44,077
9th Apr	S.F.	Hillsborough	Nottingham Forest	1	W 2-1	Aldridge 2 (1 pen)	51,627
14th May	Final	Wembley	Wimbledon	1	L 0-1		98,203
1988-89							
7th Jan	3	(a)	Carlisle United	4	W 3-0	Barnes, McMahon 2	18,556
29th Jan	4	(a)	Millwall	1	W 2-0	Aldridge, Rush	23,615
18th Feb	5	(a)	Hull City	2	W 3-2	Barnes, Aldridge 2	20,058
18th Mar	6	(h)	Brentford	3	W 4-0	McMahon, Barnes, Beardsley 2	42,376
7th May	S.F.	Old Trafford	Nottingham Forest	1	W 3-1	Aldridge, Laws o.g.	38,000
20th May	Final	Wembley	Everton	1	W 3-2aet	Aldridge, Rush 2	82,800
1989-90							
6th Jan	3	(a)	Swansea City	3	D 0-0		16,098
9th Jan	3 Rep	(h)	Swansea City	3	W 8-0	Barnes 2, Whelan, Rush 3, Beardsley, Nicol	29,194
28th Jan	4	(a)	Norwich City	1	D 0-0		23,152
31st Jan	4 Rep	(h)	Norwich City	1	W 3-1	Nicol, Barnes, Beardsley (pen)	29,339
17th Feb	5	(h)	Southampton	1	W 3-0	Rush, Beardsley, Nicol	35,961
11th Mar	6	(a)	QPR	1	D 2-2	Barnes, Rush	21,057
14th Mar	6 Rep	(h)	QPR	1	W 1-0	Beardsley	38,090
8th Apr	S.F.	Villa Park	Crystal Palace	1	L 3-4 aet	Rush, McMahon, Barnes (pen)	38,389

Date	Round	Venue	Opponents	Opponent Division	Score	Scorers	Att
1990-91							
5th Jan	3	(a)	Blackburn Rovers	2	D 1-1	Atkins o.g.	18,524
8th Jan	3 Rep	(h)	Blackburn Rovers	2	W 3-0	Houghton, Rush, Staunton	34,175
26th Jan	4	(h)	Brighton	2	D 2-2	Rush 2	32,670
30th Jan	4 Rep	(a)	Brighton	2	W 3-2 aet	McMahon 2, Rush	14,392
17th Feb	5	(h)	Everton	1	D 0-0		38,323
20th Feb	5 Rep	(a)	Everton	1	D 4-4 aet	Beardsley 2, Rush, Barnes	37,766
27th Feb	5 Rep (2)	(a)	Everton	1	L 0-1		40,201
1991-92							
6th Jan	3	(a)	Crewe Alexandra	4	W 4-0	McManaman, Barnes 3 (1 pen)	7,400
5th Feb	4	(a)	Bristol Rovers	2	D 1-1	Saunders	9,464
11th Feb	4 Rep	(h)	Bristol Rovers	2	W 2-1	McManaman, Saunders	30,142
16th Feb	5	(a)	Ipswich Town	2	D 0-0		26,140
26th Feb	5 Rep	(h)	Ipswich Town	2	W 3-2 aet	Houghton, Molby, McManaman	27,335
8th Mar	6	(h)	Aston Villa	1	W 1-0	Thomas	29,109
5th Apr	S.F.	Highbury	Portsmouth	2	D 1-1 aet	Whelan	41,869
13th Apr	S.F. Rep	Villa Park	Portsmouth	2	W 0-0 aet		40,077
			(Liverpool won 3-1 on penalties)				
9th May	Final	Wembley	Sunderland	2	W 2-0	Thomas, Rush	79,544
1992-93							
3rd Jan	3	(a)	Bolton Wanderers	2	D 2-2	Winstanley o.g., Rush	21,502
13th Jan	3 Rep	(h)	Bolton Wanderers	2	L 0-2		34,790
1993-94							
19th Jan	3	(a)	Bristol City	1	D 1-1	Rush	21,718
25th Jan	3 Rep	(h)	Bristol City	1	L 0-1		36,720
1994-95							
7th Jan	3	(a)	Birmingham City	2	D 0-0		25,326
18th Jan	3 Rep	(h)	Birmingham City	2	W 1-1aet	Redknapp	36,275
			(Liverpool won 2-0 on penalties)				
28th Jan	4	(a)	Burnley	1	D 0-0		20,551
7th Feb	4 Rep	(h)	Burnley	1	W 1-0	Barnes	32,109
19th Feb	5	(h)	Wimbledon	Prem	D 1-1	Fowler	25,124
28th Feb	5 Rep	(a)	Wimbledon	Prem	W 2-0	Barnes, Rush	12,553
11th Mar	6	(h)	Tottenham Hotspur	Prem	L 1-2	Fowler	39,592
1995-96							
6th Jan	3	(h)	Rochdale	3	W 7-0	Fowler, Collymore 3, Valentine o.g., Rush, McAteer	28,126
18th Feb	4	(a)	Shrewsbury Town	2	W 4-0	Collymore, Walton o.g., Fowler McAteer	7,752
28th Feb	5	(h)	Charlton Athletic	1	W 2-1	Fowler, Collymore	36,818
10th Mar	6	(a)	Leeds United	Prem	D 0-0		34,632
20th Mar	6 Rep	(h)	Leeds United	Prem	W 3-0	McManaman 2, Fowler	30,812
31st Mar	S.F	Old Trafford	Aston Villa	Prem	W 3-0	Fowler 2, McAteer	39,072
11th May	Final	Wembley	Manchester United	Prem	L 0-1		79,007
1996-97							
4th Jan	3	(h)	Burnley	2	W 1-0	Collymore	33,252
26th Jan	4	(a)	Chelsea	Prem	L 2-4	Fowler, Collymore	27,950

Date	Round	Venue	Opponents	Opponent Division	Score	Scorers	Att
1997-98							
3rd Jan	3	(h)	Coventry City	Prem	L 1-3	Redknapp	33,888
1998-99							
3rd Jan	3	(a)	Port Vale	1	W 3-0	Owen (pen), Ince, Fowler	16,557
24th Jan	4	(a)	Manchester United	Prem	L 1-2	Owen	54,591
1999-2000							
12th Dec	3	(a)	Huddersfield Town.	1	W 2-0	Camara, Matteo	23,678
10th Jan	4	(h)	Blackburn Rovers	1	L 0-1		32,839
2000-01							
6th Jan	3	(h)	Rotherham United	2	W 3-0	Heskey 2, Hamann	30,689
27th Jan	4	(a)	Leeds United	Prem	W 2-0	Barmby, Heskey	37,108
18th Feb	5	(h)	Manchester City	Prem	W 4-2	Litmanen (pen), Heskey, Smicer (pen), Babbel	36,231
11th Mar	6	(a)	Tranmere Rovers	1	W 4-2	Murphy, Owen, Gerrard Fowler (pen)	16,334
8th Apr	S.F.	Villa Park	Wycombe W.	2	W 2-1	Heskey, Fowler	40,037
12th May	Final	Cardiff	Arsenal	Prem	W 2-1	Owen 2	74,200
2001-02							
5th Jan	3	(h)	Birmingham City	1	W 3-0	Owen 2 ,Anelka	40,875
27th Jan	4	(a)	Arsenal	Prem	L 0-1		38,092
2002-03							
5th Jan	3	(a)	Manchester City	Prem	W 1-0	Murphy (pen)	28,586
26th Jan	4	(a)	Crystal Palace	1	D 0-0		26,054
5th Feb	4 Rep	(h)	Crystal Palace	1	L 0-2		35,109
2003-04							
4th Jan	3	(a)	Yeovil Town	3	W 2-0	Heskey, Murphy (pen)	9,348
24th Jan	4	(h)	Newcastle United	Prem	W 2-1	Cheyrou 2	41,365
15th Feb	5	(h)	Portsmouth	Prem	D 1-1	Owen	34,669
22nd Feb	5 Rep	(a)	Portsmouth	Prem	L 0-1		19,529
2004-05							
18th Jan	3	(a)	Burnley	Champ	L 0-1		19,033

FA CUP - DID YOU KNOW?

• Tony Hateley holds the record for most FA Cup goals scored in a season (8 in 1967-68).
• The 1974 final was Bill Shankly's last game in charge.
• The 1980 semi-final against Arsenal is the only one ever to go to a third replay - the Gunners finally coming out on top.
• In 1986, when Liverpool won the first-ever Merseyside FA Cup final, their starting XI did not include a single player qualified to play for England, the first time this has happened (Mark Lawrenson, although born in Preston, represented Republic of Ireland).
• Ian Rush holds the club record for scoring in FA Cup finals (5 goals).
• Liverpool won the first FA Cup semi-final to be decided on penalties, against Portsmouth in 1992.
• After beating Sunderland in the 1992 final, Liverpool were given the losers' medals and Sunderland the winners' medals - the players exchanged the medals afterwards.
• The first FA Cup final to be played outside of England was won by the Reds in 2001.

Michael Owen lifts the FA Cup after his dramatic late double against Arsenal helped the Reds to victory in 2001 (top) and Graeme Souness's team celebrate their triumph in 1992

THE LEAGUE CUP

Date	Round	Venue	Opponents	Opponent Division	Score	Scorers	Att
1960-61							
19th Oct	2	(h)	Luton Town	2	D 1-1	Leishman	10,502
24th Oct	2 Rep	(a)	Luton Town	2	W 5-2	Lewis 2, Hickson, Hunt 2	6,125
16th Nov	3	(h)	Southampton	2	L 1-2	Hunt	14,036
1967-68							
13th Sept	2	(h)	Bolton Wanderers	2	D 1-1	Thompson	45,957
27th Sept	2 Rep	(a)	Bolton Wanderers	2	L 2-3	Smith (pen), Callaghan	31,500
1968-69							
4th Sept	2	(h)	Sheffield United	2	W 4-0	Hunt, Lawler, Callaghan, Thompson	32,358
25th Sept	3	(h)	Swansea Town	4	W 2-0	Lawler, Hunt	31,051
15th Oct	4	(a)	Arsenal	1	L 1-2	Lawler	39,299
1969-70							
3rd Sept	2	(a)	Watford	2	W 2-1	Slater o.g., St John	21,149
24th Sept	3	(a)	Manchester City	1	L 2-3	A.Evans, Graham	28,019
1970-71							
8th Sept	2	(a)	Mansfield Town	3	D 0-0		12,532
22nd Sept	2 Rep	(h)	Mansfield Town	3	W 3-2 aet	Hughes, Smith (pen), A.Evans	31,087
6th Oct	3	(a)	Swindon Town	2	L 0-2		23,992
1971-72							
7th Sept	2	(h)	Hull City	2	W 3-0	Lawler, Heighway, Hall (pen)	31,612
5th Oct	3	(h)	Southampton	1	W 1-0	Heighway	28,964
27th Oct	4	(a)	West Ham United	1	L 1-2	Graham	40,878
1972-73							
5th Sept	2	(a)	Carlisle United	2	D 1-1	Keegan	16,257
19th Sept	2 Rep	(h)	Carlisle United	2	W 5-1	Keegan, Boersma 2, Lawler, Heighway	22,128
3rd Oct	3	(a)	West Bromwich Alb.	1	D 1-1	Heighway	17,756
10th Oct	3 Rep	(h)	West Bromwich Alb.	1	W 2-1 aet	Hughes, Keegan	26,461
31st Oct	4	(h)	Leeds United	1	D 2-2	Keegan, Toshack	44,609
22nd Nov	4 Rep	(a)	Leeds United	1	W 1-0	Keegan	34,856
4th Dec	5	(h)	Tottenham Hotspur	1	D 1-1	Hughes	48,677
6th Dec	5 Rep	(a)	Tottenham Hotspur	1	L 1-3	Callaghan	34,565
1973-74							
8th Oct	2	(a)	West Ham United	1	D 2-2	Cormack, Heighway	25,823
29th Oct	2 Rep	(h)	West Ham United	1	W 1-0	Toshack	26,002
21st Nov	3	(a)	Sunderland	2	W 2-0	Keegan, Toshack	36,208
27th Nov	4	(a)	Hull City	2	D 0-0		19,748
4th Dec	4 Rep	(h)	Hull City	2	W 3-1	Callaghan 3	17,120
19th Dec	5	(a)	Wolverhampton W.	1	L 0-1		15,242
1974-75							
10th Sept	2	(h)	Brentford	4	W 2-1	Kennedy, Boersma	21,413
8th Oct	3	(a)	Bristol City	2	D 0-0		25,573
16th Oct	3 Rep	(h)	Bristol City	2	W 4-0	Heighway 2, Kennedy 2	23,694
12th Nov	4	(h)	Middlesbrough	1	L 0-1		24,906

Date	Round	Venue	Opponents	Opponent Division	Score	Scorers	Att
1975-76							
10th Sept	2	(a)	York City	2	W 1-0	Lindsay (pen)	9,421
7th Oct	3	(h)	Burnley	1	D 1-1	Case	24,607
14th Oct	3 Rep	(a)	Burnley	1	L 0-1		20,022
1976-77							
31st Aug	2	(h)	West Bromwich Alb.	1	D 1-1	Callaghan	23,378
6th Sept	2 Rep	(a)	West Bromwich Alb.	1	L 0-1		22,662
1977-78							
30th Aug	2	(h)	Chelsea	1	W 2-0	Dalglish, Case	33,170
26th Oct	3	(h)	Derby County	1	W 2-0	Fairclough 2	30,400
29th Nov	4	(h)	Coventry City	1	D 2-2	Fairclough, Neal (pen)	33,817
20th Dec	4 Rep	(a)	Coventry City	1	W 2-0	Case, Dalglish	36,105
17th Jan	5	(a)	Wrexham	3	W 3-1	Dalglish 3	25,641
7th Feb	S.F.Leg 1	(h)	Arsenal	1	W 2-1	Dalglish, Kennedy	44,764
14th Feb	S.F.Leg 2	(a)	Arsenal	1	D 0-0		49,561
18th Mar	Final	Wembley	Nottingham Forest	1	D 0-0 aet		100,000
22nd Mar	Final Rep.	Old Trafford	Nottingham Forest	1	L 0-1		54,375
1978-79							
28th Aug	2	(a)	Sheffield United	2	L 0-1		35,753
1979-80							
29th Aug	2 Leg 1	(a)	Tranmere Rovers	4	D 0-0		16,759
4th Sept	2 Leg 2	(h)	Tranmere Rovers	4	W 4-0	Thompson, Dalglish 2, Fairclough	24,785
25th Sept	3	(h)	Chesterfield	3	W 3-1	Fairclough, Dalglish, McDermott	20,960
30th Oct	4	(h)	Exeter City	3	W 2-0	Fairclough 2	21,019
5th Dec	5	(a)	Norwich City	1	W 3-1	Johnson 2, Dalglish	23,000
22nd Jan	S.F.Leg 1	(a)	Nottingham Forest	1	L 0-1		32,234
12th Feb	S.F.Leg 2	(h)	Nottingham Forest	1	D 1-1	Fairclough	50,880
1980-81							
27th Aug	2 Leg 1	(a)	Bradford City	4	L 0-1		16,232
2nd Sept	2 Leg 2	(h)	Bradford City	4	W 4-0	Dalglish 2, R.Kennedy, Johnson	21,017
23rd Sept	3	(h)	Swindon Town	3	W 5-0	Lee 2, Dalglish, Cockerill o.g., Fairclough	16,566
28th Oct	4	(h)	Portsmouth	3	W 4-1	Dalglish, Johnson 2, Souness	32,021
5th Dec	5	(h)	Birmingham City	1	W 3-1	Dalglish, McDermott, Johnson	30,236
14th Jan	S.F.Leg 1	(a)	Manchester City	1	W 1-0	R.Kennedy	48,045
10th Feb	S.F.Leg 2	(h)	Manchester City	1	D 1-1	Dalglish	46,711
14th Mar	Final	Wembley	West Ham United	2	D 1-1aet	A.Kennedy	100,000
1st Apr	Final Rep	Villa Park	West Ham United	2	W 2-1	Dalglish, Hansen	36,693
1981-82							
7th Oct	2 Leg 1	(h)	Exeter City	3	W 5-0	Rush 2, McDermott, Dalglish, Whelan	11,478
28th Oct	2 Leg 2	(a)	Exeter City	3	W 6-0	Rush 2, Dalglish, Neal, Sheedy, Marker o.g.	11,740
10th Nov	3	(h)	Middlesbrough	1	W 4-1	Sheedy, Rush, Johnson 2	16,145
1st Dec	4	(a)	Arsenal	1	D 0-0		37,917
8th Dec	4 Rep	(h)	Arsenal	1	W 3-0 aet	Johnston, McDermott (pen), Dalglish	21,375
12th Jan	5	(h)	Barnsley	2	D 0-0		33,707
19th Jan	5 Rep	(a)	Barnsley	2	W 3-1	Souness, Johnson, Dalglish	29,639

Date	Round	Venue	Opponents	Opponent Division	Score	Scorers	Att

1981-82 (cont)

Date	Round	Venue	Opponents	Opponent Division	Score	Scorers	Att
2nd Feb	S.F.Leg 1	(a)	Ipswich Town	1	W 2-0	McDermott, Rush	26,690
9th Feb	S.F.Leg 2	(h)	Ipswich Town	1	D 2-2	Rush, Dalglish	34,933
13th Mar	Final	Wembley	Tottenham Hotspur	1	W 3-1 aet	Whelan 2, Rush	100,000

1982-83

Date	Round	Venue	Opponents	Opponent Division	Score	Scorers	Att
5th Oct	2 Leg 1	(a)	Ipswich Town	1	W 2-1	Rush 2	19,328
26th Oct	2 Leg 2	(h)	Ipswich Town	1	W 2-0	Whelan, Lawrenson	17,698
11th Nov	3	(h)	Rotherham United	2	W 1-0	Johnston	20,412
30th Nov	4	(h)	Norwich City	1	W 2-0	Lawrenson, Fairclough	13,235
18th Jan	5	(h)	West Ham United	1	W 2-1	Hodgson, Souness	23,953
8th Feb	S.F.Leg 1	(h)	Burnley	2	W 3-0	Souness, Neal (pen), Hodgson	33,520
15th Feb	S.F.Leg 2	(a)	Burnley	2	L 0-1		20,000
26th Mar	Final	Wembley	Manchester United	1	W 2-1 aet	Kennedy, Whelan	100,000

1983-84

Date	Round	Venue	Opponents	Opponent Division	Score	Scorers	Att
5th Oct	2 Leg 1	(a)	Brentford	3	W 4-1	Rush 2, Robinson, Souness	17,859
25th Oct	2 Leg 2	(h)	Brentford	3	W 4-0	Souness (pen), Hodgson, Dalglish, Robinson	9,902
8th Nov	3	(a)	Fulham	2	D 1-1	Rush	20,142
22nd Nov	3 Rep	(h)	Fulham	2	D 1-1 aet	Dalglish	15,783
29th Nov	3 Rep (2)	(a)	Fulham	2	W 1-0 aet	Souness	20,905
20th Dec	4	(a)	Birmingham City	1	D 1-1	Souness	17,405
22nd Dec	4 Rep	(h)	Birmingham City	1	W 3-0	Nicol, Rush 2 (1 pen)	11,638
17th Jan	5	(a)	Sheffield Wed.	2	D 2-2	Nicol, Neal (pen)	49,357
25th Jan	5 Rep	(h)	Sheffield Wed.	2	W 3-0	Rush 2, Robinson	40,485
7th Feb	S.F.Leg 1	(h)	Walsall	3	D 2-2	Whelan 2	31,073
14th Feb	S.F.Leg 2	(a)	Walsall	3	W 2-0	Rush, Whelan	19,591
25th Mar	Final	Wembley	Everton	1	D 0-0 aet		100,000
28th Mar	Final Rep	Maine Rd	Everton	1	W 1-0	Souness	52,089

1984-85

Date	Round	Venue	Opponents	Opponent Division	Score	Scorers	Att
24th Sept	2 Leg 1	(a)	Stockport County	4	D 0-0		11,169
9th Oct	2 Leg 2	(h)	Stockport County	4	W 2-0 aet	Robinson, Whelan	13,422
31st Oct	3	(a)	Tottenham Hotspur	1	L 0-1		38,690

1985-86

Date	Round	Venue	Opponents	Opponent Division	Score	Scorers	Att
24th Sept	2 Leg 1	(h)	Oldham Athletic	2	W 3-0	McMahon 2, Rush	16,150
9th Oct	2 Leg 2	(a)	Oldham Athletic	2	W 5-2	Whelan 2, Wark, Rush, MacDonald	7,719
29th Oct	3	(h)	Brighton	2	W 4-0	Walsh 3, Dalglish	15,291
26th Nov	4	(h)	Manchester United	1	W 2-1	Molby 2 (1 pen)	41,291
21st Jan	5	(h)	Ipswich Town	1	W 3-0	Walsh, Whelan, Rush	19,762
12th Feb	S.F.Leg 1	(a)	QPR	1	L 0-1		15,051
5th Mar	S.F.Leg 2	(h)	QPR	1	D 2-2	McMahon, Johnston	23,863

1986-87

Date	Round	Venue	Opponents	Opponent Division	Score	Scorers	Att
23rd Sept	2 Leg 1	(h)	Fulham	3	W 10-0	Rush 2, Wark 2, Whelan, McMahon 4, Nicol	13,498
7th Oct	2 Leg 2	(a)	Fulham	3	W 3-2	McMahon, Parker o.g., Molby (pen)	7,864
29th Oct	3	(h)	Leicester City	1	W 4-1	McMahon 3, Dalglish	20,248
19th Nov	4	(a)	Coventry City	1	D 0-0		26,385
26th Nov	4 Rep	(h)	Coventry City	1	W 3-1	Molby 3 (3 pens)	19,179
21st Jan	5	(a)	Everton	1	W 1-0	Rush	53,325
11th Feb	S.F.Leg 1	(a)	Southampton	1	D 0-0		22,818

Date	Round	Venue	Opponents	Opponent Division	Score	Scorers	Att

1986-87 (cont)

Date	Round	Venue	Opponents	Opp Div	Score	Scorers	Att
11th Feb	S.F.Leg 1	(a)	Southampton	1	D 0-0		22,818
25th Feb	S.F.Leg 2	(h)	Southampton	1	W 3-0	Whelan, Dalglish, Molby	38,481
5th Apr	Final	Wembley	Arsenal	1	L 1-2	Rush	96,000

1987-88

Date	Round	Venue	Opponents	Opp Div	Score	Scorers	Att
23rd Sept	2 Leg 1	(a)	Blackburn Rovers	2	D 1-1	Nicol	13,924
6th Oct	2 Leg 2	(h)	Blackburn Rovers	2	W 1-0	Aldridge	28,994
28th Oct	3	(h)	Everton	1	L 0-1		44,071

1988-89

Date	Round	Venue	Opponents	Opp Div	Score	Scorers	Att
28th Sept	2 Leg 1	(h)	Walsall	2	W 1-0	Gillespie	18,084
12th Oct	2 Leg 2	(a)	Walsall	2	W 3-1	Barnes, Rush, Molby (pen)	12,015
2nd Nov	3	(h)	Arsenal	1	D 1-1	Barnes	31,951
9th Nov	3 Rep	(a)	Arsenal	1	D 0-0		54,029
23rd Nov	3 Rep (2)	Villa Park	Arsenal	1	W 2-1	McMahon, Aldridge	21,708
30th Nov	4	(a)	West Ham United	1	L 1-4	Aldridge (pen)	26,971

1989-90

Date	Round	Venue	Opponents	Opp Div	Score	Scorers	Att
19th Sept	2 Leg 1	(h)	Wigan Athletic	3	W 5-2	Hysen, Rush 2, Beardsley, Barnes	19,231
4th Oct	2 Leg 2	(a)	Wigan Athletic (match played at Anfield)	3	W 3-0	Staunton 3	17,954
25th Oct	3	(a)	Arsenal	1	L 0-1		40,814

1990-91

Date	Round	Venue	Opponents	Opp Div	Score	Scorers	Att
25th Sept	2 Leg 1	(h)	Crewe Alexandra	3	W 5-1	McMahon, Gillespie, Houghton, Rush 2	17,228
9th Oct	2 Leg 2	(a)	Crewe Alexandra	3	W 4-1	Rush 3, Staunton	7,200
31st Oct	3	(a)	Manchester United	1	L 1-3	Houghton	42,033

1991-92

Date	Round	Venue	Opponents	Opp Div	Score	Scorers	Att
25th Sept	2 Leg 1	(h)	Stoke City	3	D 2-2	Rush 2	18,389
9th Oct	2 Leg 2	(a)	Stoke City	3	W 3-2	McManaman, Saunders, Walters	22,335
29th Oct	3	(h)	Port Vale	2	D 2-2	McManaman, Rush	21,553
20th Nov	3 Rep	(a)	Port Vale	2	W 4-1	McManaman, Walters, Houghton, Saunders	18,725
3rd Dec	4	(a)	Peterborough Utd	3	L 0-1		14,114

1992-93

Date	Round	Venue	Opponents	Opp Div	Score	Scorers	Att
22nd Sept	2 Leg 1	(h)	Chesterfield	3	D 4-4	Rosenthal, Hutchison, Walters Wright	12,533
6th Oct	2 Leg 2	(a)	Chesterfield	3	W 4-1	Hutchison, Redknapp, Walters Rush	10,632
28th Oct	3	(a)	Sheffield United	Prem	D 0-0		17,856
11th Nov	3 Rep	(h)	Sheffield United	Prem	W 3-0	McManaman 2, Marsh (pen)	17,654
1st Dec	4	(h)	Crystal Palace	Prem	D 1-1	Marsh (pen)	18,525
16th Dec	4 Rep	(a)	Crystal Palace	Prem	L 1-2 aet	Marsh (pen)	19,622

Date	Round	Venue	Opponents	Opponent Division	Score	Scorers	Att
1993-94							
22nd Sept	2 Leg 1	(a)	Fulham	2	W 3-1	Rush, Clough, Fowler	13,599
5th Oct	2 Leg 2	(h)	Fulham	2	W 5-0	Fowler 5	12,541
27th Oct	3	(h)	Ipswich Town	Prem	W 3-2	Rush 3	19,058
1st Dec	4	(h)	Wimbledon	Prem	D 1-1	Molby (pen)	19,290
14th Dec	4 Rep	(a)	Wimbledon	Prem	L 2-2 aet	Ruddock, Segers o.g.	11,343
			(Liverpool lost 3-4 on penalties)				
1994-95							
21st Sept	2 Leg 1	(h)	Burnley	1	W 2-0	Scales, Fowler	23,359
5th Oct	2 Leg 2	(a)	Burnley	1	W 4-1	Redknapp 2, Fowler, Clough	19,032
25th Oct	3	(h)	Stoke City	1	W 2-1	Rush 2	32,060
30th Nov	4	(a)	Blackburn Rovers	Prem	W 3-1	Rush 3	30,115
11th Jan	5	(h)	Arsenal	Prem	W 1-0	Rush	36,004
15th Feb	S.F.Leg 1	(h)	Crystal Palace	Prem	W 1-0	Fowler	25,480
8th Mar	S.F.Leg 2	(a)	Crystal Palace	Prem	W 1-0	Fowler	18,224
2nd Apr	Final	Wembley	Bolton Wanderers	1	W 2-1	McManaman 2	75,595
1995-96							
20th Sept	2 Leg 1	(h)	Sunderland	1	W 2-0	McManaman, Thomas	25,579
4th Oct	2 Leg 2	(a)	Sunderland	1	W 1-0	Fowler	20,560
25th Oct	3	(h)	Manchester City	Prem	W 4-0	Scales, Fowler, Rush, Harkness	29,394
29th Nov	4	(h)	Newcastle United	Prem	L 0-1		40,077
1996-97							
23rd Oct	3	(a)	Charlton Athletic	1	D 1-1	Fowler	15,000
13th Nov	3 Rep	(h)	Charlton Athletic	1	W 4-1	Wright, Redknapp, Fowler 2	20,714
27th Nov	4	(h)	Arsenal	Prem	W 4-2	McManaman, Fowler 2 (1 pen) Berger	32,814
8th Jan	5	(a)	Middlesbrough	Prem	L 1-2	McManaman	28,670
1997-98							
15th Oct	3	(a)	West Bromwich Alb.	1	W 2-0	Berger, Fowler	21,986
18th Nov	4	(h)	Grimsby Town	2	W 3-0	Owen 3	28,515
7th Jan	5	(a)	Newcastle United	Prem	W 2-0 aet	Owen, Fowler	33,207
27th Jan	S.F.Leg 1	(h)	Middlesbrough	1	W 2-1	Redknapp, Fowler	33,438
18th Feb	S.F.Leg 2	(a)	Middlesbrough	1	L 0-2		29,828
1998-99							
27th Oct	3	(h)	Fulham	2	W 3-1	Morgan o.g., Fowler (pen), Ince	22,296
10th Nov	4	(h)	Tottenham Hotspur	Prem	L 1-3	Owen	20,772
1999-2000							
14th Sept	2 Leg 1	(a)	Hull City	3	W 5-1	Murphy 2, Meijer 2, Staunton	10,034
21st Sept	2 Leg 2	(h)	Hull City	3	W 4-2	Murphy, Maxwell, Riedle 2	24,318
13th Oct	3	(a)	Southampton	Prem	L 1-2	Owen	13,822
2000-01							
1st Nov	3	(h)	Chelsea	Prem	W 2-1 aet	Murphy, Fowler	29,370
29th Nov	4	(a)	Stoke City	2	W 8-0	Ziege, Smicer, Babbel, Fowler 3 (1 pen), Hyypia, Murphy	27,109
13th Dec	5	(h)	Fulham	1	W 3-0 aet	Owen, Smicer, Barmby	20,144
10th Jan	S.F.Leg 1	(a)	Crystal Palace	1	L 1-2	Smicer	25,933
24th Jan	S.F.Leg 2	(h)	Crystal Palace	1	W 5-0	Smicer, Murphy 2, Biscan Fowler	41,854
25th Feb	Final	Cardiff	Birmingham City	1	W 1-1 aet	Fowler	73,500
			(Liverpool won 5-4 on penalties)				

Date	Round	Venue	Opponents	Opponent Division	Score	Scorers	Att
2001-02							
9th Oct	3	(h)	Grimsby Town	1	L 1-2 aet	McAllister (pen)	32,672
2002-03							
6th Nov	3	(h)	Southampton	Prem	W 3-1	Berger, Diouf, Baros	35,870
4th Dec	4	(h)	Ipswich Town	1	W 1-1	Diouf (pen)	26,305
			(Liverpool won 5-4 on penalties)				
18th Dec	5	(a)	Aston Villa	Prem	W 4-3	Murphy 2, Baros, Gerrard	38,530
8th Jan	S.F.Leg 1	(a)	Sheffield United	1	L 1-2	Mellor	30,095
21st Jan	S.F.Leg 2	(h)	Sheffield United	1	W 2-0 aet	Diouf, Owen	43,837
2nd Mar	Final	Cardiff	Manchester United	Prem	W 2-0	Gerrard, Owen	74,500
2003-04							
29th Oct	3	(a)	Blackburn Rovers	Prem	W 4-3	Murphy (pen), Heskey 2, Kewell	16,918
3rd Dec	4	(h)	Bolton Wanderers	Prem	L 2-3	Murphy, Smicer	33,185
2004-05							
26th Oct	3	(a)	Millwall	1	W 3-0	Diao, Baros 2	17,655
10th Nov	4	(h)	Middlesbrough	Prem	W 2-0	Mellor 2	28,176
1st Dec	5	(a)	Tottenham Hotspur	Prem	W 1-1 aet	Sinama-Pongolle (pen)	36,100
			(Liverpool won 4-3 on penalties)				
11th Jan	S.F.Leg 1	(h)	Watford	1	W 1-0	Gerrard	35,739
25th Jan	S.F.Leg 2	(a)	Watford	1	W 1-0	Gerrard	19,797
27th Feb	Final	Cardiff	Chelsea	Prem	L 2-3 aet	Riise, Nunez	71,622

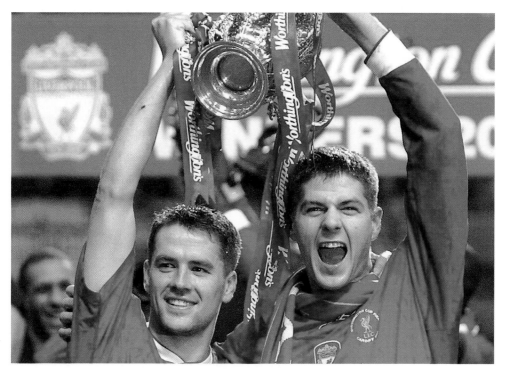

Michael Owen and Steven Gerrard celebrate the 2003 Worthington Cup

WORLD CLUB CHAMPIONSHIP

Date	Round	Venue	Opponents	Opponent Country	Score	Scorers	Att
1981							
13th Dec	Final	Tokyo	Flamengo	Bra	L 0-3		62,000
1984							
9th Dec	Final	Tokyo	Independiente	Arg	L 0-1		62,000

THE CHARITY SHIELD
(FA COMMUNITY SHIELD)

Date	Round	Venue	Opponents	Opponent Division	Score	Scorers	Att
1922							
10th May		Old Trafford	Huddersfield Town	1	L 0-1		20,000
1964							
15th Aug		Anfield	West Ham United	1	D 2-2	Wallace, Byrne	38,858
1965							
14th Aug		Old Trafford	Manchester United	1	D 2-2	Stevenson, Yeats	48,502
1966							
13th Aug		Goodison P	Everton	1	W 1-0	Hunt	63,329
1971							
7th Aug		Filbert St	Leicester City	1	L 0-1		25,014
1974							
10th Aug		Wembley	Leeds United (Liverpool won 6-5 on penalties)	1	W 1-1	Boersma	67,000
1976							
14th Aug		Wembley	Southampton	2	W 1-0	Toshack	76,500
1977							
13th Aug		Wembley	Manchester United	1	D 0-0		82,000
1979							
11th Aug		Wembley	Arsenal	1	W 3-1	McDermott 2, Dalglish	92,000
1980							
9th Aug		Wembley	West Ham United	2	W 1-0	McDermott	90,000
1982							
21st Aug		Wembley	Tottenham Hotspur	1	W 1-0	Rush	82,500
1983							
20th Aug		Wembley	Manchester United	1	L 0-2		92,000
1984							
18th Aug		Wembley	Everton	1	L 0-1		100,000
1986							
16th Aug		Wembley	Everton	1	D 1-1	Rush	88,231
1988							
20th Aug		Wembley	Wimbledon	1	W 2-1	Aldridge 2	54,887
1989							
12th Aug		Wembley	Arsenal	1	W 1-0	Beardsley	63,149
1990							
18th Aug		Wembley	Manchester United	1	D 1-1	Barnes	66,558
1992							
12th Aug		Wembley	Leeds United	Prem	L 3-4	Rush, Saunders, Strachan o.g.	61,291
2001							
12th Aug		Cardiff	Manchester United	Prem	W 2-1	McAllister (pen), Owen	70,227
2002							
11th Aug		Cardiff	Arsenal	Prem	L 0-1		67,337

Gary McAllister converts a penalty to help the Reds to the 2001 Community Shield in Cardiff

SCREEN SPORT SUPER CUP

Date	Round	Venue	Opponents	Opponent Division	Score	Scorers	Att
1985-86							
			Group stage				
17th Sept	Group	(h)	Southampton	1	W 2-1	Molby, Dalglish	16,189
22nd Oct	Group	(a)	Southampton	1	D 1-1	Walsh	10,503
3rd Dec	Group	(h)	Tottenham Hotspur	1	W 2-0	MacDonald, Walsh	14,855
14th Jan	Group	(a)	Tottenham Hotspur	1	W 3-0	Rush 2, Lawrenson	10,078
5th Feb	SF Leg 1	(a)	Norwich City	1	D 1-1	Dalglish	15,330
6th May	SF Leg 2	(h)	Norwich City	1	W 3-1	MacDonald, Molby (pen), Johnston	26,696
1986-87							
16th Sept	F Leg 1	(h)	Everton	1	W 3-1	Rush 2, McMahon	20,660
30th Sept	F Leg 2	(a)	Everton	1	W 4-1	Rush 3, Nicol	26,068

THE MARATHON MEN

CORRECT AT END OF MAY 2005 - Games played includes substitute appearances

OVERALL APPEARANCES (500+ GAMES)

1	Ian Callaghan	857
2	Ray Clemence	665
=	Emlyn Hughes	665
4	Ian Rush	660
5	Phil Neal	650
6	Tommy Smith	638
7	Bruce Grobbelaar	628
8	Alan Hansen	620
9	Chris Lawler	549
10	Billy Liddell	534
11	Kenny Dalglish	515

Most goalkeeper appearances: Legend Clem

LEAGUE APPEARANCES (400+ GAMES)

1	Ian Callaghan	640
2	Billy Liddell	492
3	Emlyn Hughes	474
4	Ray Clemence	470
5	Ian Rush	469
6	Tommy Smith	467
7	Phil Neal	455
8	Bruce Grobbelaar	440
9	Alan Hansen	434
10	Elisha Scott	430
11	Chris Lawler	406
12	Roger Hunt	404

Tommy Smith   **Billy Liddell**

EUROPE APPEARANCES (40+ GAMES)

1	Ian Callaghan	89
2	Tommy Smith	85
3	Ray Clemence	80
4	Emlyn Hughes	79
5	Phil Neal	74
6	Steve Heighway	67
7	Chris Lawler	66
8	Jamie Carragher	65
9	Sami Hyypia	62
10	Steven Gerrard	54
11	Kenny Dalglish	51
12	Dietmar Hamann	50
=	Ray Kennedy	50
=	Michael Owen	50
=	Phil Thompson	50
16	Alan Hansen	46
=	Danny Murphy	46
18	Emile Heskey	45
=	John Arne Riise	45
20	Peter Thompson	43

Loyal servant: The late Emlyn Hughes

FA CUP APPEARANCES (45+ GAMES)

1	Ian Callaghan	79
2	Bruce Grobbelaar	62
=	Emlyn Hughes	62
4	Ian Rush	61
5	Alan Hansen	58
6	Ray Clemence	54
7	Tommy Smith	52
8	John Barnes	51
9	Steve Nicol	50
=	Ron Yeats	50
11	Ian St John	49
12	Chris Lawler	47

LEAGUE CUP APPEARANCES (40+ GAMES)

1	Ian Rush	78
2	Bruce Grobbelaar	70
3	Alan Hansen	68
4	Phil Neal	66
5	Kenny Dalglish	59
6	Ray Clemence	55
7	Mark Lawrenson	50
=	Ronnie Whelan	50
9	Emlyn Hughes	46
10	Alan Kennedy	45
=	Graeme Souness	45
12	Phil Thompson	43
13	Ian Callaghan	42
=	Steve Nicol	42

Alan Hansen: The Liverpool defender with the most accumulated FA Cup and League Cup appearances

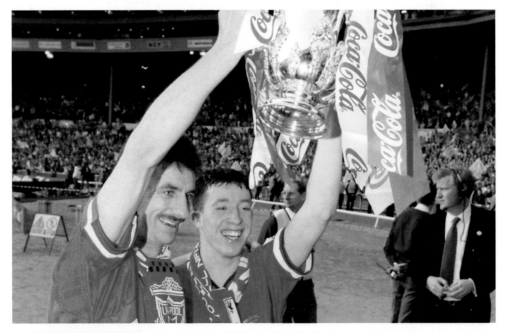

Ian Rush celebrates the Coca-Cola Cup in 1995. Rush holds the League Cup appearance record

THE RECORD GOALSCORERS

CORRECT AT END OF MAY 2005 – Games played includes substitute appearances

OVERALL (100+ GOALS)

		TIME WITH CLUB	GAMES	GOALS
1	Ian Rush	1980-87 & 1988-96	660	346
2	Roger Hunt	1959-1970	492	286
3	Gordon Hodgson	1925-1936	379	241
4	Billy Liddell	1945-1961	534	228
5	Kenny Dalglish	1977-1990	515	172
6	Robbie Fowler	1993-2001	330	171
7	Michael Owen	1997-2004	297	158
8	Harry Chambers	1919-1928	339	151
9	Jack Parkinson	1899-1914	222	130
10	Sam Raybould	1899-1907	224	127
11	Dick Forshaw	1919-1927	288	124
12	Ian St John	1961-1971	425	118
13	Jack Balmer	1935-1952	310	110
14	John Barnes	1987-1997	407	108
15	Kevin Keegan	1971-1977	323	100

LEAGUE (100+ GOALS)

1	Roger Hunt	1959-1970	404	245
2	Gordon Hodgson	1925-1936	360	233
3	Ian Rush	1980-87 & 1988-96	469	229
4	Billy Liddell	1945-1961	492	215
5	Harry Chambers	1919-1928	310	135
6	Jack Parkinson	1899-1914	203	125
7	Robbie Fowler	1993-2001	236	120
8	Sam Raybould	1899-1907	211	119
9	Kenny Dalglish	1979-1990	355	118
=	Michael Owen	1997-2004	216	118
11	Dick Forshaw	1919-1927	266	117

EUROPE (11+ GOALS)

1	Michael Owen	1997-2004	50	22
2	Ian Rush	1980-87 & 1988-96	38	20
3	Roger Hunt	1959-1970	31	17
4	Terry McDermott	1974-1982	34	15
5	Jimmy Case	1974-1981	35	13
=	Emile Heskey	2000-2004	45	13
7	Robbie Fowler	1993-2001	38	12
=	Kevin Keegan	1971-1977	40	12
=	Ray Kennedy	1974-1982	50	12
10	Kenny Dalglish	1979-1990	51	11
=	Steve Heighway	1970-1981	67	11
=	Chris Lawler	1962-1975	66	11
=	Phil Neal	1974-1985	74	11

FA CUP (10+ GOALS)

		TIME WITH CLUB	GAMES	GOALS
1	Ian Rush	1980-87 & 1988-96	61	39
2	Roger Hunt	1959-1970	44	18
3	John Barnes	1987-1997	51	16
=	Harry Chambers	1919-1928	28	16
5	Kevin Keegan	1971-1977	28	14
6	Kenny Dalglish	1979-1990	37	13
=	Billy Liddell	1945-1961	42	13
8	Jack Balmer	1935-1952	21	12
=	Robbie Fowler	1993-2001	24	12
=	Ian St John	1961-1971	49	12
11	Peter Beardsley	1987-1991	25	11
=	Billy Lacey	1911-1924	28	11
13	Willie Fagan	1937-1952	24	10

LEAGUE CUP (10+ GOALS)

1	Ian Rush	1980-87 & 1988-96	78	48
2	Kenny Dalglish	1979-1990	59	27
=	Robbie Fowler	1993-2001	32	27
4	Ronnie Whelan	1980-1994	50	14
5	Steve McMahon	1985-1991	27	13
6	Danny Murphy	1997-2004	16	11
7	David Fairclough	1975-1983	20	10
=	Steve McManaman	1990-1999	33	10

'Sir' Roger Hunt is second only to Ian Rush in the all-time Liverpool goalscoring charts

THE OLDEST/YOUNGEST

Oldest player

	Final game	Age
Ted Doig	April 11 1908	41 years & 165 days

Oldest player (post-War)

Kenny Dalglish	May 1 1990	39 years & 58 days
Billy Liddell	August 31 1960	38 years & 234 days
Gary McAllister	May 11 2002	37 years & 137 days
Paul Jones	January 17 2004	36 years & 274 days
Bruce Grobbelaar	February 19 1994	36 years & 136 days
Phil Taylor	December 25 1953	36 years & 98 days
Jack Balmer	February 16 1952	36 years & 10 days
Ian Callaghan	February 4 1978	35 years 300 days
Berry Nieuwenhuys	February 1 1947	35 years 88 days
Bob Paisley	March 13 1954	35 years 49 days

Youngest player (post-War)

	Debut	Age
Max Thompson	May 8 1974	17 years & 128 days
Michael Owen	May 6 1997	17 years & 144 days
Johnny Morrissey	September 23 1957	17 years & 158 days
Reginald Blore	October 17 1959	17 years & 213 days
Phil Charnock	September 16 1992	17 years & 215 days

Youngest player to score on debut

Michael Owen	May 6 1997	17 years & 144 days

Oldest post-War Liverpool player: Kenny Dalglish featured as a 39-year-old for the Reds

MOST GOALS FOR LIVERPOOL IN A LEAGUE SEASON

Name	Season	Division	Games	Goals	Goal average
Roger Hunt	1961-62	2	41	41	1
Gordon Hodgson	1930-31	1	40	36	1.11
Ian Rush	1983-84	1	41	32	1.28
Sam Raybould	1902-03	1	33	31	1.06
Roger Hunt	1963-64	1	41	31	1.32
Jack Parkinson	1909-10	1	31	30	1.03
Gordon Hodgson	1928-29	1	38	30	1.27
Billy Liddell	1954-55	2	40	30	1.33
Ian Rush	1986-87	1	42	30	1.4
Roger Hunt	1965-66	1	37	29	1.28
John Evans	1954-55	2	38	29	1.31
Robbie Fowler	1995-96	Prem	38	28	1.36
Dick Forshaw	1925-26	1	32	27	1.19
Gordon Hodgson	1934-35	1	34	27	1.26
Billy Liddell	1955-56	2	39	27	1.44
Gordon Hodgson	1931-32	1	39	26	1.5
John Aldridge	1987-88	1	36	26	1.38
George Allan	1895-96	2	20	25	0.8
Roger Hunt	1964-65	1	40	25	1.6
Roger Hunt	1967-68	1	40	25	1.6
Robbie Fowler	1994-95	Prem	42	25	1.68

MOST GOALS FOR LIVERPOOL IN A SEASON
- ALL COMPETITIONS

Name	Season	Games	Goals	Goal average
Ian Rush	1983-84	65	47	1.38
Roger Hunt	1961-62	46	42	1.1
Roger Hunt	1964-65	58	37	1.57
Gordon Hodgson	1930-31	41	36	1.14
Robbie Fowler	1995-96	53	36	1.47
Ian Rush	1986-87	57	35	1.63
John Evans	1954-55	42	33	1.27
Roger Hunt	1963-64	46	33	1.39
Ian Rush	1985-86	56	33	1.7
Sam Raybould	1902-03	34	32	1.06
Gordon Hodgson	1928-29	41	32	1.28
Billy Liddell	1955-56	44	32	1.38
Roger Hunt	1965-66	46	32	1.44
Billy Liddell	1954-55	44	31	1.42
Robbie Fowler	1996-97	44	31	1.42
John Aldridge	1988-89	47	31	1.52
Ian Rush	1982-83	51	31	1.65
Robbie Fowler	1994-95	57	31	1.84
Kenny Dalglish	1977-78	62	31	2

THE HAT-TRICK HEROES

(ALL TIME HAT-TRICKS BY LIVERPOOL PLAYERS - LEAGUE ONLY)

CLUB BY CLUB

ARSENAL

15/02/1908	J. HEWITT (Home)
01/01/1910	J. PARKINSON (Home)
25/02/1922	D. FORSHAW (Home)
26/08/1922	D. JOHNSON (Home)
27/10/1928	G. HODGSON (Away)
23/11/1946	J. BALMER (Home)
28/08/1994	R. FOWLER (Home)
23/12/1995	R. FOWLER (Home)

ASTON VILLA

26/09/1964	B. GRAHAM (Home)
20/01/1984	I. RUSH (Away)
21/11/1998	R. FOWLER (Away)
06/09/2000	M. OWEN (Home)

BIRMINGHAM CITY

29/08/1923	H. CHAMBERS (Home)
17/03/1934	G. HODGSON, 4 (Home)
11/10/1975	J. TOSHACK (Home)
26/04/1986	G. GILLESPIE (Home)

BLACKBURN ROVERS

17/02/1923	D. FORSHAW (Home)
22/02/1958	B. LIDDELL (Away)

BLACKPOOL

04/03/1905	J. PARKINSON (Home)
25/10/1930	J. SMITH (Away)
28/02/1931	G. HODGSON (Home)
08/04/1933	G. HODGSON (Home)

BOLTON WANDERERS

19/04/1913	J. PARKINSON (Home)
09/11/1929	H. RACE (Home)
30/09/1978	J. CASE (Home)
23/09/1995	R. FOWLER, 4 (Home)

BRISTOL ROVERS

15/09/1954	J. EVANS, 5 (Home)
04/04/1961	K. LEWIS (Away)

BURNLEY

26/12/1928	G.HODGSON (Home)
19/09/1953	L.BIMPSON, 4 (Home)
05/12/1964	R.HUNT (Away)

BURTON SWIFTS

29/02/1896	J. ROSS (Away)
29/02/1896	F. BECTON (Away)

BURY

31/08/1927	W. DEVLIN, 4 (Home)
12/03/1955	J. EVANS, 4 (Away)
10/02/1962	R. HUNT (Away)

CARDIFF CITY

15/04/1922	H. CHAMBERS (Home)

CHARLTON ATHLETIC

10/05/1947	A. STUBBINS (Away)
27/08/1988	J. ALDRIDGE (Away)
11/04/1990	R. ROSENTHAL (Away)

CHELSEA

08/01/1910	J. STEWART (Home)
13/02/1915	F. PAGNAM (Home)
27/09/1930	G. HODGSON (Home)
05/10/1997	P. BERGER (Home)

COVENTRY CITY

13/11/1982	I. RUSH (Home)
07/05/1984	I. RUSH, 4 (Home)
12/04/1986	R. WHELAN (Home)
05/05/1990	J. BARNES (Away)
17/04/1993	M. WALTERS (Home)

CREWE ALEXANDRA

28/03/1896	G. ALLAN (Away)

CRYSTAL PALACE

13/11/2004	M. BAROS (Home)

DERBY COUNTY

08/04/1899	J. WALKER (Home)
03/04/1920	D. FORSHAW (Home)
22/01/1927	G. HODGSON (Home)
19/11/1932	G. HODGSON (Home)
16/11/1946	J. BALMER, 4 (Away)
11/12/1971	J. WHITHAM (Home)
29/09/1987	J. ALDRIDGE (Home)
15/10/2000	E. HESKEY (Away)

DONCASTER ROVERS

21/08/1954	A. ROWLEY (Home)

EVERTON

07/10/1922	H. CHAMBERS (Home)
26/09/1925	D. FORSHAW (Home)
11/02/1933	H. BARTON (Home)
07/09/1935	F. HOWE, 4 (Home)
06/11/1982	I. RUSH, 4 (Away)

FULHAM

18/09/1954	B. LIDDELL (Home)

GAINSBOROUGH TRINITY

18/03/1905	S. RAYBOULD (Home)

GLOSSOP

23/12/1899	J. ('SAILOR') HUNTER (Home)

GRIMSBY TOWN

06/12/1902	S. RAYBOULD, 4 (Home)
14/09/1935	F. HOWE (Home)
12/02/1947	C. DONE (Home)

HUDDERSFIELD TOWN

19/10/1946	C. DONE (Away)
06/03/1948	A. STUBBINS, 4 (Home)
15/12/1956	A. ARNELL (Away)

IPSWICH TOWN

25/12/1954	B. LIDDELL, 4 (Home)
17/11/1973	K. KEEGAN (Home)

LEEDS UNITED

02/02/1935	G. HODGSON (Home)
26/08/1961	R. HUNT (Home)

LEICESTER CITY

01/10/1904	R. ROBINSON, 4, (Home)
17/11/1934	G. HODGSON (Home)
14/02/1987	I. RUSH (Home)
20/10/2001	R. FOWLER (Away)

LEYTON ORIENT

11/02/1961	D. HICKSON (Home)
17/11/1962	R. HUNT (Home)

LUTON TOWN

29/10/1983	I. RUSH, 5 (Home)
14/03/1989	J. ALDRIDGE (Home)

MANCHESTER CITY

01/03/1902	S. RAYBOULD (Home)
27/10/1906	R. ROBINSON (Home)
01/05/1978	K. DALGLISH (Home)
27/12/1982	K. DALGLISH (Home)
28/09/2002	M. OWEN (Away)

MANCHESTER UNITED

22/04/1905	S. RAYBOULD (Home)
25/03/1908	W. MCPHERSON (Home)
19/09/1925	D. FORSHAW (Home)
28/08/1926	D. FORSHAW (Home)
21/11/1936	F. HOWE (Away)
16/09/1990	P. BEARDSLEY (Home)

MIDDLESBROUGH

01/11/1902	S. RAYBOULD (Home)
11/11/1905	J. HEWITT (Away)
19/11/1921	D. SHONE (Home)
03/03/1934	G. HODGSON (Home)
24/02/1962	R. HUNT (Home)
14/12/1996	R. FOWLER, 4 (Home)

MIDDLESBROUGH IRONOPOLIS

07/10/1893	J. STOTT (Home)

NEWCASTLE UNITED

14/09/1895	J. ROSS (Home)
25/12/1925	H. CHAMBERS (Home)
07/02/1931	D. WRIGHT (Home)
26/08/1967	T. HATELEY (Home)
20/09/1987	S. NICOL (Away)
30/08/1998	M. OWEN (Away)
05/05/2001	M. OWEN (Home)

NORWICH CITY

09/02/1980	D. FAIRCLOUGH (Away)
01/11/1986	P. WALSH (Home)

NOTTINGHAM FOREST

18/09/1909	J. PARKINSON (Away)
20/04/1910	J. PARKINSON (Home)
17/12/1955	B. LIDDELL (Home)
11/05/1968	T. HATELEY (Home)
24/10/1998	M. OWEN, 4 (Home)

NOTTS COUNTY

09/11/1907	J. HEWITT (Home)
26/01/1982	I. RUSH (Away)
01/01/1983	I. RUSH (Home)

PORT VALE

28/09/1895	G. ALLAN, 4 (Home)
21/10/1895	F. BECTON (Away)
08/04/1905	J. PARKINSON (Home)
14/04/1956	A. ROWLEY (Home)
03/11/1956	J. WHEELER (Home)

PORTSMOUTH

01/10/1927	W. DEVLIN, 4 (Home)
01/10/1927	G. HODGSON (Home)
15/10/1932	G. HODGSON (Home)
09/11/1946	J. BALMER (Home)

PRESTON NORTH END

25/09/1920	D. JOHNSON (Home)
16/09/1922	D. FORSHAW (Home)

ROTHERHAM UNITED

04/01/1896	G. ALLAN (Away)
18/02/1896	G. ALLAN, 4 (Home)
18/02/1896	M. MCVEAN (Home)
28/03/1962	I. ST.JOHN (Home)

SHEFFIELD UNITED

18/10/1924	D. FORSHAW, 4 (Home)
11/09/1926	G. HODGSON (Home)
29/11/1930	G. HODGSON (Home)
26/11/1960	J. HARROWER (Home)
01/02/1964	I. ST.JOHN (Home)

SHEFFIELD WEDNESDAY

11/02/1911	J. PARKINSON (Home)
12/11/1927	T. REID (Home)
14/02/1931	G. HODGSON, 4 (Away)
14/02/1998	M. OWEN (Away)

SOUTHAMPTON

30/10/1993	R. FOWLER (Home)
16/01/1999	R. FOWLER (Home)

STOKE CITY

04/01/1902	A. MCGUIGAN, 5 (Home)
26/12/1963	R. HUNT, 4 (Home)

SUNDERLAND

19/01/1907	J. PARKINSON (Away)
01/01/1909	J. HEWITT (Away)
20/04/1929	H. RACE (Home)
12/02/1966	R. HUNT (Home)

SWANSEA CITY

25/11/1961	R. HUNT (Home)

TOTTENHAM HOTSPUR

30/10/1914	F. PAGNAM, 4 (Home)
01/12/1951	B. LIDDELL (Away)
27/03/1964	R. HUNT (Away)
07/09/1974	P. BOERSMA (Home)

WALSALL

09/12/1893	M. MCVEAN (Home)
14/10/1961	R. HUNT (Home)

WEST BROMWICH ALBION

02/03/1932	G. HODGSON (Home)
06/01/1968	R. HUNT (Home)
23/03/1985	J. WARK (Away)
26/04/2003	M. OWEN, 4 (Away)

WEST HAM UNITED

06/09/1965	R. HUNT (Away)
31/01/1976	J. TOSHACK (Away)
15/10/1983	M. ROBINSON (Away)

Hats off to a treble of heroes. Michael Owen scores his third against Newcastle in 2001 (top). Above: Kevin Keegan and John Aldridge both celebrated Anfield hat-tricks.

THE HAT-TRICK HEROES – COMPETITIONS

FA CUP

10/03/1906	S. RAYBOULD (v Southampton)
16/01/1909	R. ORR (v Lincoln City)
01/02/1913	A. METCALFE (at Arsenal)
02/02/1924	J. WALSH (at Bolton Wanderers)
12/01/1927	H. CHAMBERS (v Bournemouth)
23/01/1932	H. BARTON, 4 (at Chesterfield)
01/03/1947	A. STUBBINS (v Birmingham City)
04/01/1964	A. ARROWSMITH, 4 (v Derby County)
19/02/1968	T. HATELEY, 4 (v Walsall)
05/01/1980	D. JOHNSON (v Grimsby Town)
20/02/1985	J. WARK (v York City)
10/03/1985	I. RUSH (at Barnsley)
09/01/1990	I. RUSH (v Swansea City)
06/01/1992	J. BARNES (at Crewe Alexandra)
07/01/1996	S. COLLYMORE (v Rochdale)

(LEAGUE CUP)

04/12/1973	I. CALLAGHAN (v Hull City)
17/01/1978	K. DALGLISH (at Wrexham)
29/10/1985	P. WALSH (v Brighton)
23/09/1986	S. MCMAHON, 4 (v Fulham)
29/10/1986	S. MCMAHON (v Leicester City)
26/11/1986	J. MOLBY (v Coventry City)
04/10/1989	S. STAUNTON (at Wigan Athletic - played at Anfield)
09/10/1990	I. RUSH (at Crewe Alexandra)
05/10/1993	R. FOWLER, 5 (v Fulham)
27/10/1993	I. RUSH (v Ipswich Town)
30/11/1994	I. RUSH (at Blackburn Rovers)
18/11/1997	M. OWEN (v Grimsby Town)
29/11/2000	R. FOWLER (at Stoke City)

(EUROPE)

10/03/1970	A. EVANS (v Bayern Munich - UEFA Cup)
30/09/1975	J. TOSHACK (v Hibernian - UEFA Cup)
10/12/1975	J. CASE (v Slask Wroclaw - UEFA Cup)
06/12/1977	T. MCDERMOTT (v SV Hamburg - Super Cup)
01/10/1980	G. SOUNESS (v Oulu Palloseura - European Cup)
01/10/1980	T. MCDERMOTT (v Oulu Palloseura - European Cup)
04/03/1981	G. SOUNESS (v CSKA Sofia - European Cup)
03/10/1984	J. WARK (v Lech Poznan - European Cup)
24/10/1984	I. RUSH (v Benfica - European Cup)
18/09/1991	D. SAUNDERS, 4 (v Kuusysi Lahti - UEFA Cup)
11/12/1991	D. SAUNDERS (v Swarovski Tirol - UEFA Cup)
16/09/1992	I. RUSH, 4 (v Apollon Limassol - European Cup Winners' Cup)
08/08/2001	M. OWEN (at FC Haka - European Cup)
22/10/2002	M. OWEN (at Spartak Moscow - European Cup)

THE HAT-TRICK HEROES – TOTALS

30/09/1986   I. RUSH (at Everton)

HAT-TRICKS TOTAL

	At Anfield	Away	Total
LEAGUE	124	43	167
FA CUP	10	5	15
LEAGUE CUP	8	5	13
EUROPE	12	2	14
OTHER GAMES	0	1	1
TOTAL	154	56	210

Hat-tricks scored by 81 different players
up to and including 25th May 2005

A familiar sight at Anfield as Ian Rush celebrates a goal against Southampton in 1990, Rush is the greatest Liverpool goalscorer of all-time. Nobody can compare to him.

BIGGEST-EVER VICTORIES

Date	Opponents	Venue	Competition	Score
17th Sept 1974	Stromsgodset	Home	European Cup Winners' Cup	Won 11-0
16th Sept 1969	Dundalk	Home	Inter Cities' Fairs Cup	Won 10-0
23rd Sept 1986	Fulham	Home	League Cup	Won 10-0
18th Feb 1896	Rotherham Utd	Home	League	Won 10-1
1st Oct 1980	Oulu Palloseura	Home	European Cup	Won 10-1
29th Oct 1892	Newtown	Home	FA Cup	Won 9-0
12th Sept 1989	Crystal Palace	Home	League	Won 9-0
26th Dec 1928	Burnley	Home	League	Won 8-0
7th Nov 1967	TSV Munich 1860	Home	Inter Cities' Fairs Cup	Won 8-0
9th Jan 1990	Swansea City	Home	FA Cup	Won 8-0
29th Nov 2000	Stoke City	Away	League Cup	Won 8-0
6th Dec 1902	Grimsby Town	Home	League	Won 9-2
8th Apr 1905	Port Vale	Home	League	Won 8-1
29th Feb 1896	Burton Swifts	Away	League	Won 7-0
28th Mar 1896	Crewe A	Away	League	Won 7-0
4th Jan 1902	Stoke City	Home	League	Won 7-0
2nd Sept 1978	Tottenham H	Home	League	Won 7-0

BIGGEST-EVER DEFEATS

Date	Opponents	Venue	Competition	Score
11th Dec 1954	Birmingham C	Away	League	Lost 9-1
10th Nov 1934	Huddersfield T	Away	League	Lost 8-0
1st Jan 1934	Newcastle Utd	Away	League	Lost 9-2
7th May 1932	Bolton W	Away	League	Lost 8-1
1st Sept 1934	Arsenal	Away	League	Lost 8-1
7th Dec 1912	Sunderland	Away	League	Lost 7-0
1st Sept 1930	West Ham United	Away	League	Lost 7-0
19th Apr 1930	Sunderland	Home	League	Lost 6-0
28th Nov 1931	Arsenal	Away	League	Lost 6-0
11th Sept 1935	Manchester City	Away	League	Lost 6-0
26th Sept 1953	Charlton Athletic	Away	League	Lost 6-0

Famous night: John Aldridge bows out after the Reds' 9-0 defeat of Crystal Palace in 1989

THE INDIVIDUAL HONOURS

FOOTBALL WRITERS FOOTBALLER OF THE YEAR

Honours won (that season)

1974	Ian Callaghan	FA Cup
1976	Kevin Keegan	First Division, UEFA Cup
1977	Emlyn Hughes	First Division, European Cup, Charity Shield
1979	Kenny Dalglish	First Division
1980	Terry McDermott	First Division, Charity Shield
1983	Kenny Dalglish	First Division, League Cup, Charity Shield
1984	Ian Rush	First Division, League Cup, European Cup
1988	John Barnes	First Division
1989	Steve Nicol	FA Cup, Charity Shield
1990	John Barnes	First Division, Charity Shield

PFA PLAYER OF THE YEAR

1980	Terry McDermott	First Division, Charity Shield
1983	Kenny Dalglish	First Division, League Cup, Charity Shield
1984	Ian Rush	First Division, League Cup, European Cup
1988	John Barnes	First Division

PFA YOUNG PLAYER OF THE YEAR

1983	Ian Rush	First Division, League Cup, Charity Shield
1995	Robbie Fowler	League Cup
1996	Robbie Fowler	
1998	Michael Owen	
2001	Steven Gerrard	FA Cup, League Cup, UEFA Cup

EUROPEAN FOOTBALLER OF THE YEAR

2001	Michael Owen	FA Cup, League Cup, UEFA Cup

MANAGER OF THE YEAR

1973	Bill Shankly	First Division, UEFA Cup
1976	Bob Paisley	First Division, UEFA Cup
1977	Bob Paisley	First Division, European Cup, European Super Cup, Charity Shield
1979	Bob Paisley	First Division
1980	Bob Paisley	First Division, Charity Shield
1982	Bob Paisley	First Division, League Cup
1983	Bob Paisley	First Division, League Cup, Charity Shield
1984	Joe Fagan	First Division, League Cup, European Cup
1986	Kenny Dalglish	First Division, FA Cup
1988	Kenny Dalglish	First Division
1990	Kenny Dalglish	First Division, Charity Shield

PLAYER WITH MOST MEDALS

20	Phil Neal (8 League, 1 FA Cup runner-up, 4 League Cup, 1 runner-up, 5 European, 1 runner-up)

NATIONALITIES

The signing of Mauricio Pellegrino during the winter transfer window of 2004-05 took the number of different overseas nationalities (excluding the home nations and the Republic of Ireland) who have represented Liverpool in a first-team game to 24, thus players such as goalkeeper Michael Stensgaard (Denmark) and Daniel Sjolund (Finland) have been left off the list due to this rule.

The advent of overseas players has increased markedly in recent years due in part to the Bosman ruling and subsequent relaxation of rules permitting foreign players in the English league, and also due to the management of Gerard Houllier and Rafael Benitez in pursuing the signing of overseas stars. Below is a comprehensive list of those players:

COUNTRIES REPRESENTED	PLAYERS
Argentina	Mauricio Pellegrino
Australia	Harry Kewell
Cameroon	Rigobert Song
Croatia	Igor Biscan
Czech Republic	Patrik Berger, Vladimir Smicer, Milan Baros
Denmark	Jan Molby, Jorgen Nielsen, Torben Piechnik
Finland	Sami Hyypia, Jari Litmanen
France	Jean-Michel Ferri, Pegguy Arphexad, Bernard Diomede, Gregory Vignal, Nicolas Anelka, Bruno Cheyrou, Patrice Luzi, Anthony Le Tallec, Florent Sinama-Pongolle, Djibril Cisse
Germany	Karlheinz Riedle, Dietmar Hamann, Markus Babbel, Christian Ziege, Sean Dundee
Guinea	Titi Camara
Holland	Erik Meijer, Sander Westerveld, Boudewijn Zenden
Hungry	Istvan Kozma
Israel	Avi Cohen, Ronny Rosenthal
Mali	Djimi Traore, Mohamed Sissoko
Norway	Stig Inge Bjornebye, Oyvind Leonhardsen, Bjorn Tore Kvarme, Vegard Heggem, Frode Kippe, John Arne Riise
Poland	Jerzy Dudek
Portugal	Abel Xavier
Senegal	El-Hadji Diouf, Salif Diao
South Africa	Lance Carr, Hugh Gerhadi, Gordon Hodgson, Dirk Kemp, Berry Nieuwenhuys, Robert Priday, Arthur Riley, Doug Rudham, Charlie Thompson, Harman Van Den Berg
Spain	Josemi, Luis Garcia, Xabi Alonso, Antonio Nunez, Fernando Morientes, Jose Reina, Antonio Barragan
Sweden	Glenn Hysen
Switzerland	Stephane Henchoz
USA	Brad Friedel, Zak Whitbread
Zimbabwe	Bruce Grobbelaar

* Note Craig Johnston (born in South Africa) represented England at 'B' and U21 level and has not been included – likewise John Barnes (born in Jamaica) played for England.

Top 5 capped players (while at Liverpool)

England

60	Michael Owen
59	Emlyn Hughes
56	Ray Clemence
50	Phil Neal
48	John Barnes

Scotland

55	Kenny Dalglish
37	Graeme Souness
28	Billy Liddell
27	Steve Nicol
26	Alan Hansen

Wales

67	Ian Rush
26	John Toshack
18	Joey Jones
16	Maurice Parry
10	Ernest Peake

Northern Ireland (3 players only)

27	Elisha Scott
12	Billy Lacey
3	David McMullen

Republic of Ireland

51	Ronnie Whelan
38	Steve Staunton
34	Ray Houghton
33	Steve Heighway
25	Phil Babb

Ronnie Whelan: Most capped Republic of Ireland man while a Liverpool player

Phil Neal - Liverpool's most decorated player, who won 50 caps for England during his Reds career

ARSENAL

FINAL STANDINGS 04-05

		W	D	L	PTS
1	Chelsea	29	8	1	95
2	Arsenal	25	8	5	83
3	Man Utd	22	11	5	77

ALL-TIME RECORD

(League matches only)

	PL	W	D	L
Home:	81	46	14	21
Away:	81	20	26	35
Overall:	162	66	40	56

LAST 2 MEETINGS

08/05/2005

Arsenal	3-1	Liverpool
Pires 25, Reyes 29, Fabregas 90		Gerrard 51

28/11/2004

Liverpool	2-1	Arsenal
Alonso 41, Mellor 90		Vieira 57

CLUB DETAILS

Nickname: The Gunners
Ground: Highbury, capacity 38,500 (due to move to Ashburton Grove for start of 2006-07)
Manager: Arsene Wenger (app. 30/09/96)
Assistant: Pat Rice
Year formed: 1886

USEFUL INFORMATION

Website: www.arsenal.com
Address: Arsenal Stadium, Avenell Road, Highbury, London N5 1BU
Switchboard: 0207 704 4000

TRAVEL INFORMATION

By Train: Get off at Arsenal (closest to ground); Finsbury Park; Highbury or Islington.
By Bus: Take numbers 4, 19 and 236 which go along Highbury Grove to Blackstock Road. From here it is a 5-10 minute walk to turnstiles.

ASTON VILLA

FINAL STANDINGS 04-05

		W	D	L	PTS
9	Tottenham	14	10	14	52
10	Aston Villa	12	11	15	47
11	Charlton	12	10	16	46

ALL-TIME RECORD

(League matches only)

	PL	W	D	L
Home:	80	50	16	14
Away:	80	24	19	37
Overall:	160	74	35	51

LAST 2 MEETINGS

15/05/2005

Liverpool	2-1	Aston Villa
Cisse20 (p), 27		Barry 67

04/12/2004

Aston Villa	1-1	Liverpool
Solano 44		Kewell 16

CLUB DETAILS

Nickname: The Villans
Ground: Villa Park, capacity 42,602
Manager: David O'Leary (app. 20/05/03)
Assistant: Roy Aitken
Year formed: 1874

USEFUL INFORMATION

Website: www.avfc.co.uk
Address: Villa Park, Trinity Road, Birmingham B6 6HE
Switchboard: 0121 327 2299

TRAVEL INFORMATION

By Train: It is a two-minute walk from Witton Station. Aston Station is a 10-minute walk with connecting trains running from Birmingham New Street.
By Bus: The number 7 runs from Birmingham City Centre directly to the ground, while numbers 11a and 11c also serve Villa Park.

BIRMINGHAM CITY

FINAL STANDINGS 04-05

		W	D	L	PTS
11	Charlton	12	10	16	46
12	**Birmingham**	**11**	**12**	**15**	**45**
13	Fulham	12	8	18	44

ALL-TIME RECORD

(League matches only)

	PL	W	D	L
Home:	46	31	8	7
Away:	46	15	10	21
Overall:	92	46	18	28

LAST 2 MEETINGS

12/02/2005

Birmingham City	2-0	Liverpool
Pandiani 38 (p), Gray 45		

06/11/2004

Liverpool	0-1	Birmingham City
		Anderton 77

CLUB DETAILS

Nickname: Blues
Ground: St Andrews, capacity 30,000
Manager: Steve Bruce (app. 12/12/01)
Assistant: John Benson
Year formed: 1875

USEFUL INFORMATION

Website: www.bcfc.com
Address: St Andrews, Birmingham B9 4NH
Switchboard: 0871 226 1875

TRAVEL INFORMATION

By Train: Birmingham New Street and Birmingham Moor Street are around 20 minutes' walk - taxis should cost around £5.
By Bus: Numbers 56, 57, 57a, 58 and 60 run from the city centre to the ground.

BLACKBURN ROVERS

FINAL STANDINGS 04-05

		W	D	L	PTS
14	Newcastle	10	14	14	44
15	**Blackburn**	**9**	**15**	**14**	**42**
16	Portsmouth	10	9	19	39

ALL-TIME RECORD

(League matches only)

	PL	W	D	L
Home:	57	33	15	9
Away:	57	13	20	24
Overall:	114	46	35	33

LAST 2 MEETINGS

16/03/2005

Liverpool	0-0	Blackburn Rovers

30/10/2004

Blackburn Rovers	2-2	Liverpool
Bothroyd 16, Emerton 45		Riise 7, Baros 54

CLUB DETAILS

Nickname: Rovers
Ground: Ewood Park, capacity 31,367
Manager: Mark Hughes (app. 15/09/04)
Assistant: Mark Bowen
Year formed: 1875

USEFUL INFORMATION

Website: www.rovers.co.uk
Address: Ewood Park, Blackburn, Lancashire BB2 4JF
Switchboard: 01254 698888

TRAVEL INFORMATION

By Train: Blackburn Station is 1 1/2 miles away, while Mill Hill is 1 mile from the stadium.
By Bus: The central bus station is next to the railway station. Services 3, 3A, 3B, 46 and 346 all go from Blackburn to Darwen - Ewood Park is about a mile and a half along the route.

BOLTON WANDERERS

FINAL STANDINGS 04-05

		W	D	L	PTS
5	Liverpool	17	7	14	58
6	**Bolton**	**16**	**10**	**12**	**58**
7	Middlesbro	14	13	11	55

ALL-TIME RECORD

(League matches only)

	PL	W	D	L
Home:	52	26	16	10
Away:	52	16	12	24
Overall:	104	42	28	34

LAST 2 MEETINGS

02/04/2005

Liverpool	1-0	Bolton Wanderers
Biscan 86		

29/08/2004

Bolton Wanderers 1-0	Liverpool
Davies 38	

CLUB DETAILS

Nickname:	The Trotters
Ground:	Reebok Stadium, capacity 28,000
Manager:	Sam Allardyce (app. 19/10/99)
Assistant:	Sammy Lee
Year formed:	1874

USEFUL INFORMATION

Website:	www.bwfc.co.uk
Address:	Reebok Stadium, Burnden Way, Lostock, Bolton BL6 6JW
Switchboard:	01204 673673

TRAVEL INFORMATION

By Train: Horwich Parkway Station is a two-minute walk from the stadium, while Bolton Station is around 5 miles away.

By Bus: The club run buses from Bolton town centre, while the number 539 bus runs directly to the ground.

CHARLTON ATHLETIC

FINAL STANDINGS 04-05

		W	D	L	PTS
10	Aston Villa	12	11	15	47
11	**Charlton**	**12**	**10**	**16**	**46**
12	Birmingham	11	12	15	45

ALL-TIME RECORD

(League matches only)

	PL	W	D	L
Home:	26	16	4	6
Away:	26	12	2	12
Overall:	52	28	6	18

LAST 2 MEETINGS

01/02/2005

Charlton Athletic	1-2	Liverpool
Bartlett 20		Morientes 61,
		Riise 79

23/10/2004

Liverpool	2-0	Charlton Athletic
Riise 52,		
Luis Garcia 74		

CLUB DETAILS

Nickname:	Addicks
Ground:	The Valley, capacity 27,100
Manager:	Alan Curbishley (app. 24/07/91)
Assistant:	Keith Peacock
Year formed:	1905

USEFUL INFORMATION

Website:	www.cafc.co.uk
Address:	The Valley, Floyd Road, Charlton, London SE7 8BL
Switchboard:	0208 333 4000

TRAVEL INFORMATION

By Train: Trains run from Charing Cross, London Bridge and Waterloo East to Charlton Station, about two minutes walk. Turn right out of the station and left into Floyd Road. North Greenwich on the Jubilee Line has bus links to the ground.

By Bus: Numerous routes serve the ground including the 53, 54, 161, 177, 180, 422, 472 and the 486.

CHELSEA

FINAL STANDINGS 04-05

		W	D	L	PTS
1	Chelsea	29	8	1	95
2	Arsenal	25	8	5	83
3	Man Utd	22	11	5	77

ALL-TIME RECORD

(League matches only)

	PL	W	D	L
Home:	62	42	13	7
Away:	62	15	13	34
Overall:	124	57	26	41

LAST 2 MEETINGS (LEAGUE)

01/01/2005

Liverpool	0-1	Chelsea
		Cole 80

03/10/2004

Chelsea	1-0	Liverpool
Cole 64		

CLUB DETAILS

Nickname: The Blues
Ground: Stamford Bridge, capacity 42,522
Manager: Jose Mourinho (app. 02/06/04)
Assistant: Steve Clarke/Baltemar Brito
Year formed: 1905

USEFUL INFORMATION

Website: www.chelseafc.com
Address: Stamford Bridge, London SW6 1HS
Switchboard: 0207 385 5545

TRAVEL INFORMATION

By Train: Fulham Broadway (tube) is on the District Line, around 5 minutes walk. Turn left out of the station and the ground is on the left.
By Bus: Numbers 14, 414 and 211 go along Fulham Road. The 11, 14, 28, 211, 295, 391, 414 and 424 all stop near the stadium.

EVERTON

FINAL STANDINGS 04-05

		W	D	L	PTS
3	Man Utd	22	11	5	77
4	Everton	18	7	13	61
5	Liverpool	17	7	14	58

ALL-TIME RECORD

(League matches only)

	PL	W	D	L
Home:	86	36	27	23
Away:	86	27	27	32
Overall:	172	63	54	55

LAST 2 MEETINGS

20/03/2005

Liverpool	2-1	Everton
Gerrard 27,		Cahill 82
Luis Garcia 32		

11/12/2004

Everton	1-0	Liverpool
Carsley 68		

CLUB DETAILS

Nickname: The Toffees
Ground: Goodison Park, capacity 40,200
Manager: David Moyes (app. 15/03/02)
Assistant: Alan Irvine
Year formed: 1878

USEFUL INFORMATION

Website: www.evertonfc.com
Address: Goodison Park, Liverpool L4 4EL
Switchboard: 0151 330 2200

TRAVEL INFORMATION

By Train: From Liverpool Central, take any train heading for Ormskirk or Kirkby and get off at Kirkdale - from there it is a 10-minute walk.
By Bus: From Queen's Square Bus Station in Liverpool city centre, numbers 1, 2, 19, 20, 311, 345 and 350 go past the stadium.

FULHAM

FINAL STANDINGS 04-05

		W	D	L	PTS
12	Birmingham	11	12	15	45
13	**Fulham**	**12**	**8**	**18**	**44**
14	Newcastle	10	14	14	44

ALL-TIME RECORD

(League matches only)

	PL	W	D	L
Home:	18	13	5	0
Away:	18	7	6	5
Overall:	36	20	11	5

LAST 2 MEETINGS

05/02/2005

Liverpool	3-1	Fulham
Morientes 9,		Cole 16
Hyypia 63, Baros 77		

16/10/2004

Fulham	2-4	Liverpool
Boa Morte 24, 30		Knight 50 (og), Baros 71
		Alonso 79, Biscan 89

CLUB DETAILS

Nickname:	Cottagers
Ground:	Craven Cottage, capacity 22,000
Manager:	Chris Coleman (app. 17/04/03)
Assistant:	Steve Kean
Year formed:	1879

USEFUL INFORMATION

Website:	www.fulhamfc.com
Address:	Craven Cottage, Stevenage Road, Fulham, London SW6 6HH
Switchboard:	0207 893 8383

TRAVEL INFORMATION

By Train: Alight at Putney Bridge. Turn left out of station and right down Ranleigh Gardens. At the end of the road (before the Eight Bells pub) turn left into Willow Bank and right through the underpass into Bishops Park. Walk along river to ground.
By Bus: The numbers 74 and 220 both run along Fulham Palace Road.

MANCHESTER CITY

FINAL STANDINGS 04-05

		W	D	L	PTS
7	Middlesbro	14	13	11	55
8	**Man City**	**13**	**13**	**12**	**52**
9	Tottenham	14	10	14	52

ALL-TIME RECORD

(League matches only)

	PL	W	D	L
Home:	69	42	14	13
Away:	69	27	18	24
Overall:	138	69	32	37

LAST 2 MEETINGS

09/04/2005

Manchester City	1-0	Liverpool
Musampa 90		

21/08/2004

Liverpool	2-1	Manchester City
Baros 48, Gerrard 75		Anelka 45

CLUB DETAILS

Nickname:	Blues/The Citizens
Ground:	City of Manchester Stadium, capacity 48,000
Manager:	Stuart Pearce (app. 11/03/05)
First-team coach:	Derek Fazackerley
Year formed:	1887

USEFUL INFORMATION

Website:	www.mcfc.co.uk
Address:	City of Manchester Stadium, Sportcity, Manchester M11 3FF
Switchboard:	0161 231 3200

TRAVEL INFORMATION

By Train: The nearest station is Manchester Piccadilly, roughly 1 mile from the stadium.
By Bus: Numbers 216, 217, 230 and 237 run from the city centre.

MANCHESTER UNITED

FINAL STANDINGS 04-05

		W	D	L	PTS
2	Arsenal	25	8	5	83
3	**Man Utd**	**22**	**11**	**5**	**77**
4	Everton	18	7	13	61

ALL-TIME RECORD

(League matches only)

	PL	W	D	L
Home:	72	35	17	20
Away:	72	14	25	33
Overall:	144	49	42	53

LAST 2 MEETINGS

15/01/2005

Liverpool	0-1	Manchester Utd
		Rooney 21

20/09/2004

Manchester Utd	2-1	Liverpool
Silvestre 20, 66		O'Shea 54 (og)

CLUB DETAILS

Nickname:	Red Devils
Ground:	Old Trafford, capacity 68,190
Manager:	Sir Alex Ferguson (app. 06/11/86)
Assistant:	Carlos Queiroz
Year formed:	1878

USEFUL INFORMATION

Website:	www.manutd.com
Address:	Old Trafford, Manchester M16 0RA
Switchboard:	0161 868 8000

TRAVEL INFORMATION

By Train: Special services run from the clubs own railway station adjacent to the south stand.

By Bus: Numbers 114, 230, 252 and 253 all run from the city centre to the ground.

MIDDLESBROUGH

FINAL STANDINGS 04-05

		W	D	L	PTS
6	Bolton	16	10	12	58
7	**Middlesbro**	**14**	**13**	**11**	**55**
8	Man City	13	13	12	52

ALL-TIME RECORD

(League matches only)

	PL	W	D	L
Home:	63	33	17	13
Away:	63	20	19	24
Overall:	126	53	36	37

LAST 2 MEETINGS

30/04/2005

Liverpool	1-1	Middlesbrough
Gerrard 52		Nemeth 4

20/11/2004

Middlesbrough	2-0	Liverpool
Riggott 36, Zenden 62		

CLUB DETAILS

Nickname:	Boro
Ground:	Riverside Stadium, capacity 35,100
Manager:	Steve McClaren (app. 12/06/01)
Assistant:	Bill Beswick
Year formed:	1876

USEFUL INFORMATION

Website:	www.mfc.co.uk
Address:	Cellnet Riverside Stadium, Middlesbrough, Cleveland TS3 6RS
Switchboard:	01642 877700

TRAVEL INFORMATION

By Train: Middlesbrough Station is about 15 minutes walk from the stadium, take the back exit from the station, turn right then after a couple of minutes right again into Windward Way.

By Bus: Numbers 36, 37 and 38 go from the town centre close to the ground.

NEWCASTLE UNITED

FINAL STANDINGS 04-05

		W	D	L	PTS
13	Fulham	12	8	18	44
14	**Newcastle**	**10**	**14**	**14**	**44**
15	Blackburn	9	15	14	42

ALL-TIME RECORD

(League matches only)

	PL	W	D	L
Home:	70	45	14	11
Away:	70	19	23	28
Overall:	140	64	37	39

LAST 2 MEETINGS

05/03/2005

Newcastle	1-0	Liverpool
Robert 70		

19/12/2004

Liverpool	3-1	Newcastle
Bramble 35 (og),		Kluivert 32
Mellor 38, Baros 61		

CLUB DETAILS

Nickname: Magpies
Ground: St James' Park, capacity 52,387
Manager: Graeme Souness (app. 13/09/04)
Assistant: Alan Murray
Year formed: 1881

USEFUL INFORMATION

Website: www.nufc.co.uk
Address: St James' Park,
Newcastle-upon-Tyne
NE1 4ST
Switchboard: 0191 201 8400

TRAVEL INFORMATION

By Train: St James' Park is a 5-minute walk from Newcastle Central Station. The stadium is also served by its own Metro station (St James' Metro).
By Bus: Any bus from the town centre heading towards Gallowgate.

PORTSMOUTH

FINAL STANDINGS 04-05

		W	D	L	PTS
15	Blackburn	9	15	14	42
16	**Portsmouth**	**10**	**9**	**19**	**39**
17	West Brom	6	16	16	34

ALL-TIME RECORD

(League matches only)

	PL	W	D	L
Home:	25	12	9	4
Away:	25	7	4	14
Overall:	50	19	13	18

LAST 2 MEETINGS

20/04/2005

Portsmouth	1-2	Liverpool
Kamara 34		Morientes 4,
		Luis Garcia 45

14/12/2004

Liverpool	1-1	Portsmouth
Gerrard 70		LuaLua 90

CLUB DETAILS

Nickname: Pompey
Ground: Fratton Park, capacity 20,200
Manager: Alain Perrin (app. 07/04/05)
Coach: Joe Jordan
Year formed: 1898

USEFUL INFORMATION

Website: www.pompeyfc.co.uk
Address: Fratton Park,
Frogmore Road,
Portsmouth,
Hants PO4 8RA
Switchboard: 0239 273 1204

TRAVEL INFORMATION

By Train: Fratton Station is a short walk from the ground.
By Bus: 3, 13, 14, 16a, 24, 27 and 57 all run to Fratton Station.

SUNDERLAND

FINAL C'SHIP STANDINGS 04-05

		W	D	L	PTS
1	**Sunderland**	**29**	**7**	**10**	**94**
2	Wigan	25	12	9	87
3	Ipswich	24	13	9	85

ALL-TIME RECORD

(League matches only)

	PL	W	D	L
Home:	69	33	18	18
Away:	69	25	13	31
Overall:	138	58	31	49

LAST 2 MEETINGS

15/12/2002

Sunderland	2-1	Liverpool
McCann 36,		Baros 68
Proctor 85		

17/11/2002

Liverpool	0-0	Sunderland

CLUB DETAILS

Nickname:	The Black Cats
Ground:	Stadium of Light, capacity 49,000
Manager:	Mick McCarthy (app. 12/03/03)
Assistant:	Ian Evans
Year formed:	1879

USEFUL INFORMATION

Website:	www.safc.com
Address:	Stadium of Light, Sunderland, Tyne and Wear SR5 1SU
Switchboard:	0191 551 5000

TRAVEL INFORMATION

By Train: Sunderland Station is a 10-15 minute walk from the stadium. The local Metro serves nearby St Peter's and Stadium of Light stations.

By Bus: Numbers 2, 3, 4, 12, 13, 15 and 16 all stop within a few minutes walk. All main bus routes connect to the city's central bus station, Park Lane Interchange, within easy walking distance.

TOTTENHAM HOTSPUR

FINAL STANDINGS 04-05

		W	D	L	PTS
8	Man City	13	13	12	52
9	**Tottenham**	**14**	**10**	**14**	**52**
10	Aston Villa	12	11	15	47

ALL-TIME RECORD

(League matches only)

	PL	W	D	L
Home:	62	39	18	5
Away:	62	18	14	30
Overall:	124	57	32	35

LAST 2 MEETINGS

16/04/2005

Liverpool	2-2	Tottenham H.
Luis Garcia 44,		Edman 12,
Hyypia 63		Keane 55

14/08/2004

Tottenham H.	1-1	Liverpool
Defoe 71		Cisse 38

CLUB DETAILS

Nickname:	Spurs
Ground:	White Hart Lane, capacity 36,240
Manager:	Martin Jol (app. 05/11/04)
Assistant:	Chris Hughton
Year formed:	1882

USEFUL INFORMATION

Website:	www.spurs.co.uk
Address:	748 High Road, Tottenham, London N17 0AP
Switchboard:	0208 365 5000

TRAVEL INFORMATION

By Train: The nearest Underground station is Seven Sisters, which is around a 30-minute walk. The nearest station is White Hart Lane, approx 5 minutes walk, on the Liverpool Street-Enfield Town line.

By Bus: Numbers 149, 259 and 279 all go along Tottenham High Road.

WEST BROMWICH ALBION

FINAL STANDINGS 04-05

		W	D	L	PTS
16	Portsmouth	10	9	19	39
17	**West Brom**	**6**	**16**	**16**	**34**
18	C Palace	7	12	19	33

ALL-TIME RECORD

(League matches only)

	PL	W	D	L
Home:	56	30	17	9
Away:	56	21	16	19
Overall:	112	51	33	28

LAST 2 MEETINGS

26/12/2004

West Brom	0-5	Liverpool

Riise 17, 82,
S-Pongolle 51,
Gerrard 55,
Luis Garcia 89

11/09/2004

Liverpool	3-0	West Brom

Gerrard 16, Finnan 42, Luis Garcia 60

CLUB DETAILS

Nickname: Baggies/Albion
Ground: The Hawthorns, capacity 27,877
Manager: Bryan Robson (app. 09/11/04)
Assistant: Nigel Pearson
Year formed: 1878

USEFUL INFORMATION

Website: www.wba.premiumtv.co.uk
Address: The Hawthorns, Halfords Lane, West Bromwich B71 4LF
Switchboard: 0121 525 8888

TRAVEL INFORMATION

By Train: From Birmingham New Street, change for a local train or Metro to The Hawthorns from Snow Hill, which is a five-minute walk from the main station.
By Bus: Centro, the region's public transport promoter, has timetables and information. Buses from across the region stop at the stadium. The website address is: www.centro.org.uk.

WEST HAM UNITED

FINAL C'SHIP STANDINGS 04-05

		W	D	L	PTS
5	Preston	21	12	13	75
6	**West Ham**	**21**	**10**	**15**	**73**
7	Reading	19	13	14	70

ALL-TIME RECORD

(League matches only)

	PL	W	D	L
Home:	48	32	13	3
Away:	48	16	15	17
Overall:	96	48	28	20

LAST 2 MEETINGS

02/02/2003

West Ham	0-3	Liverpool

Baros 7, Gerrard 9,
Heskey 67

02/11/2002

Liverpool	2-0	West Ham

Owen 28, 55

CLUB DETAILS

Nickname: The Hammers
Ground: Upton Park, capacity 35,647
Manager: Alan Pardew (app. 20/10/03)
Assistant: Peter Grant
Year formed: 1895

USEFUL INFORMATION

Website: www.whufc.com
Address: Boleyn Ground, Green Street, Upton Park, London E13 9AZ
Switchboard: 0208 548 2748

TRAVEL INFORMATION

By Train: Upton Park Station is the closest Underground Station, around 45 minutes from Central London on the District Line. When you exit the station turn right, the stadium is then a two-minute walk.
By Bus: Routes 5, 15, 58, 104, 115, 147, 330 and 376 all serve The Boleyn Ground.

WIGAN ATHLETIC
Wigan Athletic

FINAL C'SHIP STANDINGS 04-05

		W	D	L	PTS
1	Sunderland	29	7	10	94
2	**Wigan**	**25**	**12**	**9**	**87**
3	Ipswich	24	13	9	85

ALL-TIME RECORD

(All matches - League Cup)

	PL	W	D	L
Home:	1	1	0	0
Away:	1	1	0	0
Overall:	2	2	0	0

LAST 2 MEETINGS

04/10/1989

Wigan	0-3	Liverpool
		Staunton 59, 72, 88

19/09/1989

Liverpool	5-2	Wigan
Hysen 4, Rush 64, 65,		Griffiths 17, Thompson 54
Beardsley 81, Barnes 88		

CLUB DETAILS

Nickname:	The Latics
Ground:	JJB Stadium, capacity 25,000
Manager:	Paul Jewell (app. 12/06/01)
Assistant:	Chris Hutchings
Year formed:	1932

USEFUL INFORMATION

Website:	www.wiganlatics.co.uk
Address:	JJB Stadium, Loire Drive, Wigan WN5 0UH
Switchboard:	01942 774000

TRAVEL INFORMATION

By Train: Wigan Wallgate Station is just a 10-minute walk from the stadium.
By Bus: No particular route, as the venue is within easy distance of the station.

Wigan: The JJB stadium will be a new Premiership venue in 2005/06

TICKET OFFICE
CLUB STORE
MUSEUM & TOUR CENTRE
ALL LOCATED IN THE KOP GRANDSTAND

THE ALBERT

WELCOMES FOOTBALL FANS OF THE WORLD
PASSIONES DU FOOTBALL DE BIEN VENUES DU MONDE
WILLKOMMEN FUSSBALL-VENTILATOKEN DER WELT
VÄLKOMMEN ALLA VÄRLDENS FOTBOLLS SUPPORTRAR
WELKOM AAN ALLE VOETBAL FANS IN DE WERELD

TICKET INFORMATION

MATCH DAY PROGRAMMES

M
Bus Stop
Merseytravel
0151 236 7676
AREA ZONE

LIVERPOOLFC.TV

LIVERPOOL FOOTBALL CLUB
CHAMPIONS' LEAGUE WINNERS 2005
OFFICIAL WEBSITE

USERNAME   PASSWOR

COMMEN

NEWS | MATCH | SHOP | BETTING | INTERACTIVE | MOBILE | TICKETS | TEAM | HISTORY | THE CLUB

AIN STORY   July 8, 2005   NEWS HEADLINES

Watch Stevie and th
Watch now: Rafa o
Xabi welcomes Stev
Watch our first 3 ga
In this week's LFC
Kirkland hoping for
Squad numbers for

FAN CARD

187

Name:

TICKETS

Address	Ticket Office, PO Box 204, Liverpool L69 4PQ	
Ticket enquiries	0870 220 2345 0870 444 4949 (24-hour information line) 0870 220 2151 (credit card hotline - 4 tickets maximum) 0151 261 1416 (fax)	
Opening times	Monday-Friday 8.15am-5.30pm Saturday 9.15am-1.00pm Sunday 9.15am-1.00pm Matchdays 9.15am-15 minutes after the final whistle	

Prices	CAT A	CAT B
Kop	£30	£28
Over 65's	£24	£22.50
Main Stand	£32	£30
Over 65's	£24	£22.50
Centenary	£32	£30
Over 65's	£24	£22.50
Paddock	£32	£30
Over 65's	£24	£22.50
Anfield Road	£32	£30
Over 65's	£24	£22.50

Category A matches

Arsenal, Aston Villa, Blackburn Rovers, Chelsea, Everton, Manchester City, Manchester United, Newcastle United and Tottenham Hotspur.

Family tickets

Kop/Anfield Road: 1 adult + up to 2 children = price of adult ticket for that area, plus half price for each child aged 16 and under.

Buying tickets

General sales begin 18 days before a home fixture and are available through the credit card hotline, postal application and for e-Season Ticket holders, online. A small number are often made available online on the date of general sale.

By post

Send a letter stating the match and number of tickets you require, with a stamped addressed envelope, to LFC Ticket Office, PO Box 204, Liverpool L69 4PQ. You can pay by cheque, postal order, credit or debit card. Cheques must be made payable to Liverpool Football Club. If you want to pay by credit or debit card, include your card number and expiry date, plus debit card issue number where applicable. If the number of applications exceeds the number of tickets, they will be allocated through a ballot.

By phone

You can apply for a maximum of four tickets, by calling the credit card hotline, quoting your credit or debit card number and expiry date. A minimum booking fee of 50p per ticket will be charged. Tickets booked more than three days before the match will be sent out by post, those booked after this must be collected from the credit card collections window at the ticket office, and you must produce the card used to book the tickets.

TICKETS

In person
Any remaining tickets will go on sale at the ticket office under the Kop 11 days in advance. However, tickets usually sell out through phone and postal bookings.

Away matches
Tickets for away fixtures go on sale first to Liverpool season-ticket holders. Priority will be based on a loyalty system. The number of matches attended will be determined from the information held on the ticket office database.

European/Domestic Cup matches
Tickets for home European games and domestic cup matches are generally sold based on loyalty in previous rounds. In order to apply for European away tickets you must be a Fancard holder.

Other information
There are a limited number of disabled spaces, some of which are reserved for away fans and the majority for season-ticket holders. Tickets for these go on sale 18 days prior to a fixture and are priced £24 for category A games and £22.50 for category B for those in wheelchairs, and are free for a personal assistant. There is a waiting list of several years for a season ticket in this area. There are also 40 tickets available for visually impaired fans: 24 as season tickets, 16 as match tickets - priced as for wheelchair users. Persons applying must do so 18 days in advance of the fixture, enclosing a copy of their BD8 form and the the appropriate payment.

THE LFC FANCARD

About the Fancard
Fancards are now used to record attendance and help prevent ticket fraud. If you do not have a Fancard, you can purchase from the ticket office (for a one-off fee of £2.50 for a multi-season card).

Season-ticket holders, Priority Ticket Scheme, Official Liverpool Supporters' Club and e-Season Ticket members all receive Fancard details automatically.

Buying Tickets
When purchasing tickets you must provide your Fancard customer number either by handing your Fancard to the ticket office, quoting it via the telephone booking line or by post, or using it to log in online. Further information may be requested for security reasons. Purchases made online will require your Fancard customer number and password.

Only one ticket per match will be recorded on your Fancard, e.g. should you only have 1 Fancard and purchased 2 tickets on general sale, you will only be entitled to purchase 1 ticket for future priority sales.

If applying for tickets as a group it will be necessary for you to disclose each Fancard customer number and the customer name in order for us to record the purchase history correctly.

What Happens If I Lose My Fancard?
In the event that your Fancard is lost or stolen, please let the ticket office know immediately in writing. Your Fancard will then be deactivated and a new Fancard will be issued for a fee of £2.50. The data held on your lost or stolen Fancard will be transferred onto your new Fancard.

Should you change address, please inform the ticket office in writing, quoting your old address and enclosing a copy of a utility bill (gas, electric, water or telephone) to the ticket office.

GETTING TO ANFIELD

How to get there - by car
Follow the M62 until you reach the end of the motorway. Then follow the A5058 towards Liverpool for 3 miles, then turn left at the traffic lights into Utting Avenue (there is a McDonalds on the corner of this junction). Proceed for one mile and then turn right at The Arkles pub for the ground. It is recommended that you arrive at least two hours before kick-off in order to secure your parking spec. Otherwise, you can park in the streets around Goodison Park and walk across Stanley Park to Anfield, or you can park in a secure parking area at Goodison.

How to get there - by train
Kirkdale Station is the closest to Anfield (about a mile away), although Sandhills Station the stop before has the benefit of a bus service to the ground (Soccerbus). Both stations can be reached by first getting a train from Liverpool Lime Street (which is over 3 miles from the ground) to Liverpool Central (Merseyrail Northern Line), and then changing there for trains to Sandhills (2 stops away) or Kirkdale (3 stops). Note: only trains to Ormskirk or Kirkby go to Kirkdale station. A taxi from Liverpool Lime Street should cost between £5 and £7.

How to get there - Soccerbus
There are frequent shuttle buses from Sandhills Station, to Anfield for all Liverpool home Premiership and Cup matches. Soccerbus will run for two hours before each match (last bus from Sandhills Station is approximately 15 minutes before kick-off) and for 50 minutes after the final whistle (subject to availability). You can pay as you board the bus – each single journey will cost £1. Soccerbus is FREE for those who hold a valid TRIO, SOLO or SAVEAWAY ticket or Merseytravel Free Travel Pass.

How to get there - by bus
Take a 26 (or 27) from Paradise Street Bus Station or a 17B, 17C, 17D, or 217 from Queen Square bus station directly to the ground. The 68 and 168 which operate between Bootle and Aigburth and the 14 (from Queen Square) and 19 stop a short walk away.

How to get there - by air
Liverpool John Lennon Airport is around 10 miles from the ground, and taxis should be easily obtainable. Alternatively, you can catch the 80A bus to Garston Station and change at Sandhills for the Soccerbus service.

How to get there - on foot
From Kirkdale Station, turn right and then cross the railway bridge, where you will see the Melrose Abbey pub. Walk past up Westminster Road for around 1/3 of a mile before you arrive at the Elm Tree pub. Follow the road around the right-hand bend and then turn left into Bradwell Street. At the end of the road you will come to County Road (A59). Cross over at the traffic lights and then go down the road to the left of the Aldi superstore. At the end of this road you will reach Walton Lane (A580). You should be able to see Goodison Park on your left and Stanley Park in front of you. Cross Walton Lane and either enter Stanley Park, following the footpath through the park (keeping to the right) which will exit into Anfield Road. As an alternative to going through Stanley Park, bear right down Walton Lane and then turn left down the road at the end of Stanley Park to the ground.

To check bus and train times (8am-8pm, 7 days a week):

Traveline Merseyside	0870 608 2 608
Soccerbus	0151 330 1066

MUSEUM & TOUR CENTRE

Lasting approximately 45 minutes, the tour provides a fascinating behind-the-scenes look at the club. Celebrating Liverpool's illustrious history at home and abroad, special touches include entering the centre through a special turnstile, a parade of the club's silverware - including the European Cup - and mementos from some of the club's finest players. A special 60-seat cinema shows four 10-minute films of the history of the club, while the stadium tour offers the chance to visit the dressing rooms, walk down the tunnel and sit in the team dugout.

Highlights include:	Roger Hunt's 1966 World Cup winners' medal;
	All five European Cups;
	The 'treble trophies' from 2001;
	Michael Owen's 'Ballon D'Or' trophy
Address:	Museum & Tour Centre, Anfield Road, Liverpool, L4 0TH
Telephone:	0151 260 6677 (bookings)
Opening times:	Daily 10.00-17.00 - last admission 16.00 or 1 hour before kick off on matchdays. NO STADIUM TOURS ON MATCHDAYS.
Prices	
Ground tour & museum:	£9 adults, children & OAPs £5.50, family £23.00
Museum:	£5 adults, children & OAPs £3, family £13.00
	(Contact club for family tickets)
Ground tour, museum and lunch packages	£28.95 adults, U14s £18.95, U8s £12.95 and U5s £7.95
Recommend:	Booking in advance - please arrive 15 minutes prior to tour
Facilities:	Disabled access, Gift shop, Parking, Toilets

The club museum: View the Champions League trophy plus other assorted treasures

THE WEBSITE

Launched in October 2001, the club was the last top-flight side to launch an official site. But since then, it has become the most popular in the Premiership, recording 30 million hits a year placing the site in the top 10 of sporting websites.

Address: http://www.liverpoolfc.tv

Contents: News - Latest on the club, fans' views and archive;
                        Match - Full fixture list and results, match reports plus commentary;
                        Shop - From the online store to credit card applications, all are here;
                        Interactive - Messageboards, games and songs, a variety of options;
                        Mobile - All phone-related fun including ringtones and SMS alerts;
                        Tickets - Latest availability, including away travel information;
                        Team - Squad profiles, which include academy and LFC ladies features;
                        History - The LFC story, interspersed with records and quotes;
                        The Club - Includes all LFC-related initiatives and bodies.

For as little as 11p a day, the e-Season Ticket offers live matches, press conferences, interviews, famous goals and many other features at the touch of a button - while all information is accurate and 100 per cent correct.

The eight screens contained on the e-Season Ticket are the most compelling for fans, with constant updates providing something new to watch when you log on.

Buy an e-Season ticket, which includes:

Live match coverage - Every game the Reds play will be available;
Reserve footage - Highlights from every home game - and some live - giving an unrivalled insight into the progress of tomorrow's Anfield stars at the Academy;
Exclusive interviews - You set the questions, we get the answers;
Press conferences - Step into Melwood and get Rafa's thoughts; coverage of the entire pre and post-match press conference
Liverpool FC TV - A weekly news round-up, which includes in-depth analysis and reaction from our TV pundits;
Match ticket priority (500 tickets, except Everton and Manchester United) and forum access - Priority access to online sales of match tickets and exclusive access to messageboards;
Highlights and goals - All Premier League and Champions League goals can be viewed again and again - plus every goal since 2000/01;
Kop classics - Classic action from the greats of yesteryear including a 100 Days That Shook The Kop series and rare archive footage.

Price: £39.99 for 12 months (direct debit - UK only), £2.49 for 3 months then
                        £4.49 thereafter.
                        £44.99 for 12 months (credit card), £4.49 a month.

e-Season ticket link: http://www.liverpoolfc.tv/preview/
                        Or log on to the home page and choose the tickets, option, scrolling
                        down to the e-Season Ticket option

LIVERPOOLFC.TV

COMMENTARY + KOP CHANTS

LIVERPOOL FOOTBALL CLUB
CHAMPIONS' LEAGUE WINNERS 2005
OFFICIAL WEBSITE

USERNAME   PASSWORD   GO

>> Forgotten Password
>> Need to Register
>> New to Liverpoolfc.tv?

NEWS | MATCH | SHOP | BETTING | INTERACTIVE | MOBILE | TICKETS | TEAM | HISTORY | THE CLUB | E-SEASON TICK

MAIN STORY   July 8, 2005

NEWS HEADLINES
Watch Stevie and the new boys train...
Watch now: Rafa on Stevie
Xabi welcomes Stevie u-turn
Watch our first 3 games LIVE online
In this week's LFC Magazine
Kirkland hoping for better luck wit...
Squad numbers for new boys
Parry: Carragher to sign this week
>> More News

Qualifier Tickets
Onsale >>

>> Site A-Z
>> Help / Contact Us
>> Get LFC Newsletter
>> Buy e-Season Ticket

GERRARD TO PARADE EURO CUP AT WREXHAM
Steven Gerrard is expected to start Liverpool's opening pre-
season friendly at Wrexham on Saturday and as an added
bonus for those fans travelling to the Racecourse Ground the
European Cup will also be on show.

REDS 66/1 TO WIN THE DOUBLE
Can Liverpool win a Premiership and FA Cup double
in 2006? If you think they can, a £10 bet could land
you £660!

HAVE YOU SEEN ?
Win signed Morientes shirt
LFC ticketing alerts
Apply for an LFC credit card
High class LFC prints to buy
Pay pennies for Sunderland tickets

Lowest Bid Wins!

MEDIA WATCH

Source   Headline
SKY SPORTS   Reds step up Figo hunt
ECHO   Benitez agrees terms for Figo
SKY SPORTS   Baros happy to stay
ITV   Triple boost for Liverpool
SKY SPORTS   Gerrard wants Rafa chat

THE LIVERPOOLFC.TV TRANSFER TRACKER

E-SEASON TICKET

Stevie Speaks
Steven Gerrard talks about
his decision to remain a Red

Rafa on Stevie
Rafael Benitez talks about his
captain's decision to stay with
Liverpool

>> LAUNCH E-ST CONSOLE

> FREE PREVIEW   > BUY E-ST AS A GIFT
> BUY E-ST   > TECHNICAL SUPPORT

LFC BETTING

Get $100 free

liverpoolfc.tv   liverpoolfc.tv   liverpoolfc.tv   liverpoolfc.tv   liverpoolfc.tv

NEW LFC AWAY KIT 2005/06
PRE-ORDER NOW FOR DELIVERY 4TH AUGUST*

*FREE SPORTS KIT WITH EVERY PRE-ORDER

* Terms and Conditions

ENTER LIVERPOOLFC.TV | NEW AWAY KIT RANGE

MATCHDAY PROGRAMME AND OFFICIAL MAGAZINE

Official Matchday Programme

Liverpool's award-winning official matchday programme is written and produced in Liverpool by Sport Media on behalf of the club. The traditionally sized programme includes regular features like the nostalgia-based Kop'n'Goal Years, an L4 Interview with one of Rafa's squad, a message from the manager himself plus captain's notes and an A-Z look at famous Liverpool moments from the archives.

How to subscribe

Phone: 0845 143 0001 (Monday-Friday 9am-5pm)
Website: www.liverpoolfc.tv/match/magazine
(Also available in braille and other formats - contact community department on 0151 264 2316 for details)

LFC Magazine

Liverpool are the only club boasting an official weekly magazine in the Premiership. The Sport Media-produced glossy LFC Magazine, priced £1.95, provides up-to-date news and views on all aspects of the club, from exclusive player interviews, match previews and reports to features on former players and famous Reds and stats. Popular back page feature asks fans to Spot The Kop Idol from a Liverpool crowd scene while regular columnists are Chief Executive Rick Parry, plus legendary duo Kenny Dalglish and Alan Hansen.

How to subscribe

Phone: 0845 143 0001 (Monday-Friday 9am-5pm)
Website: www.liverpoolfc.tv/match/magazine

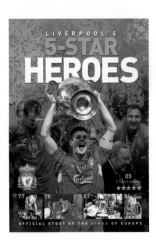

Official Champions League Book

Liverpool's 5-Star Heroes

A definitive celebration of the club's 5 European Cup successes compiled by Sport Media. Utilising a wealth of Liverpool Daily Post & Echo and club archive material and with interviews from a range of characters involved in each glorious victory from Rome to Istanbul, the publication is a must-read for all Liverpudlians. The hard-backed book costs £20 and features unique photos from the 2005 triumph.

How to order

Phone: 0845 143 0001 (Monday-Friday 9am-5pm)

CLUB STORES

Selling everything from replica kit to baby accessories, both club stores within Liverpool provide Reds fans with a wealth of souvenirs. With a new Champions of Europe range having been unveiled, there is something for everyone with fresh merchandise being added for the new season. Addresses and contact details are as follows:

Williamson Square Official Club Store
11 Williamson Square, Liverpool, L1 1EQ
United Kingdom
Tel +44 (0)151 330 3077
Opening times: Mon-Sat 9.00am - 5.30pm
Sundays 11.00am - 5.00pm

Anfield Official Club Store
Kop grandstand +44 (0)151 263 1760
Fax +44 (0)151 264 9088
Opening times Mon - Fri 9.00am - 5.00pm
Saturdays 9.00am - 5.00pm
Sundays 10.00am - 4.00pm
Match Saturdays 9.00am - 45 mins after game
Match Sundays 10.00am - 45 mins after game
Match Evenings 9.00am - 45 mins after game

Online Store
www.liverpoolfc.tv

Liverpool FC Order hotline: 0870 600 0532 **International calls:** +44 138 685 2035
Lines open 8am-9pm Mon-Sun

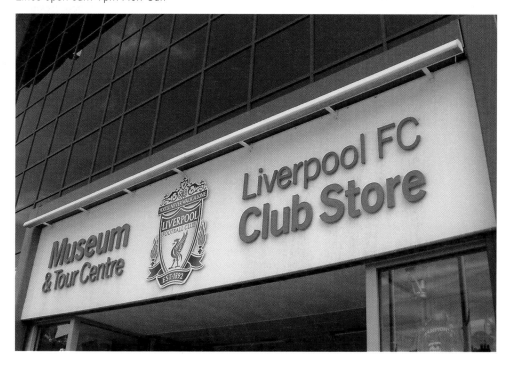

OFFICIAL LIVERPOOL SUPPORTERS CLUB

Membership of the Official Liverpool Supporters Club during the 2005-06 season can reap a wide variety of benefits.

The new package has been put together after listening to feedback from fans and taking into account research the club has undertaken on what members want.

We offer the best selection of benefits yet, having retained all the successful elements of the membership like the 10% discount in official club stores - while also building on this.

Adult and Priority Ticket Scheme (PTS) members will receive an exclusive DVD featuring the full 90 minutes of the Liverpool FC vs. Olympiakos Champions League match which saw the Reds qualify for the knockout phase and their fantastic Champions League run in 2005.

There is also a documentary giving you the manager's, players' and former players' take on the match and as a bonus, highlights of the Tsunami Match held for Soccer Aid seeing the return of legends such as Dalglish, Rush and Barnes to Anfield, to name just three.

As well as this fantastic DVD there is an exclusive Liverpool FC pennant and pin badge as well as your excellent OLSC quarterly magazine!

Junior members will get an exclusive Liverpool FC pencil case and school kit including a ruler, pencil, pencil sharpener and rubber to make sure all your class mates know you are a supporter of the best team!

There is also an exclusive Liverpool FC teddy as well as the OLSC quarterly magazine and the chance to be the mascot at an away game.

Please contact the membership office on 08707 020207 or write to Membership Dept, Liverpool FC, Anfield Road, Liverpool, L4 0TQ.

For full benefits of each scheme please see below and right. Adult and Junior Members will receive a £2 discount if you pay by Direct Debit.

PTS Scheme - Please note scheme is currently fully subscribed for 2005-06. Registrations for the PTS Waiting List are being accepted for 2006-07.

- Free Fan Card if required
- 1 in 2 chance to buy tickets for FAPL home games
- SMS and e-mail alerts on first day of sales
- Dedicated PTS helpline
- Quarterly Member Magazines including exclusive Pin badge
- Liverpool pennant
- 10% off merchandise in official club stores
- Monthly Mega Draw
- 2 for 1 museum offer
- Exclusive LFC Magazine Offers

PRICE: £50 inc P&P

Adult Membership Scheme

- Free Fan Card if required
- Quarterly Member Magazines including exclusive competitions
- DVD
- Exclusive Pin badge
- Liverpool pennant
- 10% off merchandise in official club stores
- Monthly Mega Draw
- 2 for 1 museum offer
- Exclusive LFC Magazine Offers

PRICE: £29.95 inc P&P
*£2 discount for Direct Debit

Junior Membership Scheme

- Free Fan Card if required
- Quarterly Member Magazines including exclusive competitions
- Liverpool FC teddy bear
- Liverpool pencil case and school kit
- Chance to be a mascot at an away match
- Chance to attend the Christmas Party at Anfield
- 10% off merchandise in official club stores
- Monthly Mega Draw
- 2 for 1 museum offer
- Exclusive LFC Magazine Offers

PRICE: £19.95 inc P&P
*£2 discount for Direct Debit

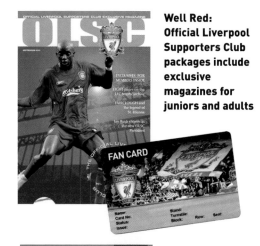

**Well Red:
Official Liverpool
Supporters Club
packages include
exclusive
magazines for
juniors and adults**

The Liverpool family: Gathering for the popular fans' day at Anfield

ASSOCIATION OF INTERNATIONAL BRANCHES

There are almost 200 Association of International Branches, and several new ones are being formed each season. Benefits of affiliating include passes to watch the first team train at the pre-season Fans Day at Anfield, an exclusive Q&A session with a Reds legend, as well as meeting like-minded supporters in your area. However, please note that new branches have restricted access to tickets.

If there isn't an AIB near you, why not form one. You'll need 25 supporters and will have to pay a small fee and sign up to AIB regulations. For further details or information on your nearest branch, please call: +44-(0)-151-261-1444 or fax 0151 261 1695.

LIVERPOOL DISABLED SUPPORTERS ASSOCIATION

The Liverpool Disabled Supporters Association (LDSA) was formed in January 2004 with help from LFC Disability Liaison Officer, Jodi Unsworth and a small group of LFC disabled supporters. The aims and objectives of this association are to act in partnership with Liverpool Football Club to promote inclusiveness for the disabled fans of the club, the disabled fans of visiting clubs as well as those individuals who support disabled people and those with impairments.

This association recognises that all fans should have an equal opportunity to participate in an enjoyable matchday experience and that people with disabilities and/or impairments must have their interests recognised and promoted by LFC with equal status to that of all other fans of the club. The LDSA committee is made up of 10 members, who are all LFC supporters. The group meets once a month with Jodi Unsworth to discuss disability issues at LFC.

If you would like anymore information about the LDSA then please send an email to LDSA@liverpoolfc.tv or write to LDSA, Liverpool Football Club, 69 Anfield Road, Liverpool, L4 0TH.

REDUC@TE

Since opening, thousands of children have now enjoyed the opportunity to learn in the exciting and inspirational environment of Liverpool Football Club. Staffed by a Centre Manager and students from the three Universities in Liverpool, Reduc@te aims to help children improve their skills in the key areas of literacy, numeracy and ICT. Resources are made available in Reduc@te on a daily basis and use football, sport and contemporary issues to help motivate young people to learn. Great emphasis is placed on rewarding achievement and building up the self-esteem of the children to give them more confidence when learning. Staff use the unique environment to make the educational experience as special as possible and groups are offered learning opportunities in the club shop, the LFC Museum, the Academy and around Anfield.

All of the curriculum materials are designed to be fun and enjoyable and study support groups attend after normal school hours on weekdays Monday to Thursday. Fridays are set aside for Special Needs schools or schools who wish to make a full day visit to the centre. Reduc@te is well equipped with ICT hardware and is always willing to embark on new and exciting projects. Recently primary schools have visited Reduc@te for French or Spanish lessons during the school day and a number of secondary schools attend Reduc@te for 'business days' where they focus on the off-field activities of the club for their GCSE and A-Level courses.

Further details on Reduc@te may be obtained from the Centre Manager, Keith White:
Tel: 0151 263 1313 **Email:** krwhite.lfc.study@talk21.com or Reducate@liverpoolfc.tv

LFC IN THE COMMUNITY

Liverpool Football Club's Community department has gone from strength to strength since it was formed in 2000. Led by Community Coaching co-ordinator Bill Bygroves, who is also Liverpool FC's club chaplain, this thriving department works very closely with the local community and are involved in a whole host of various activities both locally and world wide. Bill Bygroves works alongside former professional footballer Owen Brown and they lead a very dedicated and enthusiastic team working with the community. There are community coaches including Head Coach Eddie Sullivan, Disability Liaison Officer Jodi Unsworth and Admin Co-ordinator Tracy Boden, and six full-time coaching community staff. The community department works closely with young children and visits local schools throughout the Merseyside region giving 'Truth 4 Youth' assemblies. The slogans chosen by the Liverpool FC Community team include 'Kick Drugs into Touch', 'Give Bullying the Boot', 'Show Racism the Red Card', 'Shoot Goals, Not Guns', 'More important than being a good footballer is being a good person' and 'You'll Never Walk Alone'. Football wise, the community team take youngsters for general football coaching in mainstream schools, after school clubs, community centres, special needs schools and adult day care centres. This can involve coaches taking over PE sessions Monday-Friday, while the club also run youth club sessions three times a week in the local area.

Liverpool Football Club Community Department pioneered the SweeperZone project (pictured below), which has been tremendously successful. Liverpool FC were chosen as the first club in the Premiership to kick this project off with the aim of kicking litter off the streets, encouraging up to 25 local kids to help with this initiative on a matchday, and as a reward earning a free ticket for the match.
One of the club's most successful initiatives has also been the 'Jamie Carragher Young Person of the Year' awards night, which takes place in November each year. With categories recognising Schools, Youth and Community and Special Achievements to name but three, the night recognises good in the community and is a reward for those who have shown courage, bravery, overcome an illness or have contributed significantly in the local area. Current projects set up by Disability Liaison Officer Jodi Unsworth include a North West Wheelchair Football Premiership League, a visually impaired football team, a deaf football team, and a mini football league within special schools across Merseyside.

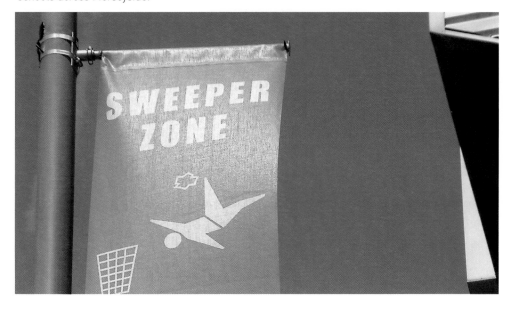

INSIDE ANFIELD

Hospitality

Heathcotes at Anfield is based at Liverpool Football Club, which has one of the regions most remarkable venues. The club is synonymous with achievement and success – great teams built on the perfect blend of skill, flair and determination, and this is highlighted in the service we offer.

Our experience in accommodating large numbers of hospitality guests – typically 2,500 people on match days – offers valuable reassurance that all events will run smoothly. And because of our considerable resources, we'll do our best to help if you are working to a tight deadline.

You'd be correct in thinking that any culinary experience that bears the name of Paul Heathcote has to be special. Under the direction of award-winning head chef Christian Grall you can enjoy a range of inspired menu options covering everything from conference luncheons to fine dining.

To find out details regarding conferencing, events and weddings and private events, further details can be obtained from the following contacts:

Telephone: 0151 263 7744
Email: events@liverpoolfc.tv
Website: www.liverpoolfc.tv/club/banqueting.htm

OUTSIDE ANFIELD

All pubs, listed alphabetically, are within 15 minutes walk of the ground, and all would be expected to be open before and after a game. This is by no means a definitive guide but might help you get around if you're looking for a certain venue pre or post-match . . .

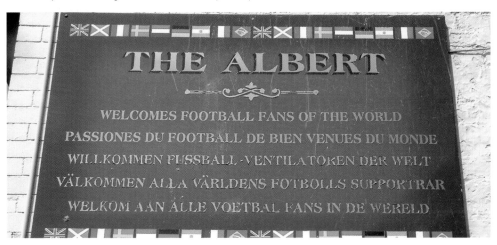

ALBERT HOTEL
Walton Breck Road (located next to the Kop).
Decorated with Liverpool memorabilia.

ARKLES
Anfield Road
Big screen TV.

BRECKSIDE (THE FLAT IRON)
Walton Breck Road
Real ale, three-room pub.

CABBAGE HALL
Townsend Lane
Big screen TV.

COCKWELL INN
Townsend Lane
One-bar pub.

GEORGE
Breck Road
Refurbished in last few years.

GROVE
Breckfield Road
Two-bar pub, safe for away fans.

LUTINE BELL
Breck Road

KING CHARLES
Thirlmere Road
One-bar pub.

KING HARRY
Blessington Road
Two-sided pub.

OAKFIELD
Oakfield Road

Two-sided pub.

PARK
Walton Breck Road
Very busy on matchdays.

RICHMOND ARMS
Breck Road
Big screen TV on Saturdays,
two-sided pub.

RYDAL
Rydal Street

SALISBURY
Walton Breck Road
Between the Albert and Stanley, a busy two-sided pub.

SAM DODDS WINE BAR
Oakfield Road

SANDON
Oakfield Road
The place where Liverpool Football Club's founder John Houlding plotted his Anfield dream. Sports memorabilia adorns the pub.

STANLEY HOTEL
Walton Breck Road
Friendly two-sided pub.

STRAWBERRY
Breckfield Road South (between West Derby Road and Breck Road)

WILLOW BANK
Townsend Lane
Big screen TV

LIVERPOOL IN THE MEDIA

LOCAL MEDIA

Liverpool Echo
Local evening daily, Monday-Saturday.
Saturday edition contains the 'Football Echo'.
Price: 38p

Liverpool Daily Post
Local morning daily, Monday-Saturday.
Price: 40p

LOCAL RADIO

BBC Radio Merseyside
Provides full coverage of all Liverpool first-team games, with Gary Gillespie the main summariser. Post-match fans' debate is a regular feature, while football is covered throughout the week, with Fridays usually previewing the weekend action.
Frequency: 95.8FM/1485AM

Radio City/Magic
Full commentary on all Liverpool matches is provided with guest summarisers including John Aldridge, who also plays a popular agony uncle to fans on the station's post-match debate.
Frequency: 96.7FM/1548AM

Century FM
Coverage of all first-team games is available, with a daily football phone-in Monday-Saturday (known as the 'Legends' phone-in), including Alan Kennedy.
Frequency: 105.4FM

OTHER UNOFFICIAL PUBLICATIONS

The KOP magazine
Important grass roots tabloid-style publication providing an alternative take on all things Red, established since 1994. On sale locally in newsagents or outside the ground on matchdays. Subscribe by calling 0845 143 0001.

Price: £1.50

The Liverpool Way
Alternative view of Liverpool FC since 1999, copies are available around Anfield on matchdays.

Price: £2

Through The Wind And Rain
Long-running publication, available on matchdays.

Price: £2

Red All Over The Land
Established in 1995, on sale at most home and away games

Price: £2

EX-REDS IN THE MEDIA

Rarely a fixture in the 'Where are they now?' sections of websites and publications, the success of the club has spawned a variety of former players in the media. From the high-profile pundits and presenters to newspaper columns and the odd guest interview on Sky Sports News, ex-Liverpool stars can be spotted on a regular basis - and not just playing football every summer in the Masters Football series.

Although not a definitive guide, the former stars are the more regularly spotted in the media:

Alan Hansen: Familiar face on the box

Alan Hansen - The doyen of pundits. A regular on BBC TV's 'Match of the Day', Alan also writes a column for the official LFC Magazine and has even presented and featured in TV documentaries.

Mark Lawrenson - Like in his Liverpool heyday, often seen partnering Hansen on 'Match of the Day', while also writing columns for the BBC Sport website and in the local media.

Phil Thompson - Utilised to the full on Sky Sports since leaving the Reds in the summer of 2004, Thommo is a regular on 'Soccer Saturday'.

John Barnes - Channel 5 stalwart, being the channel's main football presenter having previously worked for ITV as a studio guest and match analyst.

Michael Robinson - Now a huge success as a presenter on Spanish TV, Robinson's latest venue included the show El Día Después (The Day After Tomorrow) on Canal Plus.

Alan Kennedy - A fixture outside Anfield on Sky Sports News whenever there's a Reds-related story breaking, Alan can also be found on the Legends phone-in on Century FM.

John Aldridge - Often can be heard acting as a co-commentator on local radio and offering his opinions on Sky Sports.

Jim Beglin - Pundit and co-commentator for a wide variety of media, including ITV and Irish TV Channel RTE.

Ray Houghton - Presenting and commentating for Talksport gives Ray a regular national platform for his views, while as well as a brief stint as a football agent, he has worked for RTE.

Jan Molby - Another on local and national radio, Jan's stints as a lower league manager have also provided a regular dose of Danish-scouse for listeners in recent years.

David Fairclough - Will be providing commentary and studio analysis for Liverpoolfc.tv this season, while also working for Irish radio station Today FM. Appearances on Five Live and Sky are also sure to be on the agenda.

Gary Gillespie - A regular summariser for Radio Merseyside on Reds games.

Ronnie Whelan - Sky Sports News and Irish TV have been known to represent Ronnie's views since his return from managerial stints in Greece and Cyprus.

Jamie Redknapp - Has made the transition from player to pundit since his retirement in the summer, joining Sky as a match summariser.

Tommy Smith - Although no longer dishing out 'Fair tackles', 'Bounce balls' and 'Over the tops' in the Football Echo on a Saturday in Liverpool, Tommy still retains a column and pops up on Sky from time to time.

Ian St John - Achieved media fame as a partner to Jimmy Greaves on ITV's 'Saint & Greavsie' show in the 80s, and has since worked for Radio City and the written media.

2006	Jan	Feb	March	April	May	June
Monday					1	
Tuesday					2	
Wednesday		1	1		3	
Thursday		2	2		4	1
Friday		3	3		5	2
Saturday		4	4	1	6	3
Sunday	1	5	5	2	7	4
Monday	2	6	6	3	8	5
Tuesday	3	7	7	4	9	6
Wednesday	4	8	8	5	10	7
Thursday	5	9	9	6	11	8
Friday	6	10	10	7	12	9
Saturday	7	11	11	8	13	10
Sunday	8	12	12	9	14	11
Monday	9	13	13	10	15	12
Tuesday	10	14	14	11	16	13
Wednesday	11	15	15	12	17	14
Thursday	12	16	16	13	18	15
Friday	13	17	17	14	18	16
Saturday	14	18	18	15	20	17
Sunday	15	18	18	16	21	18
Monday	16	20	20	17	22	18
Tuesday	17	21	21	18	23	20
Wednesday	18	22	22	18	24	21
Thursday	18	23	23	20	25	22
Friday	20	24	24	21	26	23
Saturday	21	25	25	22	27	24
Sunday	22	26	26	23	28	25
Monday	23	27	27	24	29	26
Tuesday	24	28	28	25	30	27
Wednesday	25		29	26	31	28
Thursday	26		30	27		29
Friday	27		31	28		30
Saturday	28			29		
Sunday	29			30		
Monday	30					
Tuesday	31					

July	Aug	Sept	Oct	Nov	Dec	
						Monday
	1					Tuesday
	2			1		Wednesday
	3			2		Thursday
	4	1		3	1	Friday
1	5	2		4	2	Saturday
2	6	3	1	5	3	Sunday
3	7	4	2	6	4	Monday
4	8	5	3	7	5	Tuesday
5	9	6	4	8	6	Wednesday
6	10	7	5	9	7	Thursday
7	11	8	6	10	8	Friday
8	12	9	7	11	9	Saturday
9	13	10	8	12	10	Sunday
10	14	11	9	13	11	Monday
11	15	12	10	14	12	Tuesday
12	16	13	11	15	13	Wednesday
13	17	14	12	16	14	Thursday
14	18	15	13	17	15	Friday
15	19	16	14	18	16	Saturday
16	20	17	15	19	17	Sunday
17	21	18	16	20	18	Monday
18	22	19	17	21	19	Tuesday
19	23	20	18	22	20	Wednesday
20	24	21	19	23	21	Thursday
21	25	22	20	24	22	Friday
22	26	23	21	25	23	Saturday
23	27	24	22	26	24	Sunday
24	28	25	23	27	25	Monday
25	29	26	24	28	26	Tuesday
26	30	27	25	29	27	Wednesday
27	31	28	26	30	28	Thursday
28		29	27		29	Friday
29		30	28		30	Saturday
30			29		31	Sunday
31			30			Monday
			31			Tuesday

OTHER USEFUL CONTACTS

The Premier League
11, Connaught Place, London W2 2ET
Phone: 0207 298 1600

The Football Association
25 Soho Square, London W1D 4FA
Phone: 0207 745 4545

The Football League
Edward VII Quay, Navigation Way,
Preston, Lancashire
PR2 2YF
Phone: 01772 325800/
0870 442 0 1888
Fax: 01772 325801
Email: fl@football-league.co.uk

Professional Footballers'
Association
2, Oxford Court,
Bishopsgate,
Off Lower Mosley Street,
Manchester
M2 3WQ
Phone: 0161 236 0575

Hillsborough Family
Support Group
69, Anfield Road,
Liverpool
L4 0TH
Phone: 0151 264 2931
Email: hfsg@liverpoolfc.tv

LFC logo and crest are registered trade marks of
The Liverpoool Football Club and Athletics Grounds PLC.
Published in Great Britain in 2005 by: Trinity Mirror Sport Media, PO Box 48, Old Hall Street, Liverpool L69 3EB

ISBN: 1905266022

Printed and finished by Scotprint, Haddington, Scotland